The
New Eurasia

THE NEW EURASIA

A Guide to the Republics of the Former Soviet Union

DAVID T. TWINING

PRAEGER   Westport, Connecticut
London

Library of Congress Cataloging-in-Publication Data

Twining, David Thomas.
    The new Eurasia : a guide to the republics of the former Soviet
Union / David T. Twining.
        p.   cm.
    Includes bibliographical references and index.
    ISBN 0–275–94431–X (pbk. : alk. paper)
    1. Former Soviet republics—Guidebooks.   I. Title.
DK293.T85   1993
914.704′854—dc20   92–32670

British Library Cataloguing in Publication Data is available.

A hardcover edition of *The New Eurasia* is available from the Greenwood Press imprint of
Greenwood Publishing Group, Inc. under the title *Guide to the Republics of the Former
Soviet Union* (ISBN 0–313–28818–6).

Library of Congress Catalog Card Number: 92–32670
ISBN: 0–275–94431–X

First published in 1993

Praeger Publishers, 88 Post Road West, Westport, CT 06881
An imprint of Greenwood Publishing Group, Inc.

Printed in the United States of America

The paper used in this book complies with the
Permanent Paper Standard issued by the National
Information Standards Organization (Z39.48–1984).

10 9 8 7 6 5 4 3 2 1

The views expressed in this book are those of the author and do not necessarily reflect the
official policy or position of the Department of the Army, Department of Defense, or the
U.S. Government.

"We Are Eurasians"

We grew up with each other. The country sprawled over two continents, but it sometimes seems that in pure form it belongs neither to Europe nor to Asia. We are a kind of special formation. Whether we like it or not, we are Eurasians. We must also proceed from that premise in politics.

Izvestiya
December 14, 1991

To the rising generation of post-Soviet
scholars who have before them a new
Eurasian world to study and explore.

Contents

Maps

Preface

This work has been a labor of love, yet it chronicles events that hold such significance for the future. That we may better understand the multiple forces at work in this changing world is my intention. To those who wish to learn more about this vast land, I encourage you to consult the suggested list for further reading, because each new country needs an in-depth examination that only intense study, travel, and intellectual inquiry may provide.

The citizens of the fifteen new states have come such a long way and they have paid an enormous price for the journey. It is my very great desire that the post-Soviet world evolve in a more peaceful, beneficial manner than the Soviet world before it. The new Eurasia represents the beginning of this new era if all work to fulfill the great promise it represents.

At the same time, turbulent events since the August 1991 attempted coup have exacted a high toll within the newly independent countries. The absence of democratic institutions, combined with great social ills and devastated economies, foreshadows a future of volatility and unpredictability. In view of the great gap between popular expectations and an often harsh reality, a number of outcomes are possible. In the end, the people residing in each country must live with that which evolves. We can only hope that the freedom and welfare of all citizens are the foremost considerations motivating those now determining their fate.

Acknowledgments

I would like to thank the staff of the Army War College Library for their always cheerful assistance. I would also like to express my appreciation to my editor, Sally M. Scott, who persevered through thick and thin to produce this volume. Dr. Jim Sabin, Executive Vice President of Greenwood Publishers, deserves praise for his encouragement that something needed to be done to explain the changing world of Eurasia to others.

No work of this nature begins by itself. Indeed, people like Alvin Z. Rubinstein, Oles Smolansky, Yaroslav Bilinsky, George Ginsburgs, Don Barry, Robert Osborn, Carol Nechemias, Raj Menon, and others have provided the intellectual stimulation, example, and encouragement to assemble a work on such a contemporary subject.

My wife, Judy, and sons, Peter and Michael, have assisted at various times and have had to tolerate my hermit-like existence nearly all the time.

To my students at the U.S. Army War College and elsewhere, I owe gratitude for holding my feet to the fire and forcing me to meet their high expectations.

I have tried to cast a net as far as possible in order to capture the essence of the new Eurasian states. This broad approach is not without its risks, and I alone am responsible for any errors contained herein.

Introduction

The Eurasian continent is the largest single landmass on the globe. It commands transportation, communication, and trade routes connecting East and West. Most significantly, Eurasia is the geostrategic heartland of the world.

Until the August 1991 abortive coup attempt, the Soviet Union—the globe's largest single country—dominated this vast expanse. The failed coup accelerated the dissolution of the Soviet Union, confronting world political leaders with new post–Cold War challenges. The formation of the Commonwealth of Independent States by Russia, Ukraine, and Byelorussia (now Belarus) on December 8, 1991, and its acceptance by eight other republics on December 21, 1991, led directly to President Mikhail Gorbachev's resignation on December 25. Minutes later, the Union of Soviet Socialist Republics officially ended, with no fanfare and little acclaim.

It will be years before the far-reaching, multiple effects of these changes are fully felt, but almost at once it became clear that the single country that once so resolutely dominated the Eurasian landmass—the Soviet Union—will never again be viewed as a unified political-economic-social-geographic entity. Instead, fifteen independent states with their own customs, traditions, problems, and national interests have emerged. It is these new states—each unique in its own way—with which the world must now deal.

This account surveys and illuminates the diverse peoples, geography, and composition of the fifteen new republics of the former Soviet Union. These republics, together, were the building blocks of Soviet power for seventy-four years. After the breakup of the Soviet Union, they became sovereign states that have their own laws, police, military forces, and the like, requiring a more detailed awareness of the differences the old Soviet Union embraced and, to a large extent, concealed.

The New Eurasia—emerging from a disintegrating Soviet Union—is substantially different from the Eurasia of the past. Indeed, the many peoples and unique regions of this highly variegated area ensure a diversity of political, economic, and social relationships. Turkic, Asian, European, and Slavic peoples are seeking to establish ties beyond their traditional borders. Religious, economic, and other initiatives directed outward create a new web of relationships that are changing the existing balance of power in fundamental ways.

Until the events of December 1991, the steady erosion of central power caused authority and responsibility to devolve to the republics, giving them a virtual veto over all-union policies. This trend was spurred by the collapse of the national economy, given the weight, practices, and priorities of the administrative–bureaucratic elite that dominated all endeavors in the name of the Communist party. Beyond this, the awakening of nationalist fervor, based upon a system of ethnic regions and areas devised by Joseph Stalin, led to demands for self-determination and independence. The year 1993, proclaimed the "International Year for the World's Indigenous People" by the United Nations, has seen the indigenous peoples of the former Soviet Union dramatically assert their autonomy from the loosened grip of the old system. Now that the union itself has passed from the scene, this devolution of power has brought an unprecedented role and significance to the former republics.

At the same time, of vital import is the issue of the political center. For a country long used to the concentration of power in the hands of a few, with political direction, economic control, and military command centrally maintained, divergence from this pattern is a critical and telling change. If the Commonwealth of Independent States is to survive, this key question of the role and nature of the center (if there is one) will to a large extent define the parameters of actual independence of the constituent sovereign states.

To prepare for the many unknowns associated with the demise of the Soviet Union and the rise of fifteen sovereign states, there must be a greater knowledge of this vast region. Indeed, a new Eurasian world is developing, which will challenge existing assumptions and thinking. This book will serve as an introduction to the former republics, providing basic data on their history, populations, economic development, governments, and key issues, to orient the reader to the new states that have emerged from the former Soviet Union.

Key Terms

Political change and civil turmoil in the former Soviet Union often had as their focus political entities that were at variance with most Western terms and practice. Until the dramatic events of 1991, the Soviet Union was composed of fifteen union republics, the fundamental political unit below the national government. Each union republic was governed by a Supreme Soviet, as the highest body of state power. Because of the former Soviet Union's immense size and heterogeneous population, however, a complex series of jurisdictions was created to govern this vast land.[1]

In smaller union republics, the next subordinate political subdivision was the *raion*, which is similar to the U.S. county in rural areas. In urban areas, the raion corresponds to the borough, several of which form a city. Hence, local government in such republics is composed of raions in rural areas; a number of city governments; and governments for towns, villages, and settlements.

For larger union republics, there were a number of geopolitical subdivisions that do not overlap:

- *Krais* or *krays* (territories), responsible for large, often remote, and thinly populated areas. There were six krais in the former Soviet Union; all are in Russia.
- *Oblasts* (regions), which have larger populations but smaller territory. There were 123 oblasts in the former Soviet Union.

Other subdivisions were created to represent ethnic groups. Many such jurisdictions do not include all members of a given nationality but are artificial creations that sometimes deliberately split ethnic groups and attributed to them a falsified history.[2] All are subordinate to the union republics in which they are located, and all contain raions, cities, towns, villages, and settlements. These subdivisions include the following:

- *Autonomous Soviet Socialist Republics* (ASSRs). Autonomous soviet socialist republics were created as ethnic homelands for larger groups. They are subordinate to the union republics in which they are located, and they are governed by a Supreme Soviet. Today there are twenty-one autonomous republics in the Russian Federation, two in Georgia, one in Azerbaijan, one in Uzbekistan, and one in Ukraine.

- *Autonomous Oblasts* or regions. They are components of a union republic or rural krai. Such jurisdictions were organized for moderate-sized ethnic groups. There is one each in the Russian Federation, Azerbaijan, Georgia, and Tajikistan.

- *Autonomous Okrugs* or areas. They are found within krais or oblasts. Smaller minorities are found in these ten jurisdictions, all of which are in the Russian Federation.

The legislative bodies of the fifteen union republics were termed Supreme Soviets. They elected a Presidium, a Council of Ministers, and a Supreme Court. Corresponding Communist party bodies supervised and controlled these structures, forming a parallel government and party hierarchy at every step.

Below the union republics, all political subdivisions had elective soviets or councils, headed by *ispolkoms* (executive committees). As late as 1987, there were 52,568 soviets with 2,322,421 elected deputies throughout the country. While the 1977 Soviet Constitution declared them to have supreme authority, in practice they were dominated by local Communist party organs. The introduction of limited competitive elections in 1987 and efforts to vest the soviets with greater authority and responsibility met with mixed results.[3] Because the party largely retained its grip on the local soviets, blocking reforms and change, authorities such as Boris Yeltsin in the Russian Federation and Zviad Gamsakhurdia in Georgia, until his overthrow in January 1992, appointed officials to administer local affairs.

The political subdivisions in the former Soviet Union continue to be in flux as many entities assert their sovereignty and declare independence. Some subdivisions have acted, without authorization, to declare their independence, while others have raised their status to autonomous republics or republics. Further changes are likely as the status quo is challenged by rebellious regions or groups seeking autonomy and self-determination.

NOTES

1. Leon P. Baradat, *Soviet Political Society* (Englewood Cliffs, N.J.: Prentice-Hall, 1986), 142–51.

2. Ronald Wixman, "Forgotten Nationalisms: The Awakening of the National Minorities," paper presented at 23rd National Convention of the American Association for the Advancement of Slavic Studies, Miami, November 25, 1991. Many

excellent works detail the crude and costly manner in which the national question was addressed by Stalin. See Bohdan Nahaylo and Victor Swoboda, *Soviet Disunion: A History of the Nationalities Problem in the USSR* (New York: The Free Press, 1990); and Robert Conquest, *The Harvest of Sorrow: Soviet Collectivization and the Terror-Famine* (New York: Oxford University Press, 1986), among others.

3. Jeffrey W. Hahn, "The Soviet State System," in *Developments in Soviet Politics*, ed. Stephen White, Alex Pravda, and Zvi Gitelman (Durham, N.C.: Duke University Press, 1990), 89–97.

The
New Eurasia

Republics of the Former Soviet Union

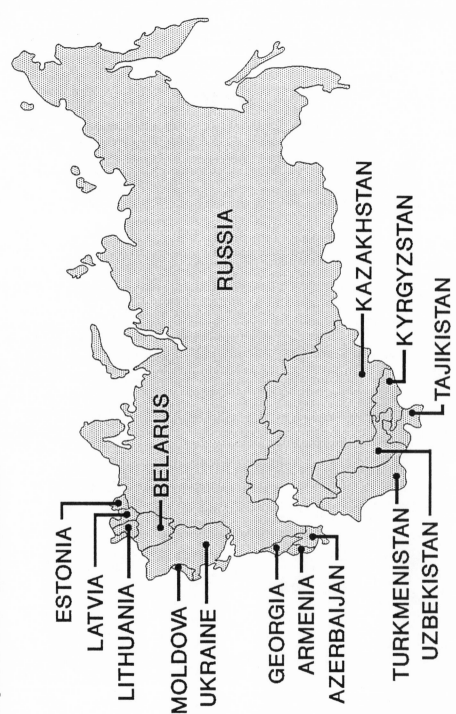

1

The Former Soviet Union

The decline and fall of the Soviet Union is the major event of the twentieth century. To a large extent, the country has been replaced by a Commonwealth of Independent States that represents a new experiment in governance for the many peoples inhabiting this vast land. The new states of Eurasia started here, with a country of a new type that set out to revolutionize the world. Its story is the precursor to all that follows.

BASIC DATA

Total Area: 8,650,000 square miles (22,402,200 square kilometers; land area, 8,599,000 square miles [22,272,000 square kilometers]). It occupied one-sixth of the globe's inhabited land and is slightly less than 2.5 times the size of the United States. Some 10 percent of the land is arable. Until December 25, 1991, the Soviet Union was the largest country in the world.

Population: 293,047,571, with an annual growth rate of 0.7 percent. The population was composed of more than 100 ethnic groups, most of them small in number. Some 72 percent of the total population were Eastern Slavs, of whom more than 70 percent (just over 50 percent of the total population) were Russians. The remainder were Belorussians and Ukrainians. Other ethnic groups belonged to Turkic, Finno-Ugric, Caucasian, Indo-European, and other linguistic families. The primary language was Russian; and for the many ethnic groups speaking languages from Turkic, Finno-Ugric, Caucasian, Indo-European, and other linguistic families, Russian was the predominant second language. The Soviet Union had the third largest population in the world, after China and India.

Religion:

Russian Orthodox	20%
Muslim	10%
Others	3%

Capital: Moscow.

Official Name: Union of Soviet Socialist Republics.

Government:

- Executive Branch: Until his resignation on December 25, 1991, the chief of state was President Mikhail S. Gorbachev, who also headed the government.
- Legislative Branch: Congress of People's Deputies and a full-time Supreme Soviet drawn from its ranks.
- Judicial Branch: Supreme Court.

Following the October Revolution of 1917 (November 7 by the new calendar) and the ensuing civil war and consolidation of power, the union was created in 1922. Its most recent constitution was approved in 1977. The union was *federal* in form, but *unitary* in practice.[1] This accounts for continuous references to the so-called center, where Moscow-based power in the hands of a few key political leaders controlled the entire country.

Economy: The national government was funded by the state monopoly of businesses and resources, and an administratively determined pricing system. Due to its inherent unsoundness, the ruble was not convertible, causing most international trade to be conducted in other currencies or by barter. Because prices had no real economic significance in determining the supply and demand of goods and services, Soviet transactions were administrative rather than economic in nature.

Given the accelerating rate of Soviet collapse following the August 19, 1991, coup attempt, President Boris Yeltsin of the Russian Federation imposed his own economic reform plan, seized oil and gas assets, and guaranteed state loans to the central government.[2] With inflation approaching 500 percent, the gross national product dropped nearly 20 percent. The country's gold reserve all but vanished, the standard of living deteriorated to that of the early 1970s, and $81 billion in gross debt forced Moscow to suspend paying the principal as of December 5. By this time, the economic crisis had become a personal issue for each citizen. The inadequate response of central authorities—principally Mikhail Gorbachev—to stem the tide and regain the political initiative resulted in the union's demise on December 25, 1991.

History: Nearly four centuries of monarchical rule ended in February 1917, when Tsar Nicholas II abdicated the throne to a provisional government formed predominantly from members of the last Duma, a quasi-representative body. By October, domestic strife and the Russian army's continued losses in World War I created chaotic conditions that led to a coup by Bolshevik revolutionaries.

Vladimir Il'ich Lenin headed the first Soviet government. The Bolsheviks acted quickly to suppress other political parties and to consolidate power, frequently by terror and force, throughout the vast country. The March 1918 Treaty of Brest–Litovsk ended Russia's participation in World War I, and all property was nationalized. After a three-year civil war, power was consolidated in the hands of what became the Communist party.

Lenin's death in 1924 caused a power struggle that lasted until 1929, ending with Joseph Stalin's complete dominance and the beginning of a dark period that brought incredible hardships and the deaths of millions of people. As World War II approached, Stalin sought to buy time by concluding, on August 23, 1939, the Molotov–Ribbentrop Pact, which provided for separate spheres of influence for Soviet and Nazi regimes: Poland and Romania were divided and Estonia, Latvia, and Lithuania eventually fell to Soviet control. Stalin attacked Finland in November 1939 and, despite heroic Finnish resistance, gained much of eastern Finland under the terms of the peace treaty of March 1940.

World War II began for the Soviet Union on June 22, 1941, when Hitler invaded his former ally, bringing untold devastation and loss of life to the Soviet Union. Four years of fighting as the eastern partner of a western anti-Hitler coalition left 27 million Soviet citizens dead and an equal number homeless. The disintegration of this coalition in the closing days of World War II was due to a variety of misunderstandings and miscues on both sides.

By March 5, 1946, Winston Churchill pronounced the beginning of the Cold War in a speech at Fulton, Missouri: "A shadow has fallen upon the scenes so lately lighted by the Allied victory. From Stettin in the Baltic to Trieste in the Adriatic an iron curtain has descended across the Continent."[3]

By the time of Stalin's death in March 1953, this pattern of Soviet–U.S. hostility was institutionalized, resulting in the most costly arms race in history, including a bomber race, a missile race, and a space race; the U.S. policy of containment, using military, economic, and political instruments of statecraft; and the comprehensive bankruptcy of the Soviet Union. Wars in Korea and Vietnam were pursued along the way, and the United States alone incurred a phenomenal $11 trillion in costs to finance this undertaking.

Successive leaders, particularly Nikita Khrushchev (1953–1964) and Leonid Brezhnev (1964–1982), continued this policy of confrontation. The initiation of détente and conclusion of SALT I's Interim Agreement, which for the first time limited strategic arms, and the Anti-Ballistic Missile Treaty in 1972, however, marked a new effort to define the limits of superpower competition. Following the brief interregnums of Yuri Andropov and Nikolai Chernenko, Mikhail Gorbachev ascended to the top party position in March 1985, ushering in a qualitatively different era of Soviet–U.S. relations. Moscow's withdrawal from Afghanistan, the opening and eventual fall of the Berlin Wall, and the gradual introduction of competitive elections and multiparty politics within the Soviet Union itself fed social and economic changes that threatened the ruling Communist party elite, the *nomenklatura*.

The abortive coup of August 19–21, 1991, discussed below, represented a last desperate attempt to preserve the Soviet Union as it was. This was a system of privilege and power for the few based upon the Communist party, the police, and the military—a triad put into place by Lenin and applied with a vengeance by Stalin. The conclusion of Gorbachev's political career coincided with that of the Soviet Union itself. The end of the Communist experiment, at the cost of untold millions of lives and rubles, is the crowning event of the twentieth century.

The Devolution of Power: After the attempted coup on August 19, 1991, historic change occurred in the organization and functioning of the central government. The Communist party was suspended on August 24 and its assets were seized. This action created an evolving political atmosphere of instability in which further change became inevitable.

The Baltic states were declared independent on September 6, 1991, by Moscow's ruling State Council. At the same time, other republics that had asserted their independence and that had proclaimed sovereignty over their affairs began to seek the realization of these goals more actively. Concurrently, the state infrastructure began to fall apart. More than 230,000 troops of the former Soviet Ministry of Internal Affairs—responsible for police functions—were transferred to the republics, and the ministry was abolished.[4] A number of KGB (Committee for State Security) forces and functions were similarly transferred, with spies in foreign countries reduced by 50 percent and the KGB overall by 90 percent.[5] The vast administrative apparatus in Moscow, which had long dominated national policy and centrally controlled the nation's economy, clearly began to wane.

Gorbachev's resignation on December 25, 1991, and the passing of the codes for initiating nuclear war to Boris Yeltsin were followed by the raising of the Russian white, red, and blue tricolor over the Kremlin. This effectively marked the end of the Soviet Union. As a consequence, the Russian Federation, which comprised 51 percent of the former country's population and 76 percent of its territory, became the dominant influence over the affairs of the newly independent states.

DEATH OF THE SOVIET UNION AND BIRTH OF THE COMMONWEALTH OF INDEPENDENT STATES

The death of the Soviet Union is a study in power, a bloodless coup that saw Mikhail Gorbachev outmaneuvered and replaced by Boris Yeltsin, who emerged from the August 1991 coup as the preeminent political figure in the country. Gorbachev's continued adherence to the "principle of socialism," his reluctance to adopt market principles and the concept of private property, and his seeming equivocation on a host of pressing issues signaled his inability to divorce himself from the past. A perceptible power vacuum appeared in Moscow, an unacceptable void, given the country's nearly four centuries of authoritarian rule.

Boris Yeltsin, with his proclivity toward action, his astute political acumen, and his keen sense of timing, recognized and converted the possibility of potential power into the reality of actual power. He was assisted in this task by those he had placed in key positions of national leadership, particularly Defense Minister Yevgeny Shaposhnikov, who replaced leading officer cadres and reorganized the armed forces to obviate any possible future challenge.

Nonetheless, Mikhail Gorbachev is a historic figure of great import. He created the atmosphere and fostered the conditions that led to epochal events within the Soviet sphere. The freeing of Eastern Europe and the Baltic states was the precursor to further demands for independence by the Soviet republics. His introduction of the secret ballot and multiple candidate elections empowered the formerly powerless masses. A willingness to explore alternative economic practices led to the turn away from central planning and fixed prices. Attempts to institutionalize the rule of law (including the creation of a bar association for attorneys), curbing the KGB, breaking the monopoly of state media, permitting the practice and teaching of religion, and making freedom of emigration and travel possible—these were done by Gorbachev.

Mikhail Gorbachev also presided over the dismantling of the Soviet empire. This group of client states ranged from Mongolia, taken over in 1921, to the countries of Eastern Europe, North Korea, and Cuba in the 1960s, to a rapidly expanding list of states in the 1970s and 1980s: Vietnam, Afghanistan, Syria, Iraq, Angola, Ethiopia, South Yemen, Nicaragua, and Grenada. At least $40 billion was expended to support this empire since the early 1960s. It may have been a good ideological investment, but it was a poor economic one. Proxy battles in Ethiopia and Angola were offset by indecisive combat in Afghanistan following the December 25, 1979, invasion. This overextended the Soviet Union and exacerbated Moscow's domestic strains.[6]

The Soviet withdrawal from Afghanistan in February 1989 and the fall of the Berlin Wall in November 1989 set the client states adrift at the same time that the Soviet Union was floundering. The seven-member, 5-million-strong, 35-year-old Warsaw Pact grew increasingly hollow; its military structure was dissolved on April 1, 1991, and its political structure was abolished three months later. The Soviet economic model of central management and the political model of monolithic Communist party rule proved inappropriate to the technological and information revolutions sweeping the globe. Mikhail Gorbachev demonstrated, by his words and deeds, that he realized that major changes were necessary if socialism was to survive. His failure to move fast or far enough led to his fall and ultimate replacement.

The social costs of some seventy-four years of communism were severe. Demonstrations in Moscow by Crimean Tatars in the summer of 1987 were precursors to violent strife between Armenians and Azerbaijanis that started in February 1989. Nationalist, irredentist, and separatist movements based on religious, geographic, economic, and social differences presented the Soviet leadership with challenges it was ill-prepared to resolve. The old system was tested on multiple fronts, and it was increasingly apparent that only radical surgery could save the ailing victim.

The August 1991 coup revealed not only how far the country had traveled but also how far it had yet to go. The attempt by conservative forces—the Communist party, the police, and the military—was a last desperate effort to grasp the remaining vestiges of power. The eight-man State of Emergency Committee, which seized control on August 19–21, claimed that it was a "patriotic act." According to former KGB chairman, Vladimir Kryuchkov, a key participant, "History will hold responsible for the fate of the Soviet Union not those who made an attempt to save it, but those who ruined our powerful and united motherland."[7]

With the coup's failure, the veneer of Marxist-Leninist mythology was finally swept away by popular demands for democratic rule. Gorbachev, a man deeply rooted in the administrative–bureaucratic structure that ruled this vast country in the name of the Communist party, was striken by caution and indecisiveness. This led *Izvestiya* in early December 1991 to lament: "Gorbachev's tragedy is a tragedy of a great person overtaken by his time."[8]

The turn from the three pillars of authoritarian oligarchic rule—the police, the Communist party, and the military—following the August coup put the country on the road to either democracy or anarchy. Top party bodies were suspended, police powers and forces devolved upon the separate republics, and the military was disillusioned. One senior Soviet officer lamented that the army "is tired of defending a country that no longer exists."[9] Communist party cells in the army, schools, and factories were disbanded, party property was seized and turned over to civil authorities, and "Iron Felix," the thirty-foot (nine-meter) statue of Felix Dzerzhinsky—founder of the dreaded KGB's predecessor, the Cheka—was removed from its perch in front of KGB headquarters by enthusiastic crowds.

Boris Yeltsin, in an effort to stem the implosion of power under way, issued presidential decrees in November seizing the Soviet Union's oil, diamonds, gold, and precious metals. This contravened an economic agreement signed by ten of the twelve remaining republics earlier in the month. Eduard

Shevardnadze, who resigned as foreign minister in December 1990 and warned of an approaching dictatorship, was reappointed to that position in November as conditions continued to deteriorate. Anatoli Sobchak, mayor of Leningrad, newly renamed St. Petersburg, aptly described this growing sense of doom: "Now we are swiftly approaching the Yugoslavization of our political life."[10]

By early December, Mikhail Gorbachev's inability to achieve agreement by republic leaders to a new union treaty binding the republics into a loose federation of sovereign states had become obvious. Boris Yeltsin acted to guarantee the loans of the near-bankrupt union, and President Gorbachev appeared on national television to warn the Soviet people of impending doom: "We shall be unable to overcome the crisis and join the civilized world and, worse still, to avoid universal catastrophe unless disintegration is arrested." This "crisis of statehood," he wrote to the parliaments of the republics, was the most dangerous situation confronting "our motherland."[11]

To contain the devolution of power to the republics and to stem the growing political weakness at the center, Gorbachev, assisted by a State Council of those republic leaders choosing to participate, established a number of bodies through which to administer a disintegrating Soviet Union. The Interstate Economic Council coordinated economic activity, and the Committee for the Operational Management of the National Economy (COMNE) was responsible for national currency, debt, and economic reform issues. The Interrepublic Security Service, headed by Vadim Bakatin, coordinated national and republic intelligence services; borders were to be controlled by the Joint Command of Border Troops; and foreign intelligence was the responsibility of the new Central Intelligence Service, headed by Yevgeniy Primakov.

Strategic air, naval, and ground-based nuclear forces were placed in a new branch of the armed forces, the Strategic Deterrence Forces. All-union military forces remained within the Ministry of Defense, but many republics began to form guards units, which were to be coordinated by the Defense Ministers Council of Republics. Foreign affairs were placed within the purview of the Ministry of Foreign Relations, a new body for coordinating and implementing trade and foreign policies agreed upon by the sovereign states.

Events, however, soon overtook Gorbachev. On December 8, 1991, leaders of Russia, Ukraine, and Byelorussia (now Belarus) jointly proclaimed the formation of the Commonwealth of Independent States at a meeting in Minsk. With renewed impetus given by Ukraine's December 1 vote for independence, this declaration was the beginning of the end of the Soviet Union. It recognized existing borders; said that military, strategic, and nuclear issues would be jointly decided; and announced that its seat would be in the Byelorussian capital of Minsk. Other functions of joint responsibility would include foreign and economic affairs, customs and immigration policy, transportation, communications, environmental affairs, and crime control.[12]

The three founding republics represented 73 percent of the former Soviet Union's population and 80 percent of its territory. They also controlled most of its economic and military strength. As a result, this agreement sealed the fates of Gorbachev and the Soviet Union. To Boris Yeltsin, "The republics have refused to voluntarily delegate to the center the powers which it has demanded of them." Because Kazakhstan, the fourth nuclear-armed republic of the former Soviet Union, was not included in the original pact, there was some concern that the agreement would unravel and threaten the control of the country's nuclear arsenal.[13]

The Central Asian republics—Kazakhstan, Kyrgyzstan, Tajikistan, Turkmenistan, and Uzbekistan—were confronted with a fait accompli. The possibility of joint action with Azerbaijan, the other Muslim republic, led to speculation that ethnic Slavs living in these regions might be threatened and that Islamic fundamentalism would spread. The leader of the Byelorussian Republic, Stanislav Shushkevich, acknowledged that other republics were welcome to join the new confederation, but the possibility existed that a Central Asian union might be created. Such a union would be conservative and Islamic, and would have growing ties to such states as Iran, Turkey, Pakistan, and Saudi Arabia.[14]

The Russian Federation, most notably in the person of Boris Yeltsin, increasingly asserted itself to fill the void of central power that had emanated from the Kremlin. By his words and deeds, he claimed Russia was the rightful inheritor of the symbols and wealth of the former Soviet state. Yeltsin called for the United States to extend diplomatic recognition to his republic as a separate, independent state on December 15. On this date, Yeltsin claimed the assets and functions of the union's Ministry of Interior as well as the buildings and accounts of the Soviet parliament.[15]

The death knell of the Soviet Union was sounded on December 21, 1991, at a summit meeting in Kazakhstan's capital, Alma-Ata. The three Slavic republics that had initiated the new commonwealth nearly two weeks earlier were now joined by eight others to create, formally, the Commonwealth of Independent States. All republics of the former Soviet Union except the Baltic states, which had become independent in September, and Georgia, embroiled in a violent civil war in Tbilisi, participated.

The Alma-Ata Declaration credited all eleven republics as cofounders. It provided for a commonwealth governed by a Council of Heads of State and a Council of Heads of Government. Membership was open to any state sharing its "goals and principles," the foremost being "to build democratic law-governed states." To defuse territorial sensitivities, the eleven leaders pledged to respect existing borders. Russia would assume the Soviet Union's seat on the UN Security Council, and full UN membership would be sought for the other signatories. Nuclear nonproliferation was pledged, with July 1, 1992, set as the date by which tactical nuclear weapons would be withdrawn to Russia from Belarus, Ukraine, and Kazakhstan. Strategic nuclear warheads in these republics were to be controlled by Russia, which will manage the nuclear arsenal subject to actions jointly agreed upon by the four nuclear republics.[16]

The issue of nuclear control, however, was never far from the thoughts of political leaders in both the East and the West. The *Nezavisimaya gazeta* (Independent Newspaper) revealed official figures on November 2 that placed the number of nuclear warheads atop intercontinental ballistic missiles at 4,278 in the Russian Republic, 1,240 in Ukraine, 1,040 in Kazakhstan, and 54 on mobile SS-25s in Belarus. In addition, air-launched cruise missiles represented another 367 warheads in Russia, 320 in Kazakhstan, and 168 in Ukraine. Many thousands of tactical nuclear warheads mounted on artillery shells, short-range battlefield missiles, and gravity bombs were in forward areas in Ukraine.[17]

The Bush–Gorbachev proposals of September–October 1991 would reduce and eliminate many of these weapons. Beyond this, Ukraine and Belarus pledged to become nuclear-free, and Kazakhstan, according to the Alma-Ata Declaration, would give up its tactical warheads. Addressing concern over nuclear control, the U.S. Congress took the unprecedented step in November 1991 of voting to appropriate $400 million to finance the dismantling of this nuclear arsenal. U.S. Secretary of State James Baker discussed nuclear issues during his December trip to Russia, Belarus, Kazakhstan, Kyrgyzstan, and Ukraine, but Gorbachev's resignation on December 25 and the Alma-Ata Declaration clearly placed key nuclear responsibilities in Boris Yeltsin's hands.

Issues concerning nuclear weapons are of continuing significance. Not only have nuclear weapons held a brooding dominance over U.S.–Soviet relations since the late 1940s but they remain an essential currency of superpower status. Fears of surprise attack in the past generated advanced states of alert for nuclear forces and caused the KGB and its military intelligence counterpart—the GRU (Main Intelligence Directorate, or *Glavnoe razvedyvatel'noe upravlenie*)—to report every two weeks from their worldwide stations the intent and actual preparations for a NATO/U.S. surprise strike. This highly secret program, begun in 1981, was abolished in November 1991.[18]

Nuclear weapons and economic and military issues required further elaboration. Yeltsin, in reviewing the historic Commonwealth agreement, denied any intention to reestablish a strong center, in Minsk or elsewhere. To Yeltsin, "Such a center, which could command every step of ours, doesn't exist and won't, that is why this appeals to all the republics."[19] The Russian president also pledged that Gorbachev would have a dignified retirement and announced that Russia's membership in NATO was a long-term goal.[20]

Gorbachev did not believe a fragmented Soviet Union would necessarily advance the cause of peace. "I don't think the transformation will be easy and simple from one partner, the Soviet Union and its leadership. Now you have to deal with 10 new politicians."[21]

Gorbachev's growing irrelevance to the new Commonwealth led him to resign on December 25, passing the briefcase containing the nuclear release codes to his successor, Boris Yeltsin. Some thirty-three minutes later, the Russian flag was raised over the Kremlin, symbolizing the death of the Soviet Union. Moscow's evening news broadcast announced the epochal event to a stunned audience: "The flag of Russia has been raised over the Kremlin. Today, it's a new day, a new state. We meet it with hope and God forbid that the sad errors of our history are repeated."[22]

Pravda observed that Gorbachev had left "an indelible mark on the annals of our society and the whole world," and *Nezavisimaya gazeta* called him "one of the key historic figures of the twentieth century and the most outstanding political leader that has ever emerged on the territory of the Soviet Union."[23]

President George Bush commemorated the event in a rare Christmas Night national television address. Bush praised Gorbachev for his "sustained commitment to world peace" and described the Soviet Union's transformation as "one of the greatest dramas of the twentieth century." He then granted diplomatic recognition as "independent states" to Russia, led by its "courageous President Boris Yeltsin," and five other republics, promising to do the same for the six remaining republics pending assurances concerning treaty compliance and democratic principles.[24]

Nonetheless, the newly created Commonwealth of Independent States was but a shell, a framework within which much substance had to be agreed upon. To address specific concerns that the original agreement did not consider, leaders of the eleven republics of the Commonwealth met on December 30, 1991, at Minsk. After difficult bargaining, it was agreed that strategic nuclear forces would remain under joint command, but individual states could form separate armies. In response to Russia's decision to decontrol most prices on January 2, 1992, Ukraine agreed to initiate a similar scheme to facilitate mutual trade.

The December 30 summit was also noteworthy for an agreement permitting individual states to create separate armed forces and to form joint armed forces and border guards subject to further discussions. Another agreement stipulated that two interstate and intergovernmental bodies would be created to coordinate Commonwealth activities. First was the Council of Heads of State, to be the supreme body at the head of state level; second was the Council of Heads of Government, consisting of each state's senior governmental executive. The Council of Heads of State will meet at least semiannually, while the Council of Heads of Government is to meet not less than every three months. In both bodies each state has one vote, meetings will be chaired in turn according to the states' alphabetical order, decisions are by consensus, and the working language is Russian. In addition, both councils may meet jointly and may establish permanent and temporary working groups.[25]

Military issues have thus far been the most contentious, with several states asserting their right, as provided in the December 30 summit agreement, to form separate armies. Russia's decision on May 7, 1992, to create a Russian army confirmed this trend and, in time, this may represent the decisive stroke cementing the CIS armed forces' irrelevance and ultimate dissolution.

The ownership of military equipment and facilities located in each republic continues to be a subject of contention, as the following chapters recount. Such claims have the potential to create nearly instant republic armies while dismembering the CIS army in the process. Ukraine has mounted a campaign to keep assets of the former Soviet state out of Russia's hands, arguing that all Soviet successor states are entitled to their fair share. As Belarus President Stanislav Shushkevich observed, "It's not easy to take apart one structure and build new ones."[26] This eventually resulted in a division of the USSR's foreign property among the former republics: 61 percent to Russia, 16 percent to Ukraine, 4 percent to Belarus, and 1.0–1.5 percent to the remaining Commonwealth states.[27]

The composition of the CIS itself has reflected the turmoil and uncertainties associated with fundamental systemic change. The Republic of Georgia did not sign the Alma-Ata agreement, yet it has continued to be represented at most CIS meetings. Azerbaijan and Moldova signed the Alma-Ata document, though their formal membership was subject to ratification by the republics' parliaments. Both governments have sent representatives to most CIS conferences and summit meetings. Nevertheless, Azerbaijan's parliament voted on October 7, 1992, against joining the CIS, bringing the organization to ten members. Moldova's final decision is pending. The resultant difficult days and issues must not conceal the central event of 1991 and probably of the twentieth century: the Commonwealth of Independent States has been formed and the Soviet Union ceased to exist. This is the new Eurasian reality with which the West and the rest of the world must deal.

THE FUTURE OF THE COMMONWEALTH OF INDEPENDENT STATES

Six themes permeate the historic record surrounding the early days of the Commonwealth of Independent States. These themes appear in the descriptions of the new countries that constitute the core of this volume. More significantly, they provide useful indicators of the future of the Commonwealth, where centripetal and centrifugal forces repeatedly conflict as the parameters of Commonwealth responsibilities and functions are better defined. In seeking to discern the future of the Commonwealth of Independent States, six themes are crucial to its eventual survival or dissolution.

1. Armed Forces/Security Issues: Perhaps the most immediate consideration for the leaders of Commonwealth countries has been the military establishment. Going from what was the largest army in the world to a host of disputes on all dimensions of military affairs has added an element of discord that seriously clouds the future of the CIS. It has raised questions concerning the composition, location, and purpose of the CIS armed forces; the command of those forces; the formation of national armies within individual member states; and intelligence operations.

Marshal of Aviation Yevgeny Shaposhnikov, commander of the Commonwealth armed forces, is confronting challenges that would test the abilities of any military leader. With Russia, Belarus, Azerbaijan, Moldova, Ukraine, and other states already forming national armies, only Russia and the Central Asian states appear firmly committed to continuing the existence of military forces serving the ten-member CIS. The republics' military and security positions have left the CIS army with little room to maneuver as new countries claim ownership of the forces and equipment of the Soviet army based on their soil. Beyond this, certain cities are trying to sell military equipment, with Omsk offering tanks and other weapons for sale as scrap and Ulyanovsk selling four mammoth An–124 transport aircraft.[28]

Marshal Shaposhnikov decried this trend in an April 1992 speech, saying that military capabilities had suffered "severe damage," funding had fallen to a record low level, small arms were being stolen, and military assets were being proffered for "self-enrichment."[29] Some three hundred thousand military families lack housing, and some military units have not been paid for months. It is little wonder that draft-dodging and desertion are rife.[30] Such upheaval has led some authorities to predict that a social explosion is in the making: "You've got the chaos already and the civil war is coming."[31]

The Soviet army has become a Commonwealth army without a state. Leonid Kravchuk, Ukraine president, has asserted that only "strategic" forces remain with the Commonwealth. "Strategic," in this view, involves only strategic nuclear forces; hence, all ground and other military forces on Ukrainian soil are considered the property of Ukraine. More than half of the seven hundred thousand servicemen manning the twenty divisions of the former Soviet army in Ukraine have taken a loyalty oath to Ukraine, and the ownership of air force and navy assets is in dispute.[32]

To prevent Ukraine's seizure of the Black Sea fleet, the carrier *Kuznetsov* was moved to Murmansk in December 1991. The fleet itself was seized by Boris Yeltsin in April 1992, in the name of the Russian Federation, to prevent its possession and possible sale by Ukrainian authorities. The issue of the Black Sea Fleet, first formed in 1783 by Catherine the Great, is inexorably connected with the ownership of the Crimean peninsula, also disputed by

Russia and Ukraine. A joint commission established to resolve the Black Sea fleet question reached no conclusion. Finally, the Russian and Ukrainian leaders settled the issue themselves by agreeing to joint control until 1995, when two separate fleets will be formed.

The ownership of former Soviet army units is being resolved on a case-by-case basis. Those units beyond the borders of Russia and not claimed by the CIS or by individual republics as a part of their separate armed forces have been claimed by the Russian Federation. According to Army General Pavel Grachev, Russia's defense minister and commander of the new Russian army, bilateral agreements will define the status of Russian troops located in the Transcaucasus and Central Asia.[33]

The status of CIS strategic, general purpose, and border forces was addressed in separate documents. Because of the vital nature of their duties, the strategic forces were the early focus. At the December 30, 1991, Minsk summit, an agreement was signed by the CIS heads of state that provided for the control and maintenance of the former Soviet strategic nuclear arsenal. Command of nuclear weapons was vested in the leaders of those states possessing them—Russia, Belarus, Ukraine, and Kazakhstan—within a joint military command. Commonwealth states pledged to observe all international agreements and to coordinate international arms control policies. In addition, tactical nuclear weapons in Kazakhstan, Ukraine, and Belarus were to be brought to Russia for dismantling by July 1, 1992.[34]

The CIS summit meeting in Minsk on February 14 further confirmed the intention of the heads of states to maintain strategic nuclear forces under joint command. They also agreed to abide by the Conventional Forces in Europe Treaty (CFE) and the Strategic Arms Reduction Treaty (START) previously signed by the Soviet Union. Marshal Yevgeny Shaposhnikov, the USSR's last minister of defense and interim commander of CIS forces, was appointed Commander-in-Chief of the CIS Joint Armed Forces. A general forces agreement was also concluded and signed by eight states—Ukraine, Azerbaijan, and Moldova did not want to imperil the status of their separate armies.

At the March 20 CIS summit in Kiev, a Joint Command of the Border Troops was established by a formal protocol signed by five states. It provided that those states forming separate border forces could participate in the CIS command by separate agreement. A CIS peacekeeping group was also created, to help member states resolve domestic disputes as well as to participate in international peacekeeping operations of the Conference on Security and Cooperation in Europe (CSCE) and the United Nations. This meeting saw agreement on the allocation of draft quotas for CIS member states and the appointment of three senior officers to serve as chief of staff and as commanders of strategic and general purpose forces of the CIS Joint Armed Forces.

Intelligence matters involving the Commonwealth of Independent States were addressed at an April 1992 session of the heads of the intelligence services of ten of the then eleven CIS states. Azerbaijan was not represented because of unrest in the republic, and Ukraine and Armenia abstained from signing the conference document because of their requirements for parliamentary authorization. The eight signatories pledged to refrain from conducting intelligence activities against CIS states. The agreement established a council of intelligence chiefs that will meet every three months, and it provided for intelligence sharing and cooperation among CIS states.[35]

The changing nature of the threat posed to CIS member states was the focus of the May 15, 1992, heads of state and heads of government summit at Tashkent. Described as the "most efficient and productive of all six summits that have been held,"[36] this session was attended by six heads of state and representatives from the other five member states. Georgia's prime minister, Tenghiz Sigua, was present as an observer.

The major result of the Tashkent summit was a collective security treaty signed by Russia, Kazakhstan, Uzbekistan, Kyrgyzstan, Armenia, and Tajikistan; other member states may join later. It went beyond the Kiev summit's agreement to form a CIS peacekeeping group by establishing a defensive alliance with a governing council for the purpose of collective protection. The pact pledged that member states would come to the aid of one another if attacked, a promise that one source termed a "tacit acknowledgment of the formation of separate armies by many states, including Russia and Ukraine."[37] It would also legitimize the stationing of Russian troops in the other republics and eventually provide a broader purpose for Russia's nuclear arms. Official statutes for the pact were later approved at the October 1992 CIS summit at Bishkek.

Ukraine was represented by Prime Minister Vitold Fokin, who said his government did not support the agreement because it did not specify the external threat the pact was directed against, and other problems were covered by existing agreements.[38] To Marshal Shaposhnikov, the general Ukrainian attitude was further evidence that it had joined the CIS solely "to bury the USSR as soon as possible, and to eventually bury the CIS itself."[39]

The Treaty on Collective Security established a Collective Security Council composed of the heads of state of signatory countries and the commander-in-chief of the CIS Joint Armed Forces. As a defensive alliance, any real or perceived aggression against a member state is considered to be aggression against all, consistent with Article 51 of the United Nations Charter. The treaty confirmed the signatories' commitment to refrain from the use of force or threatened force, and it promised that all conflicts among them and with other states would be resolved peacefully. In a tacit acknowledgment that the treaty will have a broader application than to the six new states, Article 1 observed that, should a system of collective security embracing all of Europe and Asia transpire, "for which the contracting parties will strive unswervingly," the signatories will take immediate steps to alter the treaty to accommodate the broader agreement.[40]

This action was significant to Marshal Shaposhnikov, who viewed the treaty as the basis of a permanent military alliance: "Due to the military union we have an additional chance to put an end to the process of general disintegration of the former USSR."[41] Shaposhnikov was more specific in a September 30, 1992, *Krasnaya zvezda* (Red Star) article: "Now there is a desire to create a new union on the basis of the Islamic factor in the South, incorporating the Central Asian states in the CIS. This could result in a new line of global confrontation on a 'North-South' axis. A system of collective security for the Commonwealth states could act as a stabilizing counterweight, and kind of balance to these and other systems."[42]

Efforts to create a more effective CIS political-military alliance also reflect the practical realities of the former Soviet military-industrial complex, which was a highly developed, integrated system of research institutes and manufacturing plants employing the nation's top scientists and engineers. This network, the most successful industrial undertaking of the former USSR, produced the Buran space shuttle, the SS-24 rail mobile ballistic missile, and other advanced military-space items. Its integrated nature was destroyed by the death of the Soviet Union, where, for example, fourteen factories manufactured components for self-propelled howitzers but twelve of them were in Russia and the remaining two were in Georgia and Kazakhstan. Shaposhnikov is well aware that the strategic reality of the new Eurasia requires a new approach to national security issues: "Geostrategic interests of all the CIS member states are so closely related that it would simply be foolish to disjoin them. National security of every state is part of the common geostrategic security of the CIS."[43]

Beyond this collective security treaty, a protocol governing the use of CIS multinational peacekeeping forces in "zones of interethnic conflict" was signed at Tashkent on July 16, 1992. This protocol would permit the introduction of CIS peacekeeping forces upon the consensus of the CIS Council of Heads of State, at the request of one or more CIS member states, and with the consent of the parties engaged in the conflict. The UN Security Council and the chair of the CSCE will be notified if a peacekeeping operation is approved, and possible tasks include establishing separation zones, demilitarized zones, and humanitarian corridors.[44] This permanent force, based on the UN "blue helmets," would separate warring elements, particularly the numerous violent ethnic conflicts on Russia's periphery. Russian nationalists, including Vice President Alexander Rutskoi, have pressured Boris Yeltsin to protect the 25 million–strong ethnic Russian communities living in other republics who have been threatened by ongoing ethnic disputes. This agreement enables Yeltsin to act collectively to restore the peace without raising the specter of intervention by Moscow alone.[45]

The brunt of the peacekeeping operations thus far has fallen upon the

Russian Federation. A battalion of Russian paratroopers has been deployed to support UN peacekeepers in Bosnia-Herzegovina; two ships from Russia's Pacific Fleet have sailed to the Indian Ocean to support multinational peacekeeping in the Persian Gulf; and Russian troops have been deployed in Georgia, Moldova, Tajikistan, and other new states to stem ethnic conflict. A motorized rifle division from Russia's Volga Military District has been reconfigured for what is termed "peacemaking." It is equipped with only small arms and armored personnel carriers, and has no artillery, tanks, or antiaircraft weapons. These Russian "blue helmets" are also receiving special training. To Colonel General Viktor Dubynin, chief of the General Staff, true CIS peacemaking forces must be multinational joint forces with invited participants from non-CIS countries as well. Because Russia has been the predominant contributor to these forces, the financial burden has been significant.[46]

Concern that the former USSR may fall victim to a "Lebanonization" or "Yugoslavization" has led Boris Yeltsin to pay this price, however, at a time when the Russian Federation is confronted with many other problems. To Yelena Bonner, widow of Andrei Sakharov and a human rights activist, the danger is that Russian peacekeeping troops may end up taking sides in a dispute.[47] Deputy Foreign Minister Fyodor Shelov-Kovedayev, the chief Russian diplomat responsible for relations with CIS states, has suggested a more practical reason for Russia's active peacekeeping role: "Following the disintegration of the former Soviet Union, Russia is the only state that has a smoothly running military structure. Therefore, whenever there are conflicts, the only place to look is to Russia." As a consequence, some 13,224 Russian "blue helmets" were performing peacekeeping duties as of January 1993.[48]

Peacekeeping may yet prove to be the most pressing, but also the most valuable, contribution of the CIS Joint Armed Forces. Russia's leading role could diminish over time as the structure matures and takes on an independent existence. On the other hand, the growing independence of many new states and their own nascent military structures could make the CIS Joint Armed Forces irrelevant, particularly when Russia becomes the sole post-Soviet nuclear power, de jure and de facto, in the year 2000.

The CIS is in transition as its member states adjust to the new reality of independence; it is to be expected that its military organizations reflect that uncertainty and change. Russia's acting prime minister, Yegor Gaidar, addressed this issue in a July 13, 1992 interview: "I would make forecasts with caution. It is inevitable that the CIS will have different forms of membership and some states will be interested in forming a viable system of coordination, largely of the confederation type."[49]

In the meantime, the CIS military structure is taking on more definite forms. A CIS High Command, led by Marshal of Aviation Yevgeny Shaposhnikov, commander in chief of the CIS armed forces, has been created to oversee CIS strategic and general purpose forces. Shaposhnikov is assisted by military representatives from the CIS states, who have been designated deputy chiefs of staff of the Joint Armed Forces. Strategic forces include the former Soviet Strategic Rocket Forces and those portions of the former Soviet air force, navy, air defense, and space forces having strategic responsibilities, particularly with regard to nuclear operations. General purpose forces are those troop formations, facilities, and military schools still under CIS jurisdiction as well as those national forces under CIS operational control. A Joint Armed Forces Staff controls operations, intelligence, communications, transportation, and logistics functions under the CIS High Command, which is responsible for the centralized command and control of all CIS forces.[50]

In the absence of true CIS military formations, these forces are essentially Russian forces with CIS oversight; the participation of other national armies is anticipated, once a joint military doctrine has been agreed upon and they are authorized to do so by their parliaments.

The CIS military organization is part of a still-evolving CIS political framework. The CIS Council of Heads of State is responsible for overall military policy, including nuclear strategy, military doctrine, and collective security. It is supported by the CIS Council of Heads of Government, which coordinates military and military-industrial activities, while the CIS Defense Ministers Council addresses issues of military structures and organization. The CIS Joint Armed Forces High Command is responsible for implementing the decisions of these more senior bodies. A lesser-known function of the High Command is the assistance it renders to member states in organizing and developing their own national armies.[51]

2. Nuclear Arms: The December 21, 1991, Alma-Ata declaration that formed the Commonwealth of Independent States included a pledge to eliminate all nuclear arms as well as to adhere to nuclear nonproliferation agreements. It reiterated the former Soviet Union's pledge against the first use of nuclear weapons, and promised to withdraw the three thousand tactical nuclear weapons from Ukraine, Belarus, and Kazakhstan by July 1, 1992. These pledges served as a sound basis upon which the partial denuclearization of the former Soviet Union would proceed. The significance of these initial commitments became more appreciated when the consolidation of all tactical nuclear weapons within Russia occurred as scheduled.

Some twelve thousand strategic nuclear warheads now remain to be demobilized. This is integral to the Strategic Arms Reduction Treaty (START I), which was signed by presidents Bush and Gorbachev in Moscow in July 1991 and ratified by the U.S. Senate on October 1, 1992. START I would bring the United States and the former Soviet Union down to 8,556 and 6,163 warheads, respectively, by the year 2000. In September 1991, President Bush announced a unilateral elimination of tactical warheads, which was followed by additional proposals by President Gorbachev in October.

Of significance to the strategic equation, however, was President Bush's January 1992 State of the Union Address, which proposed the deepest cuts of strategic nuclear weapons thus far. The president would reduce arsenals by approximately half, with 4,400 strategic warheads and bombs for the former Soviet Union and 4,700 for the United States. During his February visit to the United States, Boris Yeltsin offered to reduce these weapons to 2,500 and announced that U.S. cities and military facilities were no longer nuclear targets. While Bush proposed eliminating land-based multiple independently targeted reentry vehicles (MIRVs), Moscow authorities want to eliminate all MIRVed weapons. Yeltsin also suggested that the United States and Russia cooperate to construct a global Strategic Defense Initiative.[52]

Other efforts to contain nuclear weapons technology included a German proposal to create an international center to employ former Soviet nuclear scientists in more peaceful undertakings. This international center, first suggested at the January 1992 Washington conference on aid to the former Soviet Union, would receive $25 million in U.S. funds, as well as support from Japan and the European Community's European Commission.[53]

Further progress occurred in April 1992, when the Bush administration certified to Congress that U.S. funds to finance the denuclearization of the former USSR were available to three of the four nuclear states. Russia, Ukraine, and Belarus would receive the first portion of some $400 million appropriated by Congress in 1991 for that purpose because of their progress in human rights and compliance with existing arms control agreements. Kazakhstan, with some 1,410 warheads, would become eligible for the funds upon signing the Nuclear Nonproliferation Treaty, in effect promising to be a nonnuclear weapons state.[54]

The critical element in any program to denuclearize the former Soviet Union is the fact that strategic weapons are currently based in four former republics—Russia, Kazakhstan, Ukraine, and Belarus—where they will remain for some time to come. Despite some reticence by Ukraine in delivering its tactical warheads to Russia, the decision to consolidate tactical warheads within the Russian Federation for eventual disassembly and control made the issue of strategic warheads more pressing.

On May 23, 1992, this ambiguity was resolved in an arms reduction accord of great consequence. In Lisbon, the new states of Ukraine, Kazakhstan, and Belarus agreed to turn over these weapons to Russia by the end of the decade in a special protocol to the 1991 START treaty. When ratified this agreement will remove a major obstacle to the ratification of START, and it will also initiate further deep strategic arms reductions already agreed to in principle.[55] The four republics—including Kazakhstan—also agreed to formally abide by the 1968 Nonproliferation Treaty.[56]

The June 1992 Washington summit provided even greater progress in reducing U.S.–Russian nuclear arsenals. In a document of historic proportions, both nations' presidents agreed to reduce their nuclear warheads to 3,000 for Russia and 3,500 for the United States, and restrictions were imposed on multiple-warhead weapons. Yeltsin agreed to eliminate all ten-warhead SS–18s, the world's most powerful ballistic missiles, and take them off active status immediately, and Bush agreed to reduce U.S. submarine-launched missiles by half. These new limits reduced current inventories by two-thirds. Granting Russia most-favored-trading status for the first time in over forty years somehow seemed a minor concession in this strategic context.[57]

This agreement was codified by START II, which was signed by President Bush and President Yeltsin in Moscow on January 3, 1993. Boris Yeltsin called it "the treaty of the century" and promised that Russian security was not compromised: "As president and commander in chief, I can state with complete certainty that the document we have just signed will strengthen—not weaken—the security of Russia."[58] START II reductions would be achieved by Russia and the United States no later than December 31, 2003. It cannot enter into force until the Lisbon protocol to START I is ratified by all signatories, and Yeltsin himself may face opposition from the Russian parliament during START II's ratification. Nonetheless, the START II agreement brings arms control and Russian–American cooperation to new heights.

While much remains to be done to carry out the terms of the START and other agreements once formal ratification occurs, the act of reducing nuclear weapons and limiting them to two states is an advance of historic proportions. The year 2003 may find reduced arsenals of nuclear weapons held in a purely reserve retaliatory posture. The threat against which they are directed, however, remains far from clear, and the enduring legacy of distrust is still pervasive.

Reflecting on the historic turning point presented by reductions in strategic arms, Russia's Foreign Minister Andrei Kozyrev observed in June 1992 that the real issue is "how we dismantle this war machine that has been created over the past 40 years . . . not to strike the right balance of mutual threats but rather to find a technically and economically feasible way of destroying the arsenals we already have."[59] This development is a major watershed in reducing one type of weaponry, although other technologically advanced weapons lie just ahead.

While the world may rejoice that these weapons will now be consolidated in two principal nuclear weapons states—the United States and Russia—will Russia's monopoly of this most lethal of weaponry sufficiently stabilize and reassure the other members of the CIS and nonmembers Azerbaijan and Georgia? As the new states of the former Soviet Union race to develop armies in perpetuation of past patterns of investment and priority given to all things military, the CIS armed forces will command less attention and concern. Russia alone will continue to possess this currency of superpower status, and this overshadowing concern will have an imperceptible yet pervasive influence on its interaction with the other new states of Eurasia.

3. Economic Challenges: Among the issues confronting the CIS and its member states, perhaps none are as intractable as basic economic challenges. This does not ignore the fundamental political changes that must be initiated, adjusted to national conditions, and institutionalized. A viable economy is basic to success in all other endeavors. As the experience of the former Communist states of Eastern Europe testifies, there is no easy or sure method of replacing a centrally controlled command economy with a market economy based upon private enterprise.

This issue is further burdened by the necessity of cleaning up the debris left by the former Communist system, including vastly underfunded human services in health, education, and social programs; ecological devastation on a scale and of a dimension unimaginable by most; a defense infrastructure of research institutes, factories, secret installations, and schools; and a legacy of security imperatives typical of inherently insecure regimes: informant nets, tapped telephones, civil and human rights abuses, and gross injustice. While no political-social system is perfect, the substantial debris of Communist regimes will take years to overcome.

The external debt of the former Soviet Union is as much as $81 billion, mostly owed to European banks. This problem was addressed at the March 20, 1992, CIS summit in Kiev, where the member states formally acknowledged their collective responsibility for the Soviet Union's debt. A commission to study ways to resolve this problem was established in an action approved by all states except Turkmenistan.[60] When the issue was raised again at the May 15 Tashkent summit, participants complained that the resulting documents were "too complicated and poorly prepared." Staff specialists were instructed to prepare further studies for consideration by the leaders.[61]

Reorganizing the national economies of CIS states has been viewed as the supreme test of Western democracy: "It is one of the century's great turning points, and if the U.S. is to prove itself a superpower in more than military terms, it must meet the challenge with the full commitment it deserves."[62] According to one senior World Bank official, "This is the most difficult economic reconstruction job in the history of the world."[63] To the International Monetary Fund (IMF), "The magnitude of the problems facing the 15 republics is unprecedented. They go far beyond what is generally understood by the concept of economic transformation. These peoples are creating new nations, from scratch and in a very brief period."[64]

A major bellwether of the CIS's viability will be the extent to which the national economies interact. This is fundamentally the current choice facing European Community members: to perpetuate artificial barriers to free trade or to develop an integrated structure that will foster interaction and mutual prosperity.

For Russia and other CIS states, this means the development of complementary monetary, trade, taxation, and customs policies. For some states this may be easier than for others. In Turkmenistan, for example, total economic turnover in terms of imports and exports accounts for more than 75 percent of its total output; for Armenia, over 55 percent; for Estonia and Moldova, over 50 percent; for Latvia, Lithuania, Belarus, Tajikistan, Kyrgyzstan, and Azerbaijan, over 40 percent; for Ukraine and Kazakhstan, over 35 percent; and for Russia, less than 20 percent.[65] The higher the percentage of interrepublic trade, the more dependent each new state will be on its continuance; those with lower figures are more self-sufficient and, implicitly, less driven by trade considerations alone.

The IMF has been the major international institution aiding the former USSR's transition to market economics. Intent on reforming and stabilizing the new countries' economies to facilitate growth without inflation, it uses loans and technical advice as its primary instruments.[66] Its estimate of external assistance required by the fifteen former Soviet republics for 1992 alone was $24 billion for the 150 million people of Russia and $20 billion for the 147 million people of the other fourteen republics. A total of more than $100 billion would be needed through 1996, it estimated.[67]

The former republics moved much closer to economic reform when they joined the IMF on April 27, 1992. All new states except Azerbaijan (because of a paperwork delay and internal turmoil) were welcomed by the 156 members. The price of this move will be substantial, since the IMF established as prerequisites a series of sweeping reforms, among them removing price controls, reducing budget deficits, and reducing state subsidies. Yegor Gaidar, who represented Russia in the negotiations, described the required economic transformation as "a slow process, a process that is politically difficult, socially depressing."[68] IMF membership will begin the flow of most aid offered by the Group of Seven industrialized nations (France, the United Kingdom, Canada, the United States, Germany, Italy, and Japan), the World Bank, and the IMF itself.

Nowhere is the economic transition more critical than in Russia. Formerly the central cog in a vast mechanism of central planning, resource allocation, tax collection, and state expenditures, it must now endure the transition along with other former union republics. Despite inflation of 10 percent per week and an average monthly salary of 13,000 rubles,[69] IMF austerity proposals and debt repayment plans have been relaxed at Boris Yeltsin's insistence, and, as a result, Russia did not receive all of the $24 billion promised for 1992.[70]

Compounding this situation, the printing of 142 billion new rubles in July 1992—some 2.5 times the amount printed in May 1992—will produce what one Soviet newspaper termed "ferocious hyperinflation."[71] This led

Yegor Gaidar, elevated to acting prime minister, to warn the Russian parliament on July 1, 1992: "We have begun to allow ourselves to spend more than we can afford."[72]

Russia's Central Bank, controlled by the parliament rather than by President Yeltsin, has worsened the problem by issuing excessive credits to state enterprises. This has led some Russian economists to predict a monthly inflation rate as high as 60 percent. The ruble, weakened as a result, lost nearly one-half of its value in eight weeks, reaching a record low of 342 rubles to the dollar on October 6, and then falling to 660 rubles by mid-February, 1993. The end is not yet in sight.[73]

The fate of the ruble is connected to efforts to preserve the "ruble zone," in which CIS members continue mutual trade and commerce based on the common ruble. This prospect has been dimmed by the introduction of new currencies by some CIS states as well as by the explosion of printed money and credit offered by Moscow's Central Bank to the former republics. The monetary union based on the ruble is also jeopardized by the republic's central banks, which issue ruble credits to state enterprises located within their new state borders. The result has been the development of "Kazakh ruble" credit vouchers, which have a different value from "Ukraine rubles," and so forth. Since August 1992, these national rubles may only be used for trade within the issuing states, while trade with other republics is done in their ruble credits. A market has developed so that companies can buy the Belarus or Tajik rubles they need, but those republics with large trade deficits, particularly those dependent on Russia's oil and gas, are at a distinct disadvantage. To ease this pressure, in August 1992 Moscow's central bank increased the issuance of credits to other republics at the rate of 10 percent of the federation's monthly gross domestic product, which is fueling inflation and speeding the ruble's decline.[74]

Efforts to preserve a ruble zone, however, received new impetus at the October 9, 1992, CIS summit at Bishkek. A single monetary system for commercial purposes was agreed upon by Russia, Kazakhstan, Belarus, Uzbekistan, Kyrgyzstan, and Armenia. Representatives of three new states—Turkmenistan, Tajikistan, and Moldova—expressed interest in the concept but had to receive parliamentary approval before joining the coordination body. The prospect of additional participation in joint economic activity was reflected by the fact that other national currencies would be accepted in addition to the ruble. A common bank was also formed for the purpose of resolving economic disputes. According to Moscow's Central Bank chairman, the bank may eventually become a central bank, with currency-issuing and -regulating authority.[75] Increased economic cooperation among CIS member states may enhance the long-term effectiveness and viability of the CIS, particularly in areas beyond military matters.

The ability of Boris Yeltsin and other post-Soviet leaders to accommodate economic change at a time of social unrest and rising expectations is fundamental not only to their political survival but also to the survival of the new democratically based political structures they head.

4. Nationalism: If the former Soviet Union was the largest country in the world in terms of geographic size, it was also the globe's largest multiethnic country. Its legacy as a multiethnic state is derived from the collapse of the Ottoman, Austro-Hungarian, and Russian empires, which used various means to pacify and placate the highly disparate peoples living within their borders. The tsarist empire was based on Orthodoxy, a common Greek religious heritage; autocracy, the rule of the tsar over all peoples and territories; and nationality, the idea that Russians had a historic destiny to fulfill. As the chosen people, Russian rule over Slavs and non-Slavs would bring both religion and enlightenment to the empire.[76]

The disintegration of the Russian empire during World War I and the rise and consolidation of power by the Bolsheviks led to a superficial recognition of national differences. Following the suppression of a series of national independence movements by non-Russian peoples, the nationality problem was concealed by designating certain territories for the major national groups. Some twenty-two of the more than one hundred nationalities in the former Soviet Union number one million or more, and fifteen of them were given union republic or titular status. The thirty-four smaller nationalities had autonomous territorial entities named after them. Boundaries often separated similar peoples, and approximately 75 million people belong to groups that received no recognition at all. This "patchwork quilt of scattered peoples" accounts for the ethnic problems inherited by the new Eurasian states.[77]

The advent of the Soviet empire was supported by three central pillars: ideology, dictatorship, and nationalism. In the process of creating a new country on an entirely new social basis, the Communist leaders allowed the Baltic states to become independent. Other noncooperative national groups, like the Georgians and the Ukrainians, were suppressed, sometimes with a great loss of life. Russian nationalism again asserted itself after World War II, when conquered territories were occupied and their inhabitants incorporated into the mosaic of Soviet peoples. This resulted in the annexation of western Ukraine and Belorussia, southern Sakhalin and the Kuriles, and the Baltic states, along with efforts to retain northern Iran.[78]

This policy appeared successful when the domestic economy was strong. However, the legion of systemic inadequacies faced by Soviet leaders in the 1980s revealed that the forcible incorporation of diverse peoples, compounded by numerous deportations to areas far from traditional homelands during World War II, was counterproductive. Because the USSR's constitution guaranteed the independence of constituent republics—a promise with no serious basis—this independence paradoxically became an ultimate objective, with many lesser known areas and peoples clamoring for autonomy as well.

The Marxist–Leninist interpretation of what was to become of national groups failed as well. This ideological justification emphasized the international role of the proletariat, in which class distinctions were determinative. In reality, it led to policies that were distinctly antinationalist, even as the universalist ideal was repeatedly frustrated. Stalin's construction of "socialism in one country" painted the picture of voluntary unification, pretending the diverse nations and peoples had shared a common country in the tsarist past. Instead, the privileged position went to Russian nationalism as the cement by which national aspirations of other peoples were concealed. In this sense, the Russians owned the empire, and the non-Russian nationalities bore the brunt of Russian statism and its effects on language, culture, and social mobility.[79]

In many respects, early Soviet policies contributed to the virulence with which the ethnic issue has now arisen from the old union's ashes. Soviet authorities supported nation building, adding demographic and political coherence to disparate ethnic groups. They also territorialized many groups, giving them a homeland more extensive than their traditional villages, fixing the peoples to specific terrain. The seeds for later challenges were sown by the essentially imperial nature of Moscow's dealings with its subordinate political units, and the attempted Russification of native peoples led to their determination to preserve their languages and customs. Traditional cultures survived, despite the uneven effects achieved by Soviet modernization practices. Moscow's failure to resolve the "national question" effectively made matters worse, leading to a nationalist resurgence at the very time the Soviet Union itself was growing weaker. The net effect was an ethnic challenge that Mikhail Gorbachev could resolve only by yielding to nationalist demands, further contributing to the center's demise.[80]

The phenomenon of "unassimilated bilingualism," in which Russian was used for official purposes but native languages dominated social and other discourse,[81] perhaps best illustrates the failure of Soviet nationality policy. The increased usage of native languages will further fuel separatist impulses in the new CIS states.

This dominant Russian role is now reflected in the concerns of non-Russian entities over military, nuclear, and economic issues. Despite the passing of the Soviet Union as the inheritor of over 360 years of Russian expansionism, the uneasy balance of national differences and tolerance will, to a large extent, determine the future of the CIS and new states of Eurasia. According to Alexandre Benningsen, Russia has never been a melting pot; its assimilation policy of some four hundred years has largely failed, with Muslims the least Russified of all peoples of the former USSR.[82]

What gives nationalism its potency in the current Eurasian context is its potential to tear apart existing political institutions. These institutions were largely inherited from the former Soviet Union and the reforms instituted by Mikhail Gorbachev. Many are fragile, representing transitory means and methods until the new Eurasian states achieve some sort of stasis.

Nationalism, as "the world's most common ideology,"[83] is the combination of group awareness and allegiance, and the will to protect that group from external challenges.[84] Today, both within and beyond Eurasia, "techniques of nationalist agitation" are dividing nations formed in the past by similar political activity. Characteristics such as class, religion, race, and language foster this new divisiveness.[85] The exploitation of these multiple factors serves to foster exclusivity and to enhance consciousness. According to Dov Ronen, "Ethnic groups are born and arise because of the perception of oppression; if there were no perception of oppression, real or imagined, there would be no ethnic self-determination."[86]

In a place like the former Soviet Union, the list of national grievances is legion; no authoritarian system exists without injustice and arbitrariness. This has led to a fissionlike process, an endless progression of groups and leaders asserting their right to nationhood and the attendant resources and power. As Arthur Waldron has observed, "Far from being a source of cohesion, nationalism becomes an important source of intrasocietal conflict; far from simplifying politics, it adds yet another dimension of complexity."[87]

The role of the new CIS structures is thus central to the brokering of interests that must occur both within and among the new states. The Soviet Union's former prime minister, Nikolai Ryzhkov, has declared that some sort of "center" is imperative, asserting that the new states "will not survive without a new center which would balance their interests." Otherwise, the CIS is a "stillborn child born during the night."[88] To Mikhail Gorbachev, "The greatest danger is separatism."[89]

Boris Yeltsin confronted this issue at the May 15, 1992, Tashkent summit, which saw agreement to create a Commonwealth collective security body. Bristling at suggestions that the old union could be revived in some form, he said that assembled leaders were "trying to make the CIS work." "It's stupid," he observed. "Who's going to do it? Russia? Ukraine? Would we be tied together with chains, with armed coercion? These times have passed absolutely."[90]

It is clear that the future of the new Eurasia is closely associated with the development of some widely accepted formula that supports the autonomy of national groups while preserving a larger political structure within which they can thrive and develop. Will the CIS evolve to such a structure?

5. International Support and Cooperation: A key factor in the survival of the new states is the extent to which they are integrated into global institutions. Organizations such as the World Bank (which is the lead agency for coordinating international aid to the new states), the United Nations, the IMF, and the Conference on Security and Cooperation in Europe (CSCE) will support the democratic transition and serve to control conflicts. In March 1992, the new states joined the other CSCE members in agreeing to confidence-building measures in the area of sharing military information and limiting major exercises involving more than 40,000 troops or 900 tanks to once every two years.[91]

Other factors favoring enhanced global integration include Ukraine's and Russia's application to join the Council of Europe, participation by the former Soviet republics in NATO's North Atlantic Cooperation Council, and plans for joint East–West military training programs. In April, the CIS selected a battalion of Russian airborne troops to participate in UN peace-keeping efforts in Yugoslavia. This marks the first time a Russian military unit has participated in UN peacekeeping operations.[92]

In June 1992, Russia and seven other former Soviet states signed the Conventional Armed Forces in Europe accord, which reduces artillery, tanks, and other military hardware across the face of Europe. Originally signed by NATO's sixteen members and the seven member states of the Warsaw Pact in November 1990, this revalidation of intent and purpose has reallocated the reduction of some 30,000 weapons among the new countries. Now that revised figures have been agreed upon, implementation of the treaty, with its extensive inspection regime, can begin.[93]

In July 1992 a CSCE accord limited troops in many European countries except Moldova, Armenia, and Azerbaijan, which did not participate. For Russia the limit is 1,450,000, and for Ukraine the maximum is 450,000. The agreement covers political intent rather than strict legality, which would necessitate extensive verification measures. Nonetheless, it is an important advance over previous efforts to limit the size of ground forces in Europe.[94]

These agreements, and other gestures of good will, were largely responsible for the unprecedented assistance effort mounted by Western nations in 1992 to aid the new Eurasian states. In October 1992, the newly independent republics began to participate in the U.S. security assistance program of worldwide military and economic aid. This includes training foreign officers at U.S. military institutions, economic support funds to bolster the private-sector economies, foreign purchases of U.S. products, and technical and humanitarian assistance.[95] Senior Russian and Ukrainian officers, accompanied by their families, attended the U.S. Army War College in Carlisle, Pennsylvania, and other top U.S. military schools beginning in August 1992.

A key facet of any program to aid the former Soviet Union has to focus upon the dangers presented by outdated equipment and procedures associated with the country's nuclear power reactors. The former Soviet Union was the world's third-largest nuclear power generating nation, producing 13 percent of its electricity. Its forty-nine power reactors were located in Russia, Ukraine, Armenia, Kazakstan, and Lithuania, as well as additional reactors in Eastern Europe. Some twenty reactors in Russia, Ukraine, and Lithuania are RBMK (high power pressure tube) reactors of the Chernobyl type, which lack containment vessels to prevent radioactive emissions in case of an accident. Another ten first-generation VVER 440/230 (water cooled, water moderated) power reactors have no emergency or backup cooling systems. The RBMK and VVER 440/230 reactors have been judged deficient by current safety standards, and both Russian and U.S. specialists have called for their decommissioning.[96]

Many of the new states depend upon nuclear energy for much of their electricity requirements—Russia, 12 percent; Ukraine, 25 percent; and Lithuania, 45 percent[97]—and any loss of this generating capacity will be a hard blow to their struggling economies. At the same time, the combination of old technology and the absence of proper containment structures means that the protection of populations from a nuclear accident and upgrading plants and equipment are top priorities.

On May 23, 1992, the United States announced a $20 million plan to address this risk by providing technical assistance and creating regional training centers in Ukraine and Russia open to all fifteen former republics.[98] Other international assistance has also been promised.

Not only is an array of donor states now providing aid packages to address the entire spectrum of social and economic need for this vast territory, but this effort is being supplemented by private initiatives of churches, schools, sister cities, service clubs, and youth organizations worldwide. These people-to-people contacts are of fundamental importance and, in the end, may be more influential in shaping what evolves than the official desires of any foreign government.

Zbigniew Brzezinski has cautioned that Western aid programs must ensure that Russia and the other new states are not separated from the West by a *cordon sanitaire*. Instead, the West must support nation building in the new Eurasian states in such a manner that its social costs are not prohibitive, discrediting the ultimate objectives of democratic rule and market-based economies. The end of both the Russian empire and communism itself are truly historic goals. This can only take place "if the West again demonstrates strategic staying power, focused on clearheaded geopolitical—and not just on narrow socioeconomic or vaguely idealistic—aims."[99]

While many more newsworthy initiatives and crisis developments may transpire in the days ahead, the substance of programmatic efforts to aid the new countries remains crucial. Constructive assistance programs and the extent to which Russia and the other fourteen republics of the former Soviet Union are integrated into global organizations and forums will be very significant to the evolution of democratic institutions and market economies.

6. Differentiation: In fairness to the unique peoples occupying what had been the largest country in the world, other states, in their daily interaction with the new regimes, must differentiate one new state from another. This requires an appreciation of each new country's history, unique circumstances, peoples, languages, religions, cultures, and worldview. This volume is designed to convey basic knowledge in this regard, so that effective communications, policies, assistance programs, and interpersonal contacts can be undertaken.

The greatest danger in failing to differentiate each state from its fourteen brethren is a Russian-centric approach. As Turkish President Turgut Ozal told President Bush during his May 1992 state visit to Washington, failure to strengthen each state separately will create a new "center" to replace the former Soviet one. Should this occur, "Russia will pull them back as time passes."[100]

Undue emphasis on Russia could lead to a replication of large military forces and a repetition of past patterns emphasizing military programs at the expense of social ones within the other states. The former USSR cannot be treated like "Russia and branch offices." A warmer, more sensitive appreciation of each nation's independent status is required.[101] As the four nuclear republics consolidate their nuclear weapons within Russia, efforts must be made to ensure that Russia's monopoly is not used, symbolically or otherwise, to the detriment of the other new states, particularly in economic and political transactions.

If the end of the Cold War represented "a shattering of the vicious circle into which we had driven ourselves," as proclaimed by Mikhail Gorbachev at Westminster College on May 6, 1992,[102] it is now incumbent upon the global community to acknowledge the rich diversity emerging from seventy-four years of Communist obscurity. No humanitarian program, foreign policy, or social outreach effort will succeed if it fails to appreciate the distinct differences among the fifteen new states and their many peoples. This volume is dedicated to this goal.

REPUBLIC COMPARISONS BY SIZE AND POPULATION

The 1989 census revealed that while the former Soviet Union's total population increased by an average of just under 1 percent on an annual basis, the Muslim peoples of the Caucasus and Central Asia grew by approximately 2 percent annually. Their birthrates of roughly twice the national average stand in stark contrast with the Baltics, Moldova, Belarus, and Ukraine, where the population grew by 0.5 percent annually. At the same time, there had been an out-migration of Russians from Central Asia since the last census in 1979, representing a decline of from 2.5 percent to 4.4 percent. In the Baltic states, Russians increased between 0.5 and 2.4 percent. Overall, Slavic groups, which accounted for 69 percent of the Soviet population in 1989, could drop to 67 percent by 2000.[103]

The heterogeneous nature of the Soviet peoples may best be seen by

Republic	Titular Nationality (percent)	Russian (percent)	Other (percent)		Total (thous.)
Russia		82	Tatar	4	147,002
Estonia	62	30	Ukrainian	3	1,566
Latvia	52	34	Belorussian	5	2,667
Lithuania	80	9	Polish	7	3,673
Belarus	78	13	Polish	4	10,149
Ukraine	73	22	Jewish	1	51,449
Moldova	64	13	Ukrainian	14	4,332
Georgia	70	6	Armenian	8	5,396
Armenia	93	2	Azeri	3	3,304
Azerbaijan	83	6	Armenian	6	7,020
Kazakhstan	40	38	German	6	16,463
Turkmenis-tan	72	9	Uzbek	9	3,512
Tajikistan	62	8	Uzbek	24	5,090
Uzbekistan	71	8	Tajik	5	19,808
Kyrgyzstan	52	21	Uzbek	14	4,258

Republics, in Order

Size	*Population*
Russia	Russia
Kazakhstan	Ukraine
Ukraine	Uzbekistan
Turkmenistan	Kazakhstan
Uzbekistan	Belarus
Belarus	Azerbaijan
Kyrgyzstan	Tajikistan
Tajikistan	Georgia
Azerbaijan	Kyrgyzstan
Georgia	Moldova
Lithuania	Turkmenistan
Latvia	Lithuania
Estonia	Armenia
Moldova	Latvia
Armenia	Estonia

examining the composition of ethnic groups occupying the fifteen titular republics.[104]

NOTES

1. Leon P. Baradat, *Soviet Political Society* (Englewood Cliffs, N.J.: Prentice-Hall, 1986), 137. One authority has described this system as "pseudofederal": Ronald Grigor Suny, "The Soviet South: Nationalism and the Outside World," in *The Rise of Nations in the Soviet Union,* ed. Michael Mandelbaum (New York: Council on Foreign Relations Press, 1991), 66.

2. "Soviet Debt: A Surplus of Shambles," *The Economist,* November 23, 1991, 86, 88; Carey Goldberg, "Soviet Economy: Yeltsin Bankrolls Kremlin," *Harrisburg Sunday Patriot-News,* December 1, 1991, A1.

3. Francis X. Clines, "At Site of 'Iron Curtain' Speech, Gorbachev Buries the Cold War," *New York Times,* May 7, 1992, A14.

4. V. Gondusov, "V. Barannikov on Reforming the U.S.S.R. Ministry of Internal Affairs," *Krasnaya zvezda,* November 7, 1991, 3, in FBIS (Foreign Broadcast Information Service)-SOV–91–218, November 12, 1991, 18–19.

5. "Bakatin Remarks on 'Intelligence Agents,' " Moscow All-Union Radio First Program, Radio–1 Network, 1837 GMT, November 10, 1991, in FBIS-SOV–91–218, November 12, 1991, 18.

6. Justin Burke, "High Costs of Empire Sink Soviet Union," *Christian Science Monitor,* May 6, 1992, 7.

7. Justin Burke, "Jailed Conspirators Call Coup Attempt A 'Patriotic Act'," *Christian Science Monitor,* August 19, 1992, 9.

8. Laurie Hays and Elisabeth Rubinfien, "Gorbachev Struggles to Preserve Union," *Wall Street Journal,* December 10, 1991, A11.

9. Patrick E. Tyler, "U.S. Concerned That as the Union Breaks Up, So Does the Soviet Military," *New York Times,* December 10, 1991, A19.

10. Daniel Sneider, "Shevardnadze Is Back," *Christian Science Monitor,* November 21, 1991, A3.

11. Elisabeth Rubinfien, "Gorbachev, Fearing Wars and Loss of Rights, Makes Plea for Union," *Wall Street Journal,* December 4, 1991, A13; Michael Dobbs, "The Soviet Union, as We Long Knew It, Is Dead. What Next?" *Washington Post,* December 4, 1991, A27.

12. Elisabeth Rubinfien, "Russia, Ukraine, Byelorussia Establish Commonwealth," *Wall Street Journal,* December 9, 1991, A11.

13. Ibid.

14. Justin Burke, "Soviet Central Asians Weigh Status Outside Slav Commonwealth," *Christian Science Monitor,* December 12, 1991, 1, 2.

15. Daniel Sneider, "Russians Claim Soviet Mantle on Baker's Visit," *Christian Science Monitor,* December 18, 1991, 1, 2.

16. "Text of Accords by Former Soviet Republics Setting up a Commonwealth," *New York Times,* December 23, 1991, A10.

17. Daniel Sneider and Peter Grier, "Soviet Breakup Sharpens Doubts over Arms Control," *Christian Science Monitor,* December 10, 1991, 2.

18. A. Ivanko, "End of 'Surprise Nuclear Missile Attack.' Intelligence Chief Ye.

Primakov Abolishes One of the KGB's Most Secret Programs," *Izvestiya,* November 29, 1991, 1, 6, in FBIS-SOV–91–232, December 3, 1991, 36. See also David Thomas Twining, *Strategic Surprise in the Age of Glasnost* (New Brunswick, N.J.: Transaction, 1992).

19. Elisabeth Rubinfien, "Eleven Republics Lay U.S.S.R. to Rest," *Wall Street Journal,* December 23, 1991, A6.

20. Francis X. Clines, "11 Soviet States Form Commonwealth Without Clearly Defining Its Powers," *New York Times,* December 22, 1991, A1; Thomas L. Friedman, "Yeltsin Says Russia Seeks to Join NATO," *New York Times,* December 21, 1991, A5.

21. Clines, "11 Soviet States," A1.

22. James F. Clarity, "With Changing of Flags, a New, and Old, Russia," *New York Times,* December 27, 1991, A12.

23. Ibid.

24. Don Oberdorfer, "Gorbachev Resignation Ends Soviet Era; U.S. Recognizes Russia, 11 Other States," *Washington Post,* December 26, 1991, A1.

25. "Provisional Agreement on the Council of Heads of State and the Council of Heads of Government of the Commonwealth of Independent States," Moscow TASS, 0955 GMT, December 31, 1991, in FBIS-SOV–91–251, December 31, 1991, 18–20.

26. Francis X. Clines, "Joint Command Is Planned for Atom Arms," *New York Times,* December 31, 1991, A1, A6.

27. "Soviet Foreign Property Distributed Among CIS," Moscow Mayak Radio Network, 0500 GMT, July 30, 1992, in FBIS-SOV–92–147, July 30, 1992, 3.

28. John J. Fialka, "Armed Forces of Former Soviet Union Are Fast Falling Apart, Analysts Say," *Wall Street Journal,* April 13, 1992, A20.

29. Ibid.

30. Serge Schmemann, "The World: The Red Army Fights a Rearguard Action Against History," *New York Times,* March 29, 1992, E4.

31. Fialka, "Armed Forces of Former Soviet Union," A20.

32. Schmemann, "The World: The Red Army," E4.

33. V. Astafyev and V. Yermolin, "Tashkent: Military Delegations Failed to Resolve Main Tasks. Will the Politicians Succeed?" *Krasnaya zvezda,* May 15, 1992, 1, in FBIS-SOV–92–099, May 21, 1992, 10.

34. "An Agreement Between the Member States of the Commonwealth of Independent States on Strategic Forces," Moscow TASS, 0925 GMT, December 31, 1991, in FBIS-SOV–91–251, December 31, 1991, 17–18.

35. "Spokesman on Intelligence Cooperation Accords," Moscow ITAR-TASS, 1255 GMT, April 6, 1992, in FBIS-SOV–92–067, April 7, 1992, 7.

36. "Yeltsin on Security Treaty," Moscow ITAR-TASS, 1701 GMT, May 15, 1992, in FBIS-SOV–92–099, May 21, 1992, 19.

37. Steven Erlanger, "Yeltsin Angrily Assails His Critics and Gorbachev," *New York Times,* May 16, 1992, A4.

38. "Yeltsin on Security Treaty," 19–20.

39. "Shaposhnikov Comments on Tashkent Summit," Moscow INTERFAX, May 18, 1992, in FBIS-SOV–92–099, May 21, 1992, 29–30.

40. "Treaty on Collective Security," Moscow *Rossiyskaya Gazeta,* May 23, 1992, 2, in FBIS-SOV–92–101, May 26, 1992, 8–9.

41. V. Litovkin, "CIS Collective Security: A New Chance," Moscow *Priorities and Prospects*, September 1992, 15–19, in FBIS–SOV–92–183, September 21, 1992, 2.

42. Yevgeniy Shaposhnikov, "National and Collective Security in the CIS," *Krasnaya zvezda*, September 30, 1992, 2–3, in FBIS–SOV–92–190, September 30, 1992, 6.

43. Litovkin, "CIS Collective Security: A New Chance," 2.

44. Georgiy Shmelev, "Meeting Ends 16 July," Moscow ITAR-TASS, 1607 GMT, July 16, 1992, in FBIS–SOV–92–138, July 17, 1992, 10.

45. Daniel Schneider, "Deployment of Peacekeepers in Disputed Territories Boosts Russian Moderates," *Christian Science Monitor*, July 17, 1992, 1, 4.

46. Viktor Litovkin, "Peacemaking Forces Are Costing Us an Arm and a Leg," *Izvestiya*, September 2, 1992, 3, in FBIS–SOV–92–173, September 4, 1992, 24–25.

47. Daniel Schneider, "Russia's 'Peacekeeping' Raises Issue of Neutrality," *Christian Science Monitor*, September 14, 1992, 1, 4.

48. Ibid., 4; "13,244 Russian Blue Helmets Serving in Hot Spots," Moscow ITAR-TASS, 0940 GMT, January 5, 1993, in FBIS–SOV–93–002, January 5, 1993, 33.

49. Ivan Ivanov, "Gaydar Grants Interview on Ossetia, Dniester," Moscow ITAR-TASS, 1307 GMT, July 13, 1992, in FBIS–SOV–92–135, July 14, 1992, 4.

50. A. Dokuchayev, "CIS Joint Armed Forces Setting Up a Staff, But Evidently Not a General Staff," *Krasnaya zvezda*, June 25, 1992, 3, in FBIS–SOV–92–128, July 2, 1992, 5–6; V. Samsonov, "A Collective Security System Is an Objective Necessity," *Krasnaya zvezda*, July 3, 1992, 1, 2, in FBIS–SOV–92–132, July 9, 1992, 17–19; "CIS Joint Armed Forces High Command," *Krasnaya zvezda*, October 30, 1992, 1, in FBIS–SOV–92–212, November 2, 1992, 5.

51. V. Samsonov, "A Collective Security System Is an Objective Necessity," 17–18.

52. Russell Watson, "A Farewell to Arms?" *Newsweek*, February 10, 1992, 32–33.

53. Barbara Crossette, "U.S. and Russia Remain Stalled on Arms Cuts," *New York Times*, March 12, 1992, A13.

54. R. Jeffrey Smith, "3 Former Soviet Republics Meet U.S. Arms Terms," *Washington Post*, April 27, 1992, A13.

55. Don Oberdorfer, "3 Ex-Soviet States to Give up A-Arms," *Washington Post*, May 24, 1992, A1.

56. Barbara Crossette, "4 Ex-Soviet States and U.S. in Accord on 1991 Arms Pact," *New York Times*, May 24, 1992, A1.

57. Gerald F. Seib, "Bush, Yeltsin Meet, Agree on Surprise Warhead Cuts," *Wall Street Journal*, June 17, 1992, A3; Andrew Rosenthal, "Yeltsin Cheered at Capitol as He Tells of Peace Moves and Asks for Action on Aid," *New York Times*, June 18, 1992, A1; Steven Greenhouse, "Russia Is Given Most-Favored Status," *New York Times*, June 18, 1992, A19.

58. "Vesti" newscast, Moscow Russian Television Network, 2000 GMT, December 30, 1992, in FBIS–SOV–92–252, December 31, 1992; Michael Dobbs, "Yeltsin Faces Test in Ratifying Treaty," *Washington Post*, January 4, 1993, A12.

59. Don Oberdorfer, "U.S., Russia Differ on Nuclear Arsenals," *Washington Post*, June 10, 1992, A26.

60. "Decision of the Council of Heads of State of the Member-States of the Commonwealth of Independent States," Moscow TASS, 1616 GMT, March 23, 1992, in FBIS-SOV–92–056, March 23, 1992, 13.

61. "Sums up Results," Moscow ITAR-TASS, 1702 GMT, May 15, 1992, in FBIS-SOV–92–099, May 21, 1992, 21–22.

62. Bruce W. Nelan, "Is the West Losing Russia?" *Time,* March 16, 1992, 37.

63. Ibid., 35.

64. Steven Greenhouse, "$44 Billion Needed to Aid Ex-Soviet in 1992, I.M.F. Says," *New York Times,* April 16, 1992, A1, A8.

65. "Soviet Splinters," *The Economist,* September 14, 1991, 77. Figures are for 1988 interrepublic trade.

66. Caroline Rand Herron, "I.M.F. and World Bank: Lenders to the Nations," *New York Times,* April 28, 1992, A6.

67. Greenhouse, "$44 Billion Needed," A1.

68. Steven Greenhouse, "World's Lenders Offer Membership to Ex-Soviet Lands," *New York Times,* April 28, 1992, A6.

69. Celestine Bohlen, "Russia Battles with Financial Controls," *New York Times,* January 21, 1993, A7.

70. Keith Bradsher, "Anxiety and Red Tape Slow Loans to Moscow," *New York Times,* September 28, 1992, A7.

71. Celestine Bohlen, "Economic Furor Growing in Russia," *New York Times,* June 3, 1992, A11.

72. Steven Erlanger, "Ruble Floats While Russian Economy Still Sinks," *New York Times,* July 2, 1992, A8.

73. Steven Erlanger, "Russians Getting Share Vouchers but Ruble Falls," *New York Times,* October 2, 1992, A5; Serge Schmemann, "Cannily, Yeltsin Defends Program," *New York Times,* October 7, 1992, A13.

74. "The Rouble Zone: Behind the Facade," *The Economist,* September 19, 1992, 96.

75. "C.I.S. to Coordinate Economies," *Wall Street Journal,* October 12, 1992, A6; "Six CIS States to Create Common Bank," *RFE/RL Daily Report,* No. 196 (E-mail), October 12, 1992, 1.

76. Sergei Maksudov and William Taubman, "Russian-Soviet Nationality Policy and Foreign Policy: A Historical Overview of the Linkage Between Them," in *The Rise of Nations in the Soviet Union,* ed. Michael Mandelbaum (New York: Council on Foreign Relations, 1991), 18–23.

77. *Minority Rights: Problems, Parameters, and Patterns in the CSCE Context,* compiled by the staff of the Commission on Security and Cooperation in Europe (Washington, D.C.: Commission on Security and Cooperation in Europe, 1991), 28.

78. Maksudov and Taubman, "Russian-Soviet Nationality Policy" 27–36.

79. Roman Szporluk, "History and Russian Nationalism," *Survey,* Summer 1979, 1–17.

80. Ronald Grigor Suny, "The Soviet South: Nationalism and the Outside World," in *The Rise of Nations in the Soviet Union,* ed. Michael Mandelbaum (New York: Council on Foreign Relations, 1991), 67–78.

81. David D. Laitin, Roger Petersen, and John W. Slocum, "Language and the State: Russia and the Soviet Union in Comparative Perspective," in *Thinking The-*

oretically about Soviet Nationalities: History and Comparison in the Study of the USSR, ed. Alexander J. Motyl (New York: Columbia University Press, 1992), 140–49.

82. Alexandre Bennigsen, "Soviet Minority Nationalism in Historical Perspective," in *The Last Empire: Nationality and the Soviet Future,* ed. Robert Conquest (Stanford, Calif.: Hoover Institution Press, 1986), 133–47.

83. Karl W. Ryavec, *United States–Soviet Relations* (New York: Longman, 1989), 7.

84. Bennigsen, "Soviet Minority Nationalism," 131.

85. Arthur N. Waldron, "Theories of Nationalism and Historical Explanation," *World Politics* 37 (April 1985):429.

86. Dov Ronen, *The Quest for Self-Determination* (New Haven: Yale University Press, 1979), 95, cited in Waldron, "Theories of Nationalism," 431.

87. Waldron, "Theories of Nationalism," 422.

88. "Need for 'New Center' Discussed," Moscow INTERFAX, 1557 GMT, March 3, 1992, in FBIS-SOV–92–043, March 4, 1992, 23.

89. "Gorbachev Says 'Greatest Danger Is Separatism,' " Hamburg ARD Television Network, 2045 GMT, February 21, 1992, in FBIS-SOV–92–036, February 24, 1992, 21.

90. Erlanger, "Yeltsin Angrily Assails His Critics," A4.

91. Michael Z. Wise, "European Security Group Adopts New Rules to Limit Threats," *Washington Post,* March 5, 1992, A32.

92. A. Oliynik, "Direct Line: Commander in Chief of Joint Armed Forces with Russian 'Blue Berets,' " *Krasnaya zvezda,* April 4, 1992, 1, in FBIS-SOV–92–066, April 6, 1992, 7.

93. "Russia Signs European Arms Control Treaty," *Carlisle* (Pa.) *Sentinel,* June 5, 1992, A3.

94. "NATO and Eastern Lands Initial Troop Pact," *New York Times,* July 7, 1992, A8.

95. David Silverberg, "Former Soviet Republics to Join U.S. Aid Program in 1993," *Defense News International,* February 24, 1992, 36.

96. Mikhail Pogorelyy, "West Concerned about Our Nuclear Reactor Safety," *Krasnaya zvezda,* July 22, 1992, 3, in FBIS-SOV–92–143, July 24, 1992, 8; Sergey Sorokin, "Future of Nuclear Power Engineering 'Uncertain'," Moscow ITAR-TASS, 0345 GMT, June 26, 1992, in FBIS-SOV–92–126, June 30, 1992, 2.

97. Pogorelyy, "West Concerned about Our Nuclear Reactor Safety," 3.

98. "Help Offered to Russia, Ukraine," *Harrisburg* (Pa.) *Sunday Patriot-News,* May 24, 1992, A15.

99. Zbigniew Brzezinski, "The Cold War and Its Aftermath," *Foreign Affairs* 71 (Fall 1992): 48–49.

100. Gerald F. Seib, "Russian-Centered Approach of U.S. May Help to Create Instability Later," *Wall Street Journal,* May 4, 1992, A10.

101. Ibid.

102. Clines, "At Site of 'Iron Curtain' Speech," A1.

103. "USSR: Demographic Trends and Ethnic Balance in the Non-Russian Republics," Research Paper GI 90–10013U (Washington, D.C.: Directorate of Intelligence, Central Intelligence Agency, April 1990), iii–iv.

104. Ibid, 8.

2

The Russian Federation

The Russian Republic, always a significant element in the Soviet era but lacking autonomy from the center that directed it, has taken on a new life. President Boris Yeltsin, who proclaimed before the U.S. Congress on June 17, 1992, that the "idol of Communism" had "collapsed, never to rise again,"[1] has not only brought new life to what is now known as the Russian Federation, or simply Russia, but also has acted resolutely to resolve ethnic disputes that threaten the very fabric of the new Eurasia. Although other impressive national leaders are entering the political scene in the new states, none has the power and authority to achieve real change that the president of the Russian Federation has.

BASIC DATA

Total Area: 6,592,813 square miles (17,075,200 square kilometers). Russia is the largest country in the world.

Population: 150 million, with an annual growth rate of 0.4 percent. More than one hundred nationalities live in the country. The population is 82 percent Russian, 4 percent Tatar, 3 percent Ukrainian.

Religion: Russian Orthodox, Muslim, Roman Catholic, Protestant, Jewish.

Official Name: Russian Federation.

Capital: Moscow.

Government:

- Executive Branch: President Boris Yeltsin, elected on June 12, 1991, is head of state; he assumed the post of prime minister in November 1991

The Russian Federation

*Now Belarus

but promised to relinquish the position. Since June 15, chief economic reformer Yegor Gaidar had been acting prime minister, and President Yeltsin operated under increased powers granted by the 5th Congress of People's Deputies in November 1991. At the 7th session of the Congress of People's Deputies, held in December 1992, Yeltsin lost his special powers permitting rule by decree; Viktor Chernomyrdin, a former party Central Committee Staffer and oil and gas minister, was named prime minister.

- Legislative Branch: Congress of People's Deputies (1,041 members), elected in March 1990 for a five-year term, and a 242-member permanent Supreme Soviet, frequently called "parliament," elected from its ranks. The latter serves as a full-term legislature between the biannual sessions of the Congress.

- Judicial Branch: Constitutional Court, established in November 1991 to address constitutional issues.

On December 6, 1991, Hungary became the first country to establish full diplomatic relations with Russia. Foreign representation is primarily accomplished by using former Soviet embassies. In November 1991, Leningrad, the second largest city, became St. Petersburg once again. With the dissolution of the Soviet Union on December 25, 1991, Boris Yeltsin took over the Kremlin as his official residence and seat of the Soviet Union's primary successor state.

Efforts have been underway since early 1992 to replace the 1977 Soviet Constitution, which has been amended over 300 times. Because of opposition from the conservative Congress, the hammer and sickle are still the state symbols. On April 11, 1993, a referendum on principles for a new constitution was to be held that would presumably require elections for a new representative body. Its ultimate effect remains to be seen.

President Yeltsin considers issues affecting national security by means of the Russian Security Council, which met for the first time on May 20, 1992. The council's five permanent members are drawn from the executive and legislative branches, and it includes a number of senior officials as consultative members. It makes recommendations to the president on issues regarding the protection of important state and social interests. Much of the council's focus involves territorial crises and disputes; on June 3, 1992, it addressed Russian interests in the disputed Dniester region of Moldova.[2] On July 7, 1992, its charter was broadened to give it authority to coordinate the work of executive branch organizations, and, on January 13, 1993, Security Council Secretary Yury Skokov was given responsibility for coordinating foreign policy.[3]

Governmental administration in this vast region has been complicated by declarations of independence by many of the federation's thirty-two autonomous subdivisions, which occupy nearly half its territory. To better rule

Russia and to escape the grip of local soviets (councils) long headed by Communist party apparachiks, Yeltsin has appointed heads of administration to serve as chief administrators of regions and localities.

Religion is experiencing a revival in Russia; the Orthodox Christmas was celebrated on January 7, 1992, as an official holiday for the first time since Communist rule began. Boris Yeltsin and his family went to Moscow's Troitsa-Sergiyev Monastery on June 14, 1992, to celebrate the Feast of the Holy Trinity with Aleksiy II, patriarch of Moscow and all Russia. Yeltsin was blessed by the patriarch prior to his trip to Washington for the summit with George Bush.[4] Bringing religion back into the affairs of state has been welcomed by many Russians.

Economy: Despite a per capita income of $5,810, second only to Belarus, Russia faces a difficult economic future. President Yeltsin, in a late December 1991 address to the nation, said that "Russia is gravely ill," and warned that "We cannot permit a breakdown or panic. Then reform would become impossible."[5]

The Russian parliament acted decisively in this regard on January 24, 1992, when it approved an 85 percent cut in arms procurement and reduced military spending from more than 25 percent of total output to 4.5 percent.[6] When one considers that eight million people are employed in military-related activities and adds to that figure twenty-two million family members, one-fifth of Russia's population is involved in the military sector. According to a senior Yeltsin adviser, such numbers dictate that the interests of this group cannot be ignored.[7]

In view of reports that 85 percent of industrial enterprises and 90 percent of defense-related enterprises are bankrupt,[8] the Russian government increased state defense orders for 1993 over the 1992 figure to further support and stabilize the important defense sector.[9] With industrial production reduced by 27 percent for the year ending August 31, 1992, a number of plants may no longer be functioning given the disruption of needed supplies and spare parts.[10] Fears of industrial collapse caused the government to delay economic reforms; to abolish personal pensions for special categories of recipients such as outstanding sportsmen, writers, and Communist party functionaries beyond that provided by the basic pension law; and to request a postponement of repayment of its debt for up to fifteen years.[11]

The most visible evidence of economic disarray has been the profligate printing of currency by Russia's Central Bank under the control of Viktor Gerashchenko. Appointed to that position by the federation's parliament in June 1992, Gerashchenko—former head of the Soviet Central Bank— churned out more rubles in July 1992 than were printed in the last thirty years of the Soviet Union's existence. These 260 billion rubles, worth an estimated $1.6 billion, were but part of the more than one trillion rubles that the bank printed in almost four months after Gerashchenko assumed this post. By late September 1992, Acting Prime Minister Gaidar predicted a "complete crash" unless more reasonable monetary practices were adopted.[12] Sergei A. Vasiliyev, director of Russia's Government Working Center for Economic Reform, declared: "If these trends are not reversed immediately, then we will soon have hyperinflation of 50 percent a month. It's quite a realistic figure."[13]

The massive infusion of currency, new loans to floundering state enterprises, increased credits to the central banks of other former republics, and the accompanying inflation were a reversal of the tight money policies in effect prior to Gerashchenko's appointment. This policy shift was also reflected in changes in the composition of the money supply itself. Starting in July 1992, 1, 3, 5, 10 and 25 ruble notes were discontinued, along with 1, 2, 3, 5, 15, and 20 kopeck coins. Instead, coins in the denominations of 10, 20, 50, and 100 rubles bearing the two-headed Russian eagle are being minted. A new 5,000 ruble banknote was released for the first time on July 14, followed by a 10,000 ruble note on December 29.[14]

Such policies, supported by the conservative- and Communist-dominated parliament elected in March 1990, threatened to scuttle economic stabilization reforms that Russia had agreed upon with the IMF: keeping inflation below 10 percent a month and government deficit spending under 5 percent of gross domestic product by the end of 1992. With inflation running approximately 50 percent a month and deficit spending projected at 17 percent of the gross output, the stability of the currency was impossible to maintain. Any hope that the ruble would become freely convertible was abandoned in such circumstances. Beyond that, individual consumers were caught in a crisis of historic proportions, with consumer prices increasing 15.6 times from August 1991 to August 1992 while wages grew only 10.6 times.[15]

Deteriorating economic conditions have been reflected in estimates of declining oil production. Oil output in the former Soviet Union peaked in 1988, with 12.4 million barrels per day (MBD). In 1991, this figure had declined to 10.2 MBD, causing Economics Minister Andrei Nechayev to announce in late September 1992 that oil exports to the former republics would be reduced by as much as half in 1993, while export sales for hard currency would be continued.[16] On September 18, 1992, prices of oil and gas products for domestic use were nearly doubled in Russia in a move designed to prepare for complete price decontrol in 1993. One Russian institute has reported that output could fall by 50 percent by 1995. Russia, which is the globe's second largest oil producer and which produces 90 percent of all oil and gas in the former Soviet Union, could cease exporting oil entirely—at present its top earner of hard currency—should this come to pass.[17]

Other means of raising hard currency have included traditional export sales of military equipment. China purchased $1.8 billion in Russian arms in 1992, to include 24 SU–27 fighter aircraft. Additionally, Beijing is reportedly interested in purchasing advanced MIG–31 interceptors that have a multiple target capability.[18] Moscow has also sold 24 SU–24 bombers, three diesel submarines, and two 440-megawatt nuclear power reactors to Iran, leading one U.S. specialist to assert "the Russians will sell anything to anybody to earn hard currency and to keep production lines going."[19]

Such arms sales represent a significant shift from the Soviet era, when these transactions reflected the political leanings of client states. According to Petr Aven, foreign economics minister of Russia, "We start from the premise that arms are a commodity which could be sold and bought, and money could be obtained from that." The altered customer list does have some limits, however: "We have abandoned the ideological principle for exporting arms, and we cannot export them to any interested country." Among prohibited countries are those engaged in conflicts or embargoed or restricted by UN edicts.[20]

One major negative effect of weapons exports is the perpetuation of the vast military-industrial complex of arms research and production facilities. Hard currency export earnings, increased state orders for 1993, and additional credits to these enterprises from Moscow's Central Bank postpone any significant conversion to non-military purposes. The cost of this undertaking is nearly prohibitive; one Yeltsin adviser claims that it would take fifteen years and $150 billion to shift redundant defense capacities to civilian production.[21]

A more controversial means of obtaining badly needed hard currency was the decision to sell enriched uranium to its former archenemy, the United States. Under this agreement, announced on August 31, 1992, Washington would buy up to 500 metric tons of weapons-grade uranium over a twenty-year period in an unprecedented deal worth billions of dollars at current world prices. This uranium would be diluted to fuel civilian nuclear power reactors.[22] The United States, the world's leading producer of nuclear-generated electricity, possesses 110 working reactors that must be refueled every twelve to eighteen months.[23]

This long-term sales program allows Russia to earn hard currency while removing excess enriched uranium made available by the reductions in short-, intermediate-, and intercontinental-range nuclear weapons. It also reduces the possibility that this vital material may be diverted or stolen. The U.S. Congress provided $400 million in 1991 and another $400 million in 1992 to finance the denuclearization of the former Soviet Union. Some $15 million of this sum is being used to finance initial design costs associated with building a "safe, secure, and ecologically sound storage facility for fissile material derived from the destruction of nuclear weapons,"[24] the site where enriched uranium will be stored and monitored until it is purchased under the provisions of this agreement.

The prospects of stabilizing Russia's economy have been further clouded by the travails associated with the conversion to a market economy. At the

April 1992 session of the Congress of People's Deputies, Yeltsin criticized former Communist party managers who continue to head enterprises. He attacked this *"nomenklatura* privatization" by stating: "What we need is not a few millionaires but millions of owners."[25] In a similar vein, this process of top officials appropriating state property for private business purposes is known on the street as *"nomenklatura* plunderization."[26]

Such abuses have not deterred cities such as Nizhni Novgorod and St. Petersburg from selling property to private owners, with Moscow transferring 205,600 of its 3.2 million apartments and 8,000 businesses—six percent of total enterprises—to private individuals by mid-September 1992. According to Deputy Prime Minister Anatoly Chubais, there has already been significant progress in privatization. By mid-January 1993, some 146,000 private businesses had been registered with the government, and 5,600 large enterprises have been converted to joint stock companies.[27]

A more ambitious privatization program that was started on October 1, 1992, required all companies valued at more than 50 million rubles or having more than 1,000 employees to form a board of directors. At least 5,000–7,000 medium and large plants comprising 60 to 70 percent of all Russian industry will become joint stock companies that can be bought by employees and outside investors, beginning in January 1993. A primary medium of exchange will be 10,000 ruble vouchers, which were distributed to every man, woman, and child starting on October 1. The vouchers represent each person's share of state industry, and they are key to both the privatization effort and to public education in the ways of capitalism. The vouchers may be invested in specific companies, sold at exchanges, exchanged for shares in mutual funds, or used to buy land and other property.[28]

This method constitutes a necessary step if the Russian economy is to be based on the vicissitudes of market relations by private individuals owning property and selling their labor. It has met with criticism, including that of former President Gorbachev who has condemned economic reform in general and the voucher privatization plan in particular, terming it "a fraud against the people."[29] A more hopeful sign was evinced by one economist who remarked, "We're too incompetent to understand how this works. I'll get some good advice from an expert."[30] Despite the uncertainties associated with the plan, it is a positive process for doing what Lenin would have considered inconceivable.

This grand scheme must be viewed against progress in agriculture, which has been less satisfactory. Some 120,000 private farms with more than 14 million acres under cultivation were created by July 1992,[31] and 40 percent of the 26,000 state-owned farms were converted to private cooperatives. In a country where farming represents 22 percent of the gross national product and involves as much as 35 percent of the labor force, agriculture remains a significant factor.[32] Unfortunately, food production has continued to decline, with total output falling by 22 percent, on average, in the first eight months of 1992.[33] This drop exacerbates a situation already critical due to Russia's difficulties in importing food on credit since Moscow is unable to meet the overdue obligations of previous loans.

Total economic activity is still hampered by a shortage of capital and unrealistic prices. On May 18, 1992, prices of energy products were raised some five to six times. This move had the effect of increasing the cost of consumer goods by an additional 50 percent, and it came just a few months after the freeing of most retail prices on January 2, 1992. A second increase occurred in September, so that gas, oil, and coal prices would more closely approximate world market prices and thus comply with an IMF request.

East–West economic ties are on the rise, with Vladivostok now open to commercial shipping, and plans are under way to create an international air traffic control system across the vast country to provide direct transit between Europe and Asia. The increase of foreign economic activity in Russia has led one outspoken Russian nationalist, Vladimir Zhirinovsky, to proclaim that "after robbing Africa and Latin America the West has started robbing Russia."[34]

History: Moscow, which first appeared in chronicles in 1147, was an early Russian principality in Finnic territory. Its princes paid tribute to Mongol chieftains until 1380, when Moscow defeated them and rose steadily in importance. Some attribute despotic prerogatives of later Russian rulers to this period of Mongol rule. Moscow's rise to power coincided with the gathering of lands in the early sixteenth century, a process which reached the Pacific shores by the eighteenth century.

Peter the Great sought to Westernize the Slavic peoples, making St. Petersburg (his "window on the West") the capital in 1712. A succession of political struggles, economic crises, and military defeats weakened the monarchy and eventually led to its fall in February 1917 and the Bolshevik coup in October. In 1918, Lenin moved the national capital to Moscow, which served the Soviet Union during the Communist era and now serves as the seat of the Russian Federation.

THE ROAD TO INDEPENDENCE

Russia declared its sovereignty on June 12, 1990, which is celebrated as the country's independence day. Soon after the transfer of power from Mikhail Gorbachev to Boris Yeltsin in the Kremlin, Russian spokesmen reiterated Russia's adherence to arms control agreements previously concluded, assumed the Soviet Union's membership in and commitment to the International Atomic Energy Agency, replaced the USSR at the Geneva disarmament conference, accepted all rights and commitments of the former Soviet Union in the United Nations and its organizations, and requested that the Russian flag replace the Soviet flag at UN headquarters in New York, which occurred on December 28.

At this historic time a number of key issues faced Russia: the CIS charter, its mission, armed forces, and authority; the privatization of the heavily militarized and state-directed economy; the establishment of democratic institutions, policies, and procedures; and, finally, the creation of governmental structures with popular appeal, acceptance, and support. None, however, have proven as urgent as measures to ensure the viability of the Federation itself.

To prevent the disintegration of Russia due to its multitude of centrifugal influences—which include numerous ethnic groups; gold, oil, and other resources; religion; developmental status; external ties; and regional alignments—Boris Yeltsin on March 31, 1992, secured agreement to a new Federation Treaty by the vast majority of its constituent regions. This move was a deliberate effort to discourage separatist tendencies at a time when the same factors that had led to the Soviet Union's dissolution were acting upon its component parts toward the same end.

At the signing ceremony in St. George's Hall of the Kremlin, the heads of most autonomous republics, autonomous okrugs, autonomous oblasts, oblasts, and two cities—Moscow and St. Petersburg—approved the document establishing a voluntary federative state. The treaty was to become an integral part of the Federation Constitution to be approved by the Sixth Congress of People's Deputies, scheduled to convene in April 1992.

The two autonomous republics that failed to sign the document were the Chechen Republic (the Chechen-Ingush Autonomous Soviet Socialist Republic until it declared its independence in November 1991) and Tatarstan, formerly the Tatar Autonomous Soviet Socialist Republic. The Chechen Republic insists that the federation first recognize its independence, while Tatarstan holds that its ties with the larger body must be governed by separate bilateral agreements.[35] Both entities, however, are still subject to the existing constitution.

The Federation Treaty divided powers between the federation and its political subdivisions in three ways: powers reserved for the federal organs, powers jointly held, and powers reserved for the republics. The federal entity is empowered to approve and admit new republics to the Russian Federation, protect human rights, conduct foreign policy, guard the state's borders, manage key infrastructure such as railroads and nuclear power plants, coordinate foreign economic ties, levy federal taxes, and manage defense and security matters.[36]

Matters subject to joint jurisdiction of the Federation and the republics include law, order, and public safety; the use of natural resources; environmental protection; education and sports; health care and social security; disaster relief; protecting ethnic traditions; the organization of local self-government; financial and tax legislation; and administrative procedures.[37]

All remaining powers, the document stipulates, are reserved for the republics. Powers may be transferred to and from the federal authority by mutual consent, and additional amendments may be adopted with the consent of the constituent republics. Finally, relations of the constituent republics with the Federation will be conducted "on a basis of mutual respect and mutual responsibility," with disputes to be settled by mandatory conciliation.[38]

The Federation Treaty was both a tactical and a strategic victory for Boris Yeltsin. As a tactical victory, it codified in a broad way the interrelationships and division of powers between Moscow and its important subdivisions. Strategically, it presented the Congress of People's Deputies with a consensus document reflecting unity rather than disharmony and disorder. The Congress, the product of free elections held in March 1990, is dominated by Communist loyalists and conservative politicians because the party was the major political force up to the time of the August 1991 coup. The Congress is thus an obstacle to reform efforts and a standing conservative challenge to Yeltsin for the duration of its five-year term.

Yeltsin nonetheless was pleased with his victory. At the signing ceremony he addressed the delegation leaders assembled in St. George's Hall in ebullient terms: "Today we can tell our fellow citizens and peoples, who have lived together for centuries, and the whole world community, that there has been, there is, and will continue to be, a unified Russia. The course of our fatherland's history will not be severed."[39]

The Congress met on April 6, 1992, to approve the Federation Treaty and a draft constitution that had been in preparation since October. Yeltsin braced for a conservative attack on his economic reforms, and he made a number of staff changes to blunt the expected criticism. On the eve of the session, the combative and determined leader declared: "Only one way out can exist today, the continuation of radical reforms. And I shall not turn off that path, for there is no other choice today."[40]

Yeltsin said his "vision of patriotism" embraced democracy, unity, federalism, and a renewed Russia, "a civilized country capable of providing high standards of living and strict observance of human rights for its citizens." This revitalized Russia would occupy "a worthy place in the world community."[41]

The Congress of People's Deputies engaged in two weeks of often rancorous debate, with its 1,041 delegates split over draft versions of a new constitution. The Congress approved the Federation Treaty as an integral component of the Russian Federation's constitution and voted to approve the concept of constitutional reform, a preamble, and fundamental principles to establish the Russian Federation as a "sovereign, law-governed, democratic, federal, and social state."[42] In the end, the constitutional question was deferred and returned to the Constitutional Commission for revision and submission to the next session in December.

The Federation Treaty, together with continued conflicts with the parliament elected under the old regime, has encouraged Yeltsin to seek organizational solutions to what is widely perceived as governmental chaos. He has met several times with his advisory collegium to discuss reducing the number of state ministries and providing new bodies to facilitate the economic changes under way. A new constitution, with the requisite election of new representative organs, would also consolidate and streamline governmental functions.

Obtaining popular consensus for change has been difficult, however. Worsening economic conditions caused Yeltsin to admit to "serious errors" in economic planning before the October 6, 1992, session of Russia's parliament.[43] Faced with considerable opposition from Arkady Volsky, president of the Russian Union of Industrialists and Entrepreneurs, and Vice President Aleksandr Rutskoi, who claimed on July 16 that "total anarchy" ruled the country,[44] the creation of a coalitional Civic Union to contest power has made consensus even less likely. Volsky believes central planning should be reinstituted, and he holds China as a better example for Russian development than Western models, which he considers inappropriate given Russia's uniqueness. For example, he readily dismisses any talk of the Swedish model: "The problem with the Swedish model is, we don't have enough Swedes."[45]

This rise of conservative opposition—primarily former Communists (the reds), nationalists (the browns), and defense industrialists—is a serious challenge to Yeltsin and to Russia's transition to democracy. Yeltsin's decision in late October 1992 to ban the National Salvation Front, a collection of opposition groups, and to disband the parliament's private security force of some 5,000 guards, demonstrated his resolve to act decisively to protect his reforms. At the same time, Yeltsin's loss of influence at the December session of the Congress of People's Deputies, symbolized by Yegor Gaidar's ouster, has showed the tenuous position of those advocating democracy and economic reform.

Criticism from Mikhail Gorbachev has exacerbated political tensions. Gorbachev, who lost his official car, most bodyguards, and daccha, has continued to speak out against Yeltsin's reforms. On August 6, 1992, the former Soviet leader predicted that unless the Russian government changed its policies, "the existing regime will be swept aside and will be replaced by, it is easy to guess: chaos can only produce a dictatorship."[46] On October 2, the Constitutional Court, hearing the case challenging Yeltsin's ban of the Communist party and seizure of its property following the August 1991 coup, ordered Gorbachev's passport confiscated after he refused to testify in the matter. Although this move was reversed, it led Gorbachev to declare himself the Federation's first political "refusenik." On October 6, Gorbachev proclaimed that Yeltsin was not capable of ruling the country, leading Yeltsin to confiscate the Gorbachev Foundation's building and property the following day.[47] This type of wrangling has done little to instill public confidence in the political process.

Russia's new status as an independent state has raised a number of challenges regarding its foreign policy. In the past atmosphere of Cold War confrontation, ideological imperatives were dominant. Boris Yeltsin, speaking in May 1992, categorically repudiated such criteria: "[W]e dissociate ourselves from a class, national, and international struggle for domination. ... The 'cold war' climate had a considerable bearing on practical Soviet foreign policy. Russia has abandoned this legacy consciously and forever."[48]

In many respects, this has made the world much more complicated for Russian diplomats. According to Deputy Foreign Minister G. F. Kunadze, much of the difficulty lies in defining the term "national interest." No single, authoritative definition exists, he complained, and to return to past ideological clichés is impossible. In the absence of this "ideological compass," Russia's goal of "a civilized state obliges it not to accept aggression, violence, etc." Instead, Russia's interests require that it join global sanctions against Libya, Iraq, and Serbia.[49]

Foreign Minister Kozyrev, in a September 22, 1992, address to the 47th session of the UN General Assembly, made an international plea for patience and understanding toward Russia: "By locking itself away, the richest country in Eurasia has been turned into the sick man of Europe and Asia. By contrast, only an open society and an open policy will permit Russia to discover and play to the full its unique role in history."[50] Kozyrev has also proposed letting the United Nations use Russian military facilities to assist UN peacekeeping and peacekeeping training.[51]

Russia has also sought to demonstrate its break with past strictures by releasing sensitive documents related to key incidents in the nation's history. On October 14, 1992, Polish president Lech Walesa was given secret documents detailing the execution of more than 20,000 Poles, including at least 5,000 Polish military officers killed and buried in a mass grave at Katyn. Although Mikhail Gorbachev admitted Soviet guilt in April 1990, these documents provide firm evidence of Moscow's involvement in this bitterly contested and long-denied incident. A second incident—the September 1983 shootdown of South Korean airliner KAL 007—was clarified by documents released to the United States, South Korea, and families of those who died aboard the wayward flight. In both cases, a Yeltsin spokesman criticized Gorbachev for not being more forthcoming about the tragedies.[52]

Russia's new foreign policy is particularly noticeable with regard to its relations with the United States. Moscow has consulted with U.S. officials concerning possible cooperation in creating a global defense system against ballistic missile attack. The brigade of Soviet troops that has been in Cuba since 1963 will be withdrawn by mid-1993, but the electronic eavesdropping post at Lourdes, the largest signal intelligence site in the Western Hemisphere, will remain open. Travel restrictions on business people and journalists in both the United States and Russia have been mutually rescinded, and CIA Director Robert M. Gates, on October 16, 1992, provided Soviet authorities with details of the 1974 raising of a Soviet Golf II ballistic missile submarine. These changes constitute the abandonment of the final vestiges of the Cold War.[53]

This reorientation of foreign policy objectives has required a redirection of diplomatic activity. For the first time, ties with Commonwealth members are "top priority, the most difficult and important" focus of Russian diplomacy, according to an April 1992 Foreign Ministry pronouncement.[54] This has resulted in a new emphasis on bilateral relations with CIS states.

Russia's ties with the Muslim world are a particularly critical challenge. One specialist has observed that relations with the West must be accompanied by ties with the Muslim world. Russia, he observed, has the most extensive borders of all European countries with Muslim states. Rivalry between Ankara and Tehran for the loyalties of the former Soviet Union's Muslim states is complicated by the fact that some sixty-five million persons live outside their ethnic republics, including twenty-five million Russians. Russia's ties with its CIS Muslim neighbors will to a large extent define its relationship with the Muslim world.[55]

Defense issues have also received attention coincident with the continued redefinition of the CIS military role. On December 29, 1991, Boris Yeltsin announced the formation of a Russian national guard, with a force of 30,000 to 40,000 men, based on Russian tsarist traditions.[56] More significant, however, was the May 7, 1992, decision to create a Russian army, with Army General Pavel Grachev as the commander and Yeltsin himself as commander in chief and acting defense minister. Announced just before World War II Victory Day celebrations, this act gave Russia its first autonomous military force since the 1917 Revolution.

This move became inevitable as the Soviet Army disintegrated and the separate states claimed the forces and equipment based on their soil. President Yeltsin in March 1992 created a Defense Ministry and acted to claim for Russia those Soviet troops located beyond Russia's borders: the Western Group of Forces in eastern Germany and forces in Poland, Mongolia, and Cuba. While strategic forces would belong to the Commonwealth, the ownership of forces of the former Soviet Union located in other states would be subject to bilateral negotiations.[57]

General Grachev was appointed defense minister on May 18, 1992, and he began planning the armed forces' reorganization and conversion to a mixed volunteer-conscript force starting on December 1, 1992. Initial figures put the army's proposed strength at 1.5 million, but defense authorities revealed that much needs to be done before it becomes an effective combat force. Grachev noted that sweeping changes lie ahead for the army and that

"Russia will regard the dispatch of foreign troops to neighboring states and the build-up of troops and naval forces at its borders as a direct military threat to the Republic."[58]

In time, President Leonid Kravchuk of Ukraine, among others, contested the division of Soviet military spoils. Efforts to withdraw former Soviet troops from the conflict-embroiled southern states of Armenia, Azerbaijan, and Georgia were suspended on June 1, primarily at the request of Georgian and Armenian authorities. "We are there because without us, people will start killing each other," Grachev noted.[59]

A part of Defense Minister Grachev's challenge is to harness the advanced military technologies demonstrated by the United States and its allies in February 1991, during Operation Desert Storm. To accomplish this objective, he wants additional funds spent on research and development and less money spent on acquiring weapons. Modern precision weapons will not be the only advantage a Russian army would have. At a May 22 press conference, "Grachev clearly stated Russia's intention to remain a nuclear power after the rest of the former Soviet republics relinquish their weapons."[60] The CIS' control of nuclear forces during this transitional period will accommodate Ukrainian, Belarus, and Kazakh sensitivities until the weapons pass to the sole command of Russia.

The purpose and mission of Russian nuclear forces were clarified by General Grachev on June 5, 1992. In response to the statement that within the former Soviet Union only Russia will possess nuclear weapons by the year 2000, Grachev stated that Russia will provide a "nuclear umbrella" for those CIS member states which signed the May 15, 1992, collective security document at the Tashkent CIS summit. The countries party to this accord will benefit from the security and deterrence value of Russia's nuclear forces.[61]

A new branch of the Russian Army has been created as a rapid reaction force, Russian mobile forces, based upon the airborne divisions already in existence.[62] Not all is well within the Russian defense establishment, however, despite the urgency of its new peacekeeping or peacemaking responsibilities and the imperative of modernization. To many, the atmosphere within the new Russian army is chaotic, with no more than 40 percent of draftees reporting for induction, "regional princelings" forming personal militias, a legion of stolen weaponry at large, and the absence of "real borders" delineating state boundaries.[63]

Boris Yeltsin also acted to consolidate the technical services abandoned by the former Soviet Union. With the KGB's formal demise in October 1991, he assumed responsibility for the First Directorate (foreign espionage element) of the KGB, the largest foreign intelligence operation in the world. Renamed the Russian Foreign Intelligence Service (SVRR), it is directly subordinate to President Yeltsin. As had been done with the KGB, Moscow's heavy investment in space operations and research was codified with the formation of the Russian Space Agency on February 25, 1992.[64]

A final challenge confronting the new Russia concerns its people, who have paid a high price for years of malnourishment, medical neglect, and social malaise. According to Russia's top drug enforcement official, "Drug abuse is dramatically on the rise in Russia."[65] Some one million addicts are supplied by up to 100,000 opium poppy fields and 2.5 million acres of marijuana. This has led to gang violence and a 15 percent increase in drug-related crime in 1991 alone.[66] Only 25 percent of children finishing school are considered in good health, 50 percent of the water supply is not safe to drink, most Russian rivers are badly polluted, and more than one third of Russia's 150 million people live in urban areas where air pollution exceeds the clean air standard by 10 times.[67] In time, this may be Boris Yeltsin's greatest challenge of all.

Such matters can only suggest the extent to which the fledgling democrats of Russia require outside assistance. Concern that the momentum of discord has outpaced the momentum of unity has led some observers to view the future pessimistically, while a self-absorbed West barely grasps what is at stake in the world's largest country. The possibility of disintegration and reversion to more authoritarian forms causes us to speculate what may occur in this long-troubled land of vastness, beauty, sacrifice, and emotion: "Russia was never there to be 'lost,' but it is heading in a direction the West may one day soon, in this fast-forward century, come to regret."[68]

SEPARATIST/TERRITORIAL DISPUTES

1. Ethnic Disputes

Russia faces a plethora of ethnic disputes that threaten to consume the security and future of its many disparate peoples. This grave concern led Foreign Minister Kozyrev, on September 22, 1992, to request that the United Nations consider establishing international trusteeships to supervise the transition to independence of many republics of the former Soviet Union. Speaking of the rise of discrimination against Russians, Ukrainians, Belorussians, Jews, and others, Kozyrev urged the world body to protect minorities living in Estonia, Latvia, and other newly independent states. Such "aggressive nationalism," he observed, has become a "new global threat."[69]

2. Baltic and Western Region

a. An irredentist movement has developed in Karelia, ranging from Vyborg to Pechenga, in areas now occupied by ethnic Finns. These borderlands were ceded to the Soviet Union under the terms of the March 1940 peace treaty that ended the Winter War with Finland.

b. The border region between Pskov Oblast in the Russian Federation and Estonia is disputed by Estonia, based upon Lenin's signature on the 1920 Peace of Tartu.

c. The Russian government, urged on by members of parliament, has protested what it views as discriminatory practices against ethnic Russians living in Estonia and Latvia, where Russians constitute a significant percentage of the population. President Yeltsin halted troop withdrawals from the three Baltic states on October 20, 1992, to protest the treatment of Russians living there. Two weeks later, he requested that the United Nations intervene to protect their human rights. While this issue will eventually be resolved, Yeltsin's actions highlight the sensitivity with which Moscow views this problem.

d. The soviet (council) of Kaliningrad Oblast, located southwest of Lithuania, acted in mid-November 1991 to assert autonomy over its affairs from the Russian Federation.[70] This outpost is part of former East Prussia; Kaliningrad, a city of 400,000, was the former German city of Königsburg. The area was lost to Moscow in 1945.

e. The presence of substantial numbers of Russian troops and remnants of the former Soviet army seeking allegiance to the new states, Russia, or the CIS has added an element of unpredictability to Baltic security. All Baltic republics want the Russian troops to leave as soon as possible.

f. Russia is threatened with becoming further embroiled in the efforts of ethnic Russians and Ukrainians intent on maintaining a separate Trans-Dniester Republic on the left (or east) bank of the Dniester River in eastern Moldova.

3. The Caucasus

a. The Chechen-Ingush autonomous republic, a predominantly Sunni Muslim area of 1.4 million Turkic-speaking people in the northern Caucasus, has been in turmoil since nationalist leaders declared independence in November 1991. President Yeltsin deployed troops to its capital of Grozny to halt the insurgency, but the Russian parliament failed to endorse the move, causing him to withdraw them. Dzhokhar Dudayev, a former one-star Soviet general, was inaugurated as president of the "Republic of Checheniya" on November 9, 1991, after an election that was largely boycotted by the Ingush minority.[71] He organized a national guard and a small air force under the direction of a Defense Council, and in June 1992 he announced plans to form a ten thousand-man army composed primarily of Chechens.[72]

Given the Chechen Republic's new claim to autonomy and demarcation of original borders with Ingushetia based on their pre-1934 separate status, the Ingush minority, also Sunni Muslim, has supported the formation of a separate Ingush Republic within the Russian Federation. This status was granted by the Russian parliament on June 4, 1992. The law that authorized the new Republic of Ingushetia provides a period of eighteen months, until March 1994, for it to establish a government and to determine its borders.

The Ingush, however, claim some 1,000 square kilometers of territory now located to the west, in North Ossetia's Prigorodnyy district, where many Ingush lived prior to their deportation by Stalin in 1944. It has been the site of armed clashes between Ossetians and Ingush for several years. New clashes broke out in late October 1992, leading Boris Yeltsin to proclaim a state of emergency on November 2 and to send troops to halt the fighting. This marks the first serious outbreak of ethnic fighting within Russia itself. A former Ossetian official has compared this conflict with the ongoing war between Armenia and Azerbaijan: "It is the Karabakh syndrome, so the war is unavoidable."[73]

b. The North Ossetian autonomous republic, the smallest autonomous republic in the Russian Federation, is located in the northern Caucasus between the newly proclaimed republics of Checheniya and Balkariya. More than one hundred nationalities live there. North Ossetia wishes to unite with South Ossetia, an autonomous oblast located across the border in Georgia. Some 100,000 refugees from fighting in Georgia and conflict between Georgia and South Ossetia live in North Ossetia, and the situation is aggravated in the east by the insurgency being conducted by Ingush nationalists.[74]

North Ossetia and South Ossetia have threatened to annul the new Federation Treaty and form an independent state of Alaniya if Russia does not enforce a cease-fire between Georgia and South Ossetia.[75] North Ossetia has conducted a gas pipeline and transport blockade against Georgia. Direct negotiations between President Boris Yeltsin and Georgia's State Council Chairman Eduard Shevardnadze led to the Dagomys accord, which ended three years of hostilities. It instituted a ceasefire between belligerents on June 29, 1992, and established a disengagement zone maintained by Russian, Georgian, and Ossetian "peacemaking" forces. Georgia continues to oppose Ossetian independence.

c. In mid-November 1991, the Republic of Balkariya was proclaimed as an independent state within the Kabardino-Balkar Autonomous Soviet Socialist Republic in the North Caucasus. Its influence is countered by groups opposing separatism, particularly the Kabards.[76] The Balkar and Kabard peoples, both Sunni Muslims, were deported by Stalin to Central Asia in 1944, but were subsequently rehabilitated in 1957 when the autonomous republic, originally established in 1922, was reactivated. In late September 1992, civil disorders involving thousands of armed demonstrators led to the imposition of emergency rule and the introduction of Russian interior troops in the capital of Nalchik.

d. The north Caucasian Republic of Dagestan, formerly the Dagestan Autonomous Soviet Socialist Republic, is disputing some 3,000 hectares (7,500 acres) of land along its common border with Checheniya, to the west. Checheniya has declared that it will protect the rights of Chechens living in Dagestan. Russian troops moved into the border region in September 1992 and established a buffer zone between the Republic of Dagestan and Checheniya to the west, and Dagestan and Azerbaijan to the south, where 100,000 refugees from the fighting in Nagorno-Karabakh have temporarily relocated.[77] Dagestan's more than 2 million residents range from half a million Avars to 12,000 Aguls. Most are Sunni Muslim, but Shiites, Jews, and small groups of Christians live there as well.

e. The Karachayevo-Cherkess autonomous oblast in the northern Caucasus seeks recognition as the Karachay Republic under the green banner of Islam.[78]

f. The Confederation of Mountain Peoples, created in November 1991 to represent more than twenty separate ethnic groups including the Abkhazes, Shapsugs, Adyges, Abazins, Cherkesses, Kabardins, Ossetians, and Chechens, have formed an army called the "Green Helmets." Their ostensible purpose is to settle ethnic disputes in the Caucasus and to protect the mountain peoples from outside attacks, particularly from armed Cossacks.[79] In October 1992, the group changed its name to Confederation of Caucasian Peoples, with a parliament based in Grozny, Checheniya. Its involvement in fighting in Abkhazia has further incited ethnic conflict in western Georgia.

g. The situation in Nagorno-Karabakh and Nakhichevan, located in Azerbaijan and Armenia, respectively, remains volatile. Threats by Turkey to intervene to support its ethnic compatriots reflect the great danger of possible escalation. Following CSCE and Iranian mediation efforts, a ceasefire was negotiated by Russian, Armenian, and Azerbaijani defense ministers in late September 1992, in part based upon the principles of the Dagomys accord. It is the best hope yet of defusing this violent conflict.

4. Central Russia

a. Bashkir, an autonomous soviet socialist republic east of Moscow predominantly occupied by Sunni Muslims, changed its name in February 1992 to the Republic of Bashkortostan. Its economic sovereignty was ensured through a special annex to the Federation Treaty;[80] it is holding further talks with Russia to better regulate bilateral relations. Tatar residents of the region are alarmed at Bashkir assertiveness.

b. Tatar nationalists have established the Tatarstan Republic, with Kazan its capital, as an independent state. Currently an autonomous republic, its parliament approved a green, red, and white flag on December 1, 1991. By refusing to sign the Russian Federation Treaty, this region, the largest among Russia's autonomous republics and site of the giant Kama River truck factory, threatens to upset Boris Yeltsin's vision of a resurgent Russia. The movement for sovereignty in the republic of four million people (48 percent Muslim Turkic peoples and 43 percent Russians) began in 1988 but has taken on new vigor since a March 21, 1992, referendum asserting Tatar sovereignty. On November 6, 1992, Tatarstan's Supreme Council adopted a new constitution that provides for citizenship and ties with foreign states. The Volga Tatars cite the Chechen Republic, which also refused to sign the Federation Treaty, as an example they seek to emulate.[81]

Tatarstan, which considers itself completely autonomous and independent, wishes to maintain relations with Russia by means of bilateral treaties. An economic treaty was signed in August 1992 that ended a Russian economic blockade.[82] Similar treaties in other areas are under negotiation. Kazan was host to the first World Congress of Tatars in June 1992, and the republic is actively seeking economic ties with other nations. Tatarstan has also proposed the formation of a Confederation of the Peoples of the Volga and Ural Regions, an organization similar to the Confederation of the Caucasian Peoples. Its purpose would be primarily economic and social, however.[83]

c. The Union of Cossack Republics, with its own bank, mission, and commodity exchange in Moscow, was created in November 1991. Designed to protect the interests, "honor and dignity" of Cossacks throughout southern Russia, it is forming a national guard. Cossacks in Moscow, Ukraine, Siberia, the Far East, and Sakhalin are represented on the Great Council of Atamans. On June 15, 1992, President Yeltsin signed a decree rehabilitating Cossacks and their direct descendants following the repressions of the past. It also gave them the right to form Cossack military and other traditional associations. The Russian Defense Ministry has been instructed to draft proposals for Cossack military units and Cossack public service missions, such as border protection and maintaining public order.[84]

While the exact number of Cossacks is unknown, some estimates place it at as many as thirty-five million. Cossacks have volunteered to protect fellow Slavs seeking to establish a Trans-Dniester Republic in Moldova.

d. Ethnic Germans are advocating the creation of a German Autonomous Republic in the central Volga region. Leonid Kravchuk has invited the Germans to settle in the Crimea, a move that would exacerbate an already tense situation there. Boris Yeltsin signed a decree on March 2, 1992, establishing a German national *okrug* in Volgograd and Saratov oblasts.[85] Many who previously supported this concept have emigrated to Germany.

5. Central Asia

a. Gorno-Altay Soviet Socialist Republic changed its name to the Gornyy Altay Republic in February 1992. In May, the republic's Supreme Soviet changed the name again, to the Altay (or golden mountains) Republic.

b. The division of assets of the Caspian Sea Flotilla, formerly a part of the Soviet Navy based in Baku, Azerbaijan, has led Russia to establish a naval base at Astrakhan. As a result of the breakup of the USSR, "Astrakhan has unexpectedly become a border town."[86]

c. Moscow continues to sponsor talks with China and Kazakhstan, Kyrgyzstan, and Tajikistan regarding their common borders. Limits on troops and weapons, as well as the marking of boundaries, are under discussion.

6. Siberia and the Far East

a. The Irkutsk Oblast soviet on November 17, 1991, declared itself an independent autonomous state within the Russian Republic, asserting that this was a new type of statehood.[87]

b. In the Far East, the city soviet of Petropavlovsk-Kamchatka, the major political center on the Kamchatka Peninsula, voted to oppose any settlement that would transfer to Japan the four southern islands of the Kuril chain. Ths islands are considered an "inseparable part of Russia." Of particular sensitivity is the right to fish in the 200-mile economic zone surrounding the islands, which is viewed as critical to Kamchatka's economy.[88] Opposition by Russian nationalists and local political leaders to possible territorial concessions caused President Yeltsin to postpone a planned mid-September 1992 visit to Japan.

c. The Jewish Autonomous Oblast in the Far East—Evrey Oblast, based at Birobidzhan—voted in late October 1991 to become an autonomous republic within Russia, in an effort to increase its status and independence. Persons claiming Jewish ancestry constitute less than 4 percent of its total population.[89]

d. In eastern Siberia, the Yakut Autonomous Soviet Socialist Republic, now the Sakha-Yakutia Republic (the center of diamond mining for the former USSR), declared itself a nuclear-free zone in November 1991. This move by Russia's largest autonomous republic was a reaction against nuclear testing, which had been conducted there for years. The other two nuclear testing ranges were Semipalatinsk in Kazakhstan and Zapolyarnyy on the northern island of Novaya Zemlya.[90]

e. To protect Siberian interests, a movement is under way to convene a Siberian People's Congress. This followed the March 1992 session of the Siberian territories' Deputies' Congress, held in Krasnoyarsk. Fears that Siberia will continue to be robbed in a colonial manner by outsiders have generated new interest and support for the Siberian Independence Party, established in 1990.[91] Interest in Siberian separatism has led to the formation of two additional political movements, the Union for Siberian Revival and the Union for Siberian Unification, which both advocate greater autonomy for the vast region.[92]

f. An independence movement has emerged in the Tuvinian autonomous republic, an area occupied by 300,000 non-Muslim Turkic peoples who live along the border with China. The conclusion of the Federation Treaty has granted the republic greater autonomy, but some inhabitants wish to secede from Russia entirely.

g. The Chukhotka Autonomous Okrug, which borders Alaska across the

Bering Strait, was granted direct membership in the Russian Federation on June 17, 1992, by the decree of President Yeltsin.[93]

h. Korean peoples deported by Stalin from Far East coastal areas to Central Asia in the 1930s are seeking to create an autonomous "free Korean national economic zone" in Russia's Far East. Local residents are opposed, citing the absence of free land and shortages of food and housing.[94]

i. The Far Eastern Republican party claims to have formed a provisional government that will petition the United Nations and the World Court to reestablish the Far Eastern Republic, which existed from 1920 to 1922. It then merged with the Russian Soviet Federated Socialist Republic. Another group, the North Pacific Forum, seeks to form a North Pacific Federative Republic to unite Far Eastern citizens in a new Pacific nation. While the chances of either group achieving their objectives are slim, they do reflect dissatisfaction with rule from Moscow, some 4,000 miles (6,400 kilometers) away.[95]

7. Russian Diaspora

A new concern has been expressed both within and outside of the Russian Federation for those 25 million ethnic Russians who now find themselves beyond Russia's borders. In some new states, language tests are required for citizenship; in others, the Turkic or tomanian language is being adopted, together with the Latin script. As a result, ethnic Russians in these states find themselves without a country or in a society in which it is difficult to function. This concern led the Foreign Affairs Committee of the Russian Federation's Supreme Soviet to declare in late November 1992: "Russian foreign policy must be based on a doctrine that proclaims the entire geopolitical space of the former Union, a sphere of vital interest.... Russia must secure...the role of political and military guarantor of stability on all territory of the former USSR." This theme, articulated at various times by President Yeltsin's conservative opponents as justification for the evacuation of ethnic Russians from unstable areas, poses a serious danger to the development of peaceful ties with these new states.[96]

In early January 1993, Foreign Minister Kozyrev proclaimed that "the real challenge to our security today lies in regional conflicts," listing those in Tajikistan, South Ossetia, Abkhazia, and Moldova as examples. Rapid deployment forces intended for regional conflicts and peacekeeping were suggested as the focus for Russia's military preparedness.[97] Should Russian intervention in ethnic disputes assume the distinctly narrow mission of protecting or evacuating ethnic Russians, this could raise tensions and augur ill for the future.

NOTES

1. Andrew Rosenthal, "Yeltsin Cheered at Capitol as He Tells of Peace Moves and Asks for Action on Aid," *New York Times,* June 18, 1992, A1.

2. Vasily Kononenko, "What the Russian Security Council Discussed at Its First Session," *Izvestiya*, May 21, 1992, 1, in FBIS-SOV–92–099, May 21, 1992, 49–50; "Yeltsin Chairs Security Council Session 3 June," Moscow ITAR-TASS, 1521 GMT, June 3, 1992, in FBIS-SOV–92–108, June 4, 1992, 34.

3. Aleksey Kirpichnikov, "Yuriy Skokov: New Top Man," Moscow *Kommersant*, July 6–13, 1992, 2, in FBIS-SOV–92–137, July 16, 1992, 37. Suzanne Crow, "Foreign Policy Commission Approved," *RFE/RL Daily Report*, No. 8 (E-mail), January 14, 1993, 3. Comparisons of the new structure with the Communist party's former ruling Politburo have not been lost on keen observers. To Kirpichnikov, "whereas previously the question of washing powder could be investigated in the Politburo as a 'political question,' it is now investigated in the Security Council as a question of 'vitally important interests'." Ibid.

4. "Yeltsin Holds Talks with Moscow Patriarch," Moscow ITAR-TASS, 1155 GMT, June 14, 1992, in FBIS-SOV–92–115, June 15, 1992, 15.

5. Serge Schmemann, "Yeltsin Tells Russia of Hardship to Come," *New York Times*, December 30, 1991, A3.

6. Celestine Bohlen, "New Russian Budget Is Strong Medicine," *New York Times*, January 25, 1992, A3.

7. "Novosti" newscast, Moscow Ostankino First Program Network, 1300 GMT, January 18, 1992, in FBIS-SOV–92–015, January 23, 1992, 56.

8. Justin Burke, "Russian Industrialists Face Down Reformer," *Christian Science Monitor*, August 14, 1992, 4; "Novosti" newscast, Moscow Ostankino Television First Program Network, 1100 GMT, July 9, 1992, in FBIS-SOV–92–136, July 15, 1992, 43.

9. "Government Endorses 1992 State Defense Order," Moscow ITAR-TASS, 1400 GMT, September 10, 1992, in FBIS-SOV–92–177, September 11, 1992, 29.

10. Keith Bradsher, "Anxiety and Red Tape Slow Loans to Moscow," *New York Times*, September 28, 1992, A7.

11. Tatyana Khudyakova, "Russian Government Abrogates USSR Government Resolutions on Personal Pensions," *Izvestiya*, August 27, 1992, 1, in FBIS-SOV–92–168, August 28, 1992, 29; Keith Bradsher, "Talks on Rescheduling Moscow's Debt Pit U.S. and Russia against Germany," *New York Times*, September 21, 1992, A9.

12. "Russia Churns Out Rubles," *Wall Street Journal*, August 7, 1992, A6; Serge Schmemann, "Russians Warned of Monetary Peril," *New York Times*, September 23, 1992, A17.

13. Steven Erlanger. "Russia Aide Faults the Central Bank," *New York Times*, September 15, 1992, A7.

14. "Novosti" newscast, Moscow Ostankino Television First Program Network, 1400 GMT, July 30, 1992, in FBIS-SOV–92–148, July 31, 1992, 21; "Circulation of 5,000 Ruble Note Begins," Moscow ITAR-TASS, 1200 GMT, July 13, 1992, in FBIS-SOV–92–135, July 14, 1992, 17. "Vesti" newscast, Moscow Russian Television Network, 0525 GMT, December 28, 1992, in FBIS-SOV-92-252, December 31, 1992, 23.

15. Steven Greenhouse, "Ruble Support May Be Delayed to '93," *New York Times*, July 13, 1992, A8; Schmemann, "Russians Warned of Monetary Peril," A17.

16. Scott Pendleton, "Drop in Soviet Oil Output Results in Worldwide Bind,"

Christian Science Monitor, September 17, 1991, 1; "Russia Modifies Oil Sales to Raise Money," *Harrisburg* (Pa.) *Sunday Patriot News,* September 27, 1992, A17.

17. "World Wire: Dire Outlook for Russian Oil," *Wall Street Journal,* January 28, 1992, A11.

18. "Novosti" newscast, Moscow Ostankino Television First Program, 1500 GMT, December 18, 1992, in FBIS-SOV-92-145, December 21, 1992, 12. Jim Mann, "China's Military: China Pursues Russian Arms, Sources Warn," *Harrisburg* (Pa.) *Sunday Patriot News,* July 12, 1992, A17.

19. Michael R. Gordon, "Russia Selling Submarines to Teheran's Navy," *New York Times,* September 24, 1992, A9.

20. Nikolay Gelitka, "Minister Discusses Conditions for Arms Sales," Moscow Radio World Service, 1300 GMT, July 13, 1992, in FBIS-SOV–92–137, July 16, 1992, 33.

21. Brigitte Sauerwein, "Defense Conversion: Russia's 'Strategic Imperative'," *International Defense Review,* August 1992, 733–34.

22. William J. Broad, "Deal With Russia is Said to Involve More Uranium than Believed," *New York Times,* September 5, 1992, 3.

23. William J. Broad, "Russians Offering Nuclear Arms Fuel for U.S. Reactors," *New York Times,* July 22, 1992, A9.

24. "Agreement Between the Department of Defense of the United States of America and the Ministry of the Russian Federation for Atomic Energy Concerning Technical Assistance for Design of a Safe, Secure, and Ecologically Sound Storage Facility for Fissile Material Derived from the Destruction of Nuclear Weapons," Washington, D.C.: U.S. Dept. of State, October 6, 1992, 1–6.

25. Steven Erlanger, "Yeltsin Defends Reforms to Lawmakers," *New York Times,* April 8, 1992, A3.

26. Schmemann, "Cannily, Yeltsin Defends Program," A13.

27. "Yeltsin Signs Oil Decree," *Wall Street Journal,* September 18, 1992, A10; Celestine Bohlen, "Russia Battles Inflation with Financial Controls," *New York Times,* January 21, 1993, A7.

28. Celestine Bohlen, "Citizens of Russia to be Given Share of State's Wealth," *New York Times,* October 1, 1992, A1; "Russian Privatization: Free For All," *The Economist,* July 18, 1992, 70; Neela Banerjee, "Yeltsin Criticizes Cabinet Moves Toward Reform," *Wall Street Journal,* October 7, 1992, A13.

29. Steven Erlanger, "Russians Getting Share Vouchers but Ruble Falls," *New York Times,* October 2, 1992, A5.

30. Ibid.

31. Serge Schmemann, "Free-Market Ideas Grow on Russian Farms," *New York Times,* October 6, 1992, A10.

32. "Russian Farming: The Least Likely Agricultural Miracle," *The Economist,* April 11, 1992, 71–72.

33. Yevgeniy Kleshkov, "Situation Deteriorates in Food Market," Moscow ITAR-TASS, 1629 GMT, September 9, 1992, in FBIS-SOV–92–176, September 10, 1992, 27.

34. "Zhirinovsky Warns of West 'Robbing Russia,' " Moscow INTERFAX, 0938 GMT, May 7, 1992, in FBIS-SOV–92–089, May 7, 1992, 30.

35. " 'Historic Significance' Eyed," Moscow ITAR-TASS, 1848 GMT, March 31, 1992, in FBIS-SOV–92–063, April 1, 1992, 26–27.

36. "Federation Treaty Initialed," *Federatsiya*, March 18–24, 1992, 2, in FBIS-SOV–92–056, March 23, 1992, 40–41.

37. Ibid., 42.

38. Ibid.

39. "Yeltsin Gives Opening Address," Moscow Russian Television Network, 1200 GMT, March 31, 1992, in FBIS-SOV–92–063, April 1, 1992, 25.

40. Steven Erlanger, "Yeltsin Talks of Cushioning Effects of Economic Change," *New York Times,* April 6, 1992, A12.

41. Ibid.

42. "Preamble, First Part of Constitution Adopted," Moscow Mayak Radio Network, 1000 GMT, March 25, 1992, in FBIS-SOV–92–058, March 25, 1992, 51.

43. Schmemann, "Cannily, Yeltsin Defends Program," A13.

44. "Rutskoy Says 'Total Anarchy' Prevails," Moscow ITAR-TASS, 1821 GMT, July 16, 1992, in FBIS-SOV–92–138, July 17, 1992, 27.

45. Steven Erlanger. "Chaos Gives Russian Lobbyist Power," *New York Times,* August 2, 1992, A10.

46. Nataliya Kirsanova, "Russia 'Near the Brink' of Totalitarianism," Moscow ITAR-TASS, 0627 GMT, August 7, 1992, in FBIS-SOV–92–153, August 7, 1992, 32.

47. Steven Erlanger, "Yeltsin Transfers Gorbachev Foundation Property," *New York Times,* October 8, 1992, A5.

48. "The Beginnings of Russian Democracy," Warsaw *Rzeczpospolita,* May 22, 1992, 1, 10, in FBIS-SOV–92–108, June 4, 1992, 19.

49. "Does Russia Have a Foreign Policy?" Moscow Russian Television Network, 1445 GMT, June 3, 1992, in FBIS-SOV–92–109, June 5, 1992, 24.

50. "Kozyrev Speech to UN General Assembly," Moscow ITAR-TASS, 0955 GMT, September 22, 1992, in FBIS-SOV–92–185, September 23, 1992, 8.

51. Aleksandr Shalnev, "A. Kozyrev Criticizes Human Rights Violations in Estonia and Latvia from the UN Rostrum," *Izvestiya,* September 24, 1992, 4, in FBIS-SOV–92–190, September 30, 1992, 16.

52. Celestine Bohlen, "Russian Files Show Stalin Ordered Massacre of 20,000 Poles in 1940," *New York Times,* October 15, 1992, A1; Celestine Bohlen, "Russia Turns Over Data from KAL 007," *New York Times,* October 15, 1992, A9. Complete tapes were turned over to Korean authorities two months after Yeltsin's visit to Seoul.

53. Valentin Gorkayev, "Moscow to Relinquish Cuban Listening Post," Moscow Radio World Service, 2010 GMT, September 20, 1992, in FBIS-SOV–92–183, September 21, 1992, 19–20; Igor Ignatyev, "Consultations Begin with U.S. on Global Defense." Moscow ITAR-TASS, 0855 GMT, September 21, 1992, in FBIS-SOV–92–185, September 23, 1992, 2; Serge Schmemann, "Russia, U.S. Lift Curbs on Trade and News Travel," *New York Times,* September 26, 1992, A4; "U.S. Tells Russia of Bodies in Its Sunken Sub," *New York Times,* October 17, 1992, A4. Pascal Fletcher, "Russia Keeps Ear Tuned In Cuba: Listening Post Stays Under New Accords," *The Washington Post,* November 4, 1992, A47.

54. Gennadiy Chartodeyev, "The New Priority Area of Russian Diplomacy Is Relations with 'Close Neighbors Abroad,'" *Izvestiya,* April 2, 1992, 4, in FBIS-SOV–92–066, April 6, 1992, 19.

55. Aleksey Vasilyev, "Russia and the Muslim World—Partners or Opponents?" *Izvestiya,* March 11, 1992, 6, in FBIS-SOV–92–053, March 18, 1992, 22–24.

56. Michael Dobbs, "Russia to Create National Guard, Yeltsin Declares," *Washington Post,* December 30, 1991, A1.

57. "Troops Abroad Under Russian Jurisdiction," Moscow TASS, 0715 GMT, March 16, 1992, in FBIS-SOV–92–051, March 16, 1992, 47.

58. "Grachev on Army's 'Sweeping Changes,' Threats," Moscow ITAR-TASS, 1417 GMT, June 1, 1992, in FBIS-SOV–92–106, June 2, 1992, 14.

59. "Russia Postpones Troop Pullout from Three Troubled Republics," *Washington Post,* June 2, 1992, A15.

60. Daniel Sneider, "Turning Russia's Army into a Lean Machine," *Christian Science Monitor,* June 9, 1992, 7.

61. Vladimir Solntsev, "Russia to Provide CIS with 'Nuclear Umbrella,' " Moscow ITAR-TASS, 0402 GMT, June 5, 1992, in FBIS-SOV–92–110, June 8, 1992, 2.

62. Anatoliy Dokuchayev, "This Issue's Interview," *Krasnaya zvezda,* August 1, 1992, 1, in FBIS-SOV–92–155, August 11, 1992, 33–34.

63. Steven Erlanger, "Russian Military Men Deny Any Thought of Coup," *New York Times,* July 9, 1992, A5.

64. "Yeltsin Decree on Formation of Space Agency," Moscow *Rossiyskaya gazeta,* February 28, 1992, 2, in FBIS-SOV–92–041, March 2, 1992, 28–29.

65. Alexander Ivanko, "Drugs, Addictions Surging Across Former Soviet Union," *Harrisburg* (Pa.) *Sunday Patriot News,* September 27, 1992, A19.

66. Ibid.

67. "Russia's Blight Hurts Health," *Wall Street Journal,* October 8, 1992, A10.

68. Steven Erlanger, "In Russia, a Familiar Chill in the Political Air," *New York Times,* August 9, 1992, E3.

69. Thomas L. Friedman, "Russian Appeals to U.N. To Safeguard Minorities," *New York Times,* September 23, 1992, A17.

70. "Kalingrad Oblast Soviet Decisions on Oblast's Status," *Krasnaya zvezda,* November 14, 1991, 1, in FBIS-SOV–91–223, November 19, 1991, 69.

71. Michael Dobbs, "Yeltsin Cracks Down on Russian Region," *Washington Post,* November 9, 1991, A20.

72. R. Khazhiyev, "Vesti" newscast, 1600 GMT, June 24, 1992, in FBIS-SOV–92–123, June 25, 1992, 54.

73. Lyudmila Leontyeva, "Another Autonomous Republic Inside Russia," *Moscow News,* June 21–28, 1992, 5.

74. "Ossetian Official Cited on Escalating Violence," Moscow TASS, 0939 GMT, December 21, 1991, 47, in FBIS-SOV–91–247, December 24, 1991.

75. S. Knyazkov, "Lifting of Blockade on Georgia Military Highway Delayed. Ossetians Ready to Defend Themselves...with Weapons Captured from Army," *Krasnaya zvezda,* June 3, 1992, 1, in FBIS-SOV–92–108, June 4, 1992, 57.

76. " 'Republic of Balkariya' Proclaimed at Congress," Moscow Central Television Vostok Program and Orbita Networks, 1630 GMT, November 18, 1991, in FBIS-SOV–91–223, November 19, 1991, 68–69.

77. "Yeltsin Orders Troops to Border with Azerbaijan," Moscow Radio World Service, 1100 GMT, September 9, 1992, in FBIS-SOV–92–176, September 10, 1992, 19; "Checheniya, Dagestan Agree to Buffer Zone," Moscow Radio Rossii Network, 1600 GMT, September 14, 1992, in FBIS-SOV–92–179, September 15, 1992, 21.

78. L. Leontyeva, "Karachayevo-Cherkess: Situation Threatens to Get out of Control," Moscow *Rossiyskaya gazeta,* November 23, 1991, 1, in FBIS-SOV–91–229, November 27, 1991, 53–54.

79. "Military News," Moscow POSTFACTUM, 1804 GMT, March 30, 1992, in FBIS-SOV–92–064, April 2, 1992, 64.

80. "Bashkirtostan Gains Economic Sovereignty," Moscow POSTFACTUM, 1853 GMT, April 2, 1992, in FBIS-SOV–92–065, April 3, 1992, 47.

81. "Tatarstan Nationalists Want Independence," Moscow INTERFAX, 1838 GMT, November 18, 1991, in FBIS-SOV–91–223, November 19, 1991, 74; "Passes Law on Referendums," Moscow INTERFAX, 2143 GMT, December 1, 1991, in FBIS-SOV–91–231, December 2, 1991, 53; Daniel Sneider, "Yeltsin Struggles to Keep Russian Federation Intact," *Christian Science Monitor,* March 25, 1992, 1, 4.

82. "Russia, Tatarstan Achieve Economic Accord," Moscow INTERFAX, 1629 GMT, August 27, 1992, in FBIS-SOV–92–169, August 31, 1992, 27–28; Ivan Ivanov, "Government Collegium Discusses Tatarstan, Estonia," Moscow ITAR-TASS, 1401 GMT, September 29, 1992, in FBIS-SOV–92–190, September 30, 1992, 19.

83. Nikolay Sorokin, "World Congress of Tatars Opens in Kazan," Moscow ITAR-TASS, 0942 GMT, June 12, 1992, in FBIS-SOV–92–121, June 23, 1992, 7. Ann Sheehy, "Tatar Calls for Volga–Ural Confederation," *RFE/RL Daily Report,* No. 233 (E-mail), December 4, 1992, 3.

84. "Union of Cossack Republics Created," Moscow TASS, 1719 GMT, November 17, 1991, in FBIS-SOV–91–223, November 19, 1991, 67; "Yeltsin Signs Decree on Cossacks' Rehabilitation," Moscow INTERFAX, 1211 GMT, June 15, 1992, in FBIS-SOV–92–116, June 16, 1992, 29.

85. "Novosti" newscast, Moscow Television First Program Network, 1800 GMT, March 2, 1992, in FBIS-SOV–92–042, March 3, 1992, 33.

86. O. Sosnovskaya, "Vesti" newscast, Moscow Television Network, 1900 GMT, August 7, 1992, in FBIS-SOV–92–155, August 11, 1992, 5.

87. "Irkutsk Congress Calls for Republic Recognition," Moscow Radio Rossii Network, 1800 GMT, November 17, 1991, in FBIS-SOV–91–223, November 19, 1991, 69.

88. "Further on Island Transfer," Moscow INTERFAX, 1515 GMT, December 5, 1991, in FBIS-SOV–91–235, December 6, 1991, 65–66.

89. Yelena Matveyeva, "The Far East: A Pacific Nation With Its Own Currency," *Moscow News,* October 11–18, 1992, 5.

90. Nikolay Belyy, "Yakutia Is a Nuclear-Free Zone," Moscow *Rossiyskaya gazeta,* November 22, 1991, 7, in FBIS-SOV–91–228, November 26, 1991, 1.

91. "Politics" section, Moscow POSTFACTUM, 1859 GMT, April 29, 1992, in FBIS-SOV–92–085, May 1, 1992, 37.

92. Mikhail Podshibyakin, "In Parties and Movements: Siberia Will Revive," Moscow *Rossiyskaya gazeta,* September 17, 1992, 1, in FBIS-SOV–92–184, September 22, 1992, 36.

93. "Yeltsin Signs Decree on Status of Chukhotka," Moscow *Rossiyskaya gazeta,* July 9, 1992, 2, in FBIS-SOV–92–133, July 10, 1992, 33.

94. Yelena Matveyeva, "Russia's Far East: Locals Say No to Korean Autonomy in the Maritime Territory," *Moscow News,* September 20–27, 1992, 5.

95. Matveyeva, "The Far East," 5.

96. Henry R. Huttenbach, "The Sudeten Syndrome: The Emergence of A Post-Soviet Principle for Russian Expansionism." *Analysis of Current Events*, Association for the Study of Nationalities (Year 4, No. 3), December 1992, 1–3.

97. Suzanne Crow, "Kozyrev on Rapid Deployment Forces," *RFE/RL Daily Report*, No. 4 (E-mail), January 8, 1993, 1.

The Baltic States

3

The Baltic States

The three Baltic states of Estonia, Latvia, and Lithuania represent special cases, in that they were occupied as a result of the August 23, 1939, Molotov–Ribbentrop Pact, which contained a secret protocol dividing Europe into German and Soviet spheres of influence. This German–Soviet alliance, termed an agreement of neutrality and nonaggression, ended the three small states' brief interwar period of independence. By June 1940 they had become constituent republics of the Soviet Union.

Hitler attacked the Soviet Union on June 22, 1941; after four costly years of savage fighting, the defeat of Germany brought the reoccupation of the Baltic states by Soviet forces. The United States never recognized Soviet sovereignty over the three republics, and on September 6, 1991, after each had proclaimed independence and steadfastly insisted it was a sovereign state, the USSR State Council granted them their official freedom.

Acquiring full statehood, however, has proven to be more difficult. After more than fifty years of Soviet control, the Russian presence in all three Baltic states is not easily eliminated given the many Russians, both military and civilian, who live there. Starting in 1940, large numbers of Baltic peoples were arrested and deported to the east while Soviet authorities assumed complete control of each country. As a result, Russians today constitute 30 percent of Estonia's population, 34 percent of Latvia's population, and 9 percent of Lithuania's population; there are also 50,000 former Soviet troops present in the region. Each Baltic state has made its language the sole official language, and Estonia and Latvia have prepared citizenship laws that would exclude most Russians.

Hostility against the Russians has been mounting. In June 1992, attacks on Russian forces and their families led Moscow to authorize military authorities to take necessary measures to protect themselves, including shooting at the perpetrators.[1] Ruslan Khasbulatov, speaker of the Russian parliament, declared on July 9, 1992, that the rights of the 2 million Russians living in the Baltic states would be protected: "We cannot turn a blind eye to what's happening."[2] During that same month, the Russian parliament threatened to impose economic sanctions against Estonia if rights violations continued, and Foreign Minister Kozyrev offered to withdraw all troops by 1994 if certain conditions were met.[3]

At the same time, the July 1992 Helsinki Follow-Up Meeting, the first summit of CSCE states since the signing of the Charter of Paris in November 1990, saw repeated efforts by the Baltic states to pressure Russia into withdrawing its troops. This persistence found its way into the formal Helsinki Summit Declaration, "The Challenges of Change," which explicitly called for the peaceful removal of foreign forces from Baltic territories.[4]

A troop withdrawal agreement has been concluded with Lithuania, but on October 7, 1992, Boris Yeltsin made it clear that no such agreements are possible with Estonia and Latvia while the rights of Russian minorities are violated.[5] This presaged his halt of Russian troop withdrawals on October 20 and his appeal to the UN on behalf of Russians residing in the Baltic countries. As long as most Russians are viewed as occupation forces from the Soviet era—particularly in the states with a large Russian presence—peaceful relations and social tranquility will be difficult to achieve.

Estonia

BASIC DATA

Total Area: 17,413 square miles (45,100 square kilometers). Estonia is the third smallest of the fifteen former Soviet republics, after Armenia and Moldova.

Population: 1.6 million, with an annual growth rate of 0.7 percent. The population is 62 percent Estonian, 30 percent Russian, and 3 percent Ukrainian. The Estonians are related, ethnically and linguistically, to the Finns.

Religion: Lutheran, Russian Orthodox.

Official Name: Republic of Estonia.

Capital: Tallinn.

Government:

- Executive Branch: Lennart Meri, former foreign minister, was elected as Estonia's new president on October 5, 1992. The government is headed by a prime minister.
- Legislative Branch: State Assembly, advised by the Estonian Congress. On June 28, 1992, Estonian voters overwhelmingly approved a draft constitution and a new legislative entity, the State Assembly, was elected on September 20, 1992. Estonia is the first of the new Eurasian republics to adopt a new constitution.
- Judicial Branch: Supreme Court.

Economy: Estonia was the most industrialized Soviet republic and had the highest standard of living in the USSR. Ninety-five percent of its exports went to the Russian Republic, from which it received most of its raw ma-

Estonia

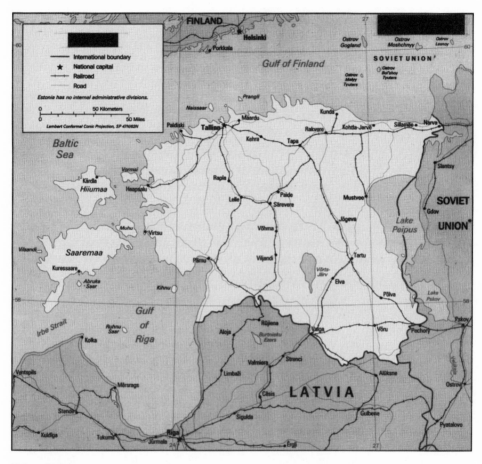

*Now Russia

terials and oil. Exports to Russia virtually stopped following independence, and the the tiny country lacks the hard currency with which to purchase Russian oil. The result has been an energy and food crisis of severe proportions, causing Prime Minister Edgar Savisaar to resign in mid-January 1992.[6] The IMF's September 1992 decision to offer its first financial assistance to Estonia of $41 million reflects confidence in the new country's economic future.[7]

History: Following Danish, German, Polish, and Swedish control during the Middle Ages, and Russian rule since 1721, Estonia enjoyed a brief period of independence from 1918 to 1940, when it was forcibly incorporated into the Soviet Union as a part of the 1939 Molotov–Ribbentrop Pact. Estonia suffered terribly under Soviet rule; agriculture was collectivized and some 10 percent of its population was deported.

THE ROAD TO INDEPENDENCE

Estonia was the first republic to declare its sovereignty, doing so on November 16, 1988. It formally declared independence on March 30, 1990, but after the attempted coup of August 19, 1991, it proclaimed its immediate independence. On September 6, 1991, the USSR State Council formally approved Estonia's independence, along with that of the other two Baltic republics. Because all three new nations were facing similar problems, they formed an interparliamentary Baltic Assembly on November 8. One of its first major decisions was the March 1, 1992, formation of the Baltic Investment Bank. The most pressing concern, however, involves foreign policy, particularly relations with the former Soviet Union.[8]

A major issue involving the former "center" is the continued presence of Russian armed forces within Estonia's borders. They numbered about 24,000 in September 1992, and included the sailors at the naval base at Paldiski, a primarily Russian town of 10,000. The base is closed to Estonian citizens, and crews of Soviet nuclear submarines are trained on a full-scale mock-up of an actual submarine. A large air base near Tartu is used by long-range bombers; attack aircraft are at three bases; there are several missile bases; and near Tallinn, there is an underground command bunker for controlling combat operations throughout the northern Baltic area.[9]

The Estonian government has insisted that the Russians leave, and NATO has been asked to assist with removing the nuclear training reactor from the Paldiski naval base, for its return to Russia.[10] Estonia wants the Russians to leave the country before the end of 1993, but Russia says the withdrawal will occur in phases from 1994 to 1997.[11]

Three major obstacles prevent a hasty Russian withdrawal, according to the commander of the Baltic Border District. First, the Baltic states want Soviet military property to remain, while Russian authorities wish to sell some of it to finance new border posts and troop housing. Second, the Russians want to privatize service housing by giving it to the occupants, who can then sell it or exchange it for housing elsewhere. Finally, the deadline for leaving—now the summer of 1993—will be very difficult to meet.[12]

Negotiations thus far to secure the withdrawal of Russian troops have been inconclusive. In July 1992, the Estonian government created two commissions to oversee Russian military activities: One will focus on the naval training center at Paldiski with its nuclear reactor and two nuclear waste facilities, while the other will supervise the property left behind.[13]

As of July 1992, borders were being guarded by Russian and Estonian guards. A March 13, 1992, decree by President Yeltsin transferred the Baltic Border District to Russia. Now CIS citizens have their documents reviewed by Russian district border troops, while Estonian citizens are checked by Estonian authorities. As soon as a final agreement is reached regarding the withdrawal of the Russian troops, the Baltic states will take on this responsibility solely.[14]

The Russian military has also been caught up in Estonia's assumption of the vestiges of statehood. Russian servicemen are unable to obtain Estonian passports. As the Bank of Estonia prepared to issue the country's new currency, the kroon, on June 20, 1992, the requirement that permanent citizens register in order to receive the currency excluded servicemen and most other Russian residents, though they were promised the right to exchange a limited amount of rubles.[15]

The citizenship issue has been particularly grating. Only those who had resided in Estonia from before June 16, 1940, could vote in the September 1992 national elections, and this excluded a large number of Russian adults, estimated by Moscow as 42 percent of total voters.[16] Russian authorities believe that the presence of Russians in Estonia as of the date of the Russian–Estonian Treaty of January 12, 1991, which regulates mutual relations, should determine citizenship, but the newly approved Estonian constitution uses the day before Soviet troops invaded the country—June 16, 1940—as the cutoff for citizenship. A knowledge of Estonian is also required.[17]

Estonia, along with Latvia and Lithuania, signed the Paris Charter for a New Europe in December 1991, in conjunction with acquiring membership in the CSCE. In another step toward statehood, the Republic of Estonia has established a Ministry of Defense, with a light brigade and main staff that will eventually consist of up to 13,000 persons. In March 1992, the first two units of the force, two infantry battalions, started forming at Voru, arrayed with standards in use prior to the 1940 Soviet takeover.[18] A small volunteer paramilitary organization, the Kaitselit (Defense Union), has also been formed. In June and July 1992 it was involved in armed incidents with Russian troops.

Estonia, like its two small Baltic neighbors, is well aware of the difficulty in organizing a defense force when there are so many other pressing issues. The area of defense cooperation has been a fruitful one. Although first meetings of the three defense ministers involved discussions of the air defense problem, on June 2, 1992, the ministers signed a protocol of defense cooperation designed to establish a single defense system. Specific agreements addressed information exchange, military-technical cooperation, a military attaché system, emergency planning, and forming a single air defense network.[19]

At the Baltic defense meeting in July 1992, the ministers discussed plans for guarding their borders. This is a sensitive area, and there was some concern for Russia's reaction to these developments. Latvia's defense minister, Talavs Jundzis, believed the West would see this as a positive sign. As for Russia, he was not so sure: "[I]t is very difficult, as I have told you on a number of occasions, to predict the action of Russia. I only want to say that Russia should not become alarmed about this agreement, but, to my mind, it should be pleased that there will be neighboring states that will take care of the security of their borders."[20]

SEPARATIST/TERRITORIAL DISPUTES

1. The Republic of Estonia has consistently asserted that the Tartu Treaty with Russia, dated February 2, 1920, and other agreements give it the right to claim areas now included in Pskov and Leningrad oblasts.[21] The disputed region stretches about ten kilometers (six miles) from the Narva River into Russia; there is also a thirty-kilometer (eighteen-mile) tract reaching into Russia from Petseri, at the junction of the Estonian, Latvian, and Russian borders. Russia does not accept the legitimacy of the Tartu Treaty, which it considers to be inequitable. Former President Arnold Ruutel has spoken with Presidents Gorbachev and Yeltsin about this matter.[22]

2. The large proportion of Estonia's population that is Russian considerably complicates the transition to statehood and has left many questions unanswered. Russians who have lived and worked in Estonia for many years claim that Estonia's restrictive citizenship policy is an issue of human rights. In addition, in some regions of the country, particularly in the the northeast, where the Russian Democratic Movement is strong and most of the population is Russian-speaking, there have been warnings that another Dniester-like crisis of separatist unrest could develop. Estonia's newly elected government has waived language requirements for some 40,000 Russians who sought citizenship status before February 1990, and other compromises are likely.[23]

Latvia

*Now Russia

**This territory is now split between Russia (to the north) and Belarus (to the south), just north of the 56th parallel.

Latvia

BASIC DATA

Total Area: 24,595 square miles (64,100 square kilometers).

Population: 2.7 million, with an annual growth rate of 0.6 percent. The population is 52 percent Latvian, 34 percent Russian, and 5 percent Belorussian. Latvians are descendants of the ancient Letts.

Religion: Predominantly Lutheran, Roman Catholic, Russian Orthodox.

Capital: Riga.

Official Name: Republic of Latvia.

Government:

- Executive Branch: The senior elected official is Anatolijs Gorbunovs, chairman of the Supreme Council since October 1988. The government is headed by a prime minister, and the Council of Ministers is the senior executive body.
- Legislative Branch: Supreme Council.
- Judicial Branch: Supreme Court.

A discussion has been under way for some time regarding revisions of the Latvian Constitution of 1922.

Economy: The country produces electronics, machinery, and various consumer goods. Like Estonia, it is dependent upon imported energy and raw materials. Food prices were freed on December 10, 1991, but privatization has been a slow process. The Latvian currency, the lat, was introduced in

March 1993 following the July 1992 adoption of the Latvian ruble as an interim currency. In September 1992, the IMF offered Latvia an $81 million loan, that organization's first financial assistance to the Riga government.[24]

History: Latvia has been part of Russia since 1795. Independent from 1918 to 1940, the country was forcibly incorporated into the Soviet Union by Stalin under the Molotov–Rippentrop Pact of 1939. After World War II, Latvia was reoccupied by Soviet troops, and the country experienced a painful, tragic Russification campaign, which was very costly in terms its national culture and institutions.

THE ROAD TO INDEPENDENCE

The parliament issued a declaration of sovereignty on July 28, 1989, and declared its independence on May 4, 1990; the Supreme Council voted for immediate independence on August 20, 1991, following the abortive coup during which Soviet troops seized strategic positions in all three Baltic republics. The USSR State Council formally recognized and approved Latvia's independence on September 6, 1991.

Latvia has been a key member of the Baltic Assembly, and it is proceeding to implement the protocol it signed with Estonia and Lithuania on June 2, 1992, regarding defense cooperation. Within the nation itself, a Defense Ministry has been created, headed by a civilian. Most of its forces will be border troops, with total strength estimated at 9,000 to 10,000. A navy was formed, with thirty-five ships in its fleet. The scarcity and high cost of fuel have hindered its operations.[25]

The police will fall within the jurisdiction of the Ministry of Internal Affairs. A people's militia, a military reserve force, will be formed under the control of the Supreme Council.[26]

Settlement of issues concerning the Russian military presence continues to require top-level attention. More than two hundred buildings and other sites in Riga were occupied by the Soviet military, since the city was the headquarters of the former Soviet Union's Baltic Military District (now renamed the Northwestern Group of Forces).[27] By January 1993, some 16,000 Russian military personnel were in Latvia, which claims that there is no legal basis for their presence. Latvia has insisted they must leave Riga by the end of 1992, and the entire country by the end of 1993, but Russian authorities have said that some soldiers will remain until 1999.[28] Negotiations on this sensitive issue are continuing.

The troop issue is a serious one for Moscow, not because of the security vacuum that may be left behind but because the Russian Federation is unable to accommodate the returning troops. Russia's Defense Minister, Gen. Pavel Grachev, has addressed the withdrawal issue in these terms: "I have already said that I will not withdraw my officers and soldiers from the Baltic and other states to open fields. The withdrawal could be accelerated only if the

Baltic States give us financial assistance or practical assistance in building houses and barracks."[29]

The issue is a difficult and complex one, both for Russia and for each of the Baltic states. According to Andrey Fyodorov, Vice President Rutskoi's foreign policy adviser, "We would be bringing an explosion into Russia by agreeing to withdraw from the Baltics." Instead, authorities in Moscow hope to lease ports in Latvia and Estonia and to secure concessions for ethnic Russians who wish to remain there.[30]

SEPARATIST/TERRITORIAL DISPUTES

1. The issue of Russian residents in this republic, the most heavily Russian populated of the three Baltic states, continues to be a sensitive problem. Questions on such issues as language, passports, and citizenship must take into account the large number of ethnic Russians living in Latvia. Citizens are expected to know Latvian, and a series of language tests has been given to state employees, with as many as 200,000 to be tested.[31] The exact requirements for citizenship have yet to be determined, although many Latvians seek to exclude those who entered Latvia after the Soviet invasion of June 17, 1940. Boris Yeltsin's firm stance will undoubtedly put pressure on Riga to yield on citizenship requirements.

2. The town of Abrene and six volosts of Abrene Uyezd, which were lost to the Soviet Union upon the reoccupation of Latvia after World War II, are contested by Latvia. The area is part of Pytalov raion in Russia's Pskov Oblast,[32] and Riga has laid claim to it based on the Russian–Latvian Treaty of 1920.

Lithuania

*Now Russia
**Now Belarus

Lithuania

BASIC DATA

Total Area: 25,174 square miles (65,200 square kilometers).

Population: 3.8 million, with an annual growth rate of 0.8 percent. The population is 80 percent Lithuanian, 9 percent Russian, and 8 percent Polish.

Religion: Roman Catholic, Russian Orthodox.

Official Name: Republic of Lithuania.

Capital: Vilnius.

Government:

- Executive Branch: Algirdas Brazauskas, leader of the Democratic Labor Party, which is composed of former Communists, became chairman of the Seimas and acting president following the October 25, 1992, national elections. Brazauskas was elected as the country's first president on February 14, 1993, under the terms of a new constitution adopted in the October 25 parliamentary elections. A prime minister heads the government. A National Security Council coordinates defense matters.
- Legislative Branch: Seimas. In the national elections, half the deputies were elected by majority vote and half by geographic region.
- Judicial Branch: Supreme Court.

Economy: Lithuania is an advanced manufacturing country that produces amber, paper, and a host of manufactured and electronic goods. It is also known for its construction and shipbuilding. The country's dependence on nuclear power for 45 percent of its electricity requirements has required it

to continue to operate two graphite-moderated, water-cooled (RBMK) reactors of the Chernobyl type at Ignalia.[33] Lithuanian ruble coupons will be
used as an interim currency prior to the introduction, by the Bank of Lithuania, of a new national monetary unit, the lit. The nation's economy has
suffered greatly since independence, primarily due to the inability to pay
hard currency for Russian oil.

History: Ruled by Russia since 1795, Lithuania was briefly independent
from 1918 to 1940, when it was forcibly incorporated into the Soviet Union
as a part of the 1939 Molotov-Ribbentrop Pact. Following the Soviet reoccupation of Lithuania after World War II, an armed nationalist resistance
continued to oppose the Red Army for several years.

THE ROAD TO INDEPENDENCE

The Lithuanian parliament declared its sovereignty on May 18, 1989,
and independence on March 11, 1990, precipitating a prolonged crisis with
Moscow leading to armed confrontations in and around Vilnius in January
1991. KGB "Alfa" commandos were involved in these confrontations, and
its deputy commander considered this distasteful experience the primary
reason why the Alfa group refused to storm the Russian White House during
the August 1991 coup.[34] After the sea change in Soviet affairs brought about
by the failed coup of August 1991, the USSR State Council formally approved Lithuania's independence on September 6, 1991.

The issue of Russia troops in Lithuania, as well as in Estonia and Latvia, continues to vex local authorities. As early as November 1991, Moscow's Ministry of Defense declared that troop withdrawal could not
begin before the end of 1994. By December 1991, Lithuania claimed all
Soviet army property based on the republic's soil.[35] In September 1992,
20,500 Russian troops were in Lithuania, based in nearly 180 separate
compounds.[36]

A referendum of Lithuanian citizens held on June 14, 1992, concerning
the "unconditional and immediate withdrawal of the Army in the current
year and compensation for the damage caused to Lithuania," received overwhelming support: some 91 percent were in favor. While some withdrawals
have taken place, there is strong sentiment in favor of ending the presence
of what most consider to be an occupying force.[37] Agreement in principle
was reached between Vilnius and Moscow on September 8, 1992, calling
for the removal of all Soviet troops by August 31, 1993. This was seen by
parliamentary leader Landsbergis as the start of normalized relations with
Russia.[38]

Moscow is also heavily dependent upon the defense plants of the former
Soviet Union located in Lithuania. Of twenty-four plants in the country,

twenty-one produced unique items for Soviet forces, ranging from radio location devices to laser equipment. Prior to the Soviet Union's collapse, Soviet airborne divisions were based in Kaunas and Jonava, and motorized rifle divisions in Vilnius and Klaipeda made a substantial military presence for Moscow.[39]

Boris Yeltsin has indicated that he will adhere to the troop withdrawal agreement, despite having voiced his displeasure with Estonia and Latvia for their tough citizenship laws. The small Russian and Polish minorities in Lithuania have been granted citizenship by Vilnius, and the Russian president reportedly told Lithuanian authorities that he was not dissatisfied with their treatment of ethnic minorities.[40]

Lithuania is forming a small armed force based upon volunteer troops, a rapid reaction unit, civil defense, a small aviation unit, naval elements, and border guards. A small coastal patrol unit is also being established. According to the Defense Ministry's chief of staff, the new army will remain outside politics.[41]

SEPARATIST/TERRITORIAL DISPUTES

1. Russia's Kaliningrad Oblast, formerly part of East Prussia, is immediately to the southwest of Lithuania. Cut off from the Russian Federation proper, it is dependent upon Vilnius for free transit to support the many Soviet troops and sailors stationed there. It serves as headquarters of the former Soviet Union's Baltic Fleet. In November 1991, servicemen meeting in Baltiysk voted to refuse orders moving them from the oblast unless there were suitable living conditions at new locations. Some Lithuanian officials have spoken in favor of incorporating Kaliningrad into Lithuania.[42]

2. There continue to be concerns among the Russian and Polish minorities whether their status will be protected by the new Lithuanian state. The Vilnius and Salnicinkai regions have significant Polish populations. According to the Polish foreign minister, "There are many problems with the Poles in Lithuania."[43] A Union of Poles in Lithuania has been formed as a political party to represent the interests of those of Polish ancestry, to include the possible formation of a Polish district as a legal entity within Lithuania. A January 1989 law mandating Lithuanian as the state language and requiring its use within two years has made Russians feel similarly insecure. As a result, Russians living in the port city of Klaipeda, concerned over the withdrawal of Russian troops, have formed a defense committee that seeks to arm themselves and to create an independent republic.[44]

3. There is a twenty-kilometer (twelve-mile) stretch of the border with Latvia that remains unclarified. It was not appropriately identified in the Lithuanian–Latvian Treaty of 1922.[45]

4. Lithuania's border with Belarus has never been marked, and considerable problems are associated with finding and agreeing upon the new international boundary. A working group was established in September 1992 for delineating the border and building customs posts. It hopes to conclude the project by the autumn of 1993.[46]

NOTES

1. "Baltics Army Units Can Retaliate If Attacked," Moscow ITAR-TASS, 1420 GMT, June 25, 1992, in FBIS-SOV–92–124, June 26, 1992, 9.

2. "Khasbulatov on Russians' Rights in Baltics," Moscow INTERFAX, 1417 GMT, July 9, 1992, in FBIS-SOV–92–133, July 10, 1992, 58.

3. Celestine Bohlen, "Why Are Russians Still Here? the Free Baltics Ask," *New York Times,* August 7, 1992, A3.

4. Conference on Security and Cooperation in Europe, *CSCE Helsinki Document 1992: The Challenges of Change* (Washington: U.S. Government Printing Office, 1992), 5.

5. John Lepingwell, "Yeltsin Warns Estonia, Latvia on Troop Withdrawals," *REF/RL Daily Report,* No. 194 (E-mail), October 8, 1992, 1.

6. Margaret Shapiro, "Hunger and Hardship from the Baltic to the Caucasus," *Washington Post,* January 28, 1992, A1, A16.

7. "I.M.F. to Aid 2 Baltic States," *New York Times,* September 14, 1992, D2.

8. "Presidium Discusses Banks, Nuclear Inspections," Moscow BALTFAX, 1843 GMT, March 2, 1992, in FBIS-SOV–92–042, March 3, 1992, 13; "Official Views New Baltic Assembly's Role," BALTFAX, 1400 GMT, November 11, 1991, in FBIS-SOV–91–218, November 12, 1991, 36.

9. "Report of Tallinn Nuclear Submarine Training Base," Stockholm Sveriges Radio Network, 1130 GMT, December 1, 1991, in JPRS (Joint Publications Research Service)-UMA–92–005, February 12, 1992, 29–30; Mert Kubu, "Russian Bases Stay," Stockholm *Dagens nyheter,* February 23, 1992, A9, in FBIS-SOV–92–037, February 25, 1992, 82–83.

10. Dmitriy Gorokhov, "Prime Minister Insists on Withdrawal in 1992," Moscow ITAR-TASS, 0915 GMT, March 30, 1992, in FBIS-SOV–92–062, March 31, 1992, 68.

11. Igor Porshnev, "Diplomatic Panorama," Moscow INTERFAX, 1146 GMT, June 10, 1992, in FBIS-SOV–92–113, June 11, 1992, 83.

12. S. Knyazkov, "On Foreign Borders," *Krasnaya zvezda,* May 27, 1992, 1, 2, in JPRS-UMA–92–021, June 10, 1992, 44–45.

13. "Estonian Commissions Formed to Monitor Russian Military," Moscow *Nezavisimaya gazeta,* July 8, 1992, 3, in JPRS-UMA–92–028, July 29, 1992, 17.

14. Knyazkov, "On Foreign Borders," 46.

15. "Money Exchange Offices Open Nationwide," Moscow BALTFAX, 1334 GMT, May 4, 1992, in FBIS-SOV–92–089, May 7, 1992, 66.

16. "Vesti" newscast, Moscow Television Network, 1000 GMT, September 19, 1992, in FBIS-SOV–92–183, September 21, 1992, 73.

17. Justin Burke, "Still Bitter Toward Russia, Estonia Reluctant to Nourish Vital Economic Cooperation," *Christian Science Monitor,* July 15, 1992, 1, 4; "Disagreements Remain on Citizenship," Moscow BALTFAX, 1355 GMT, September 12, 1992, in FBIS-SOV–92–179, September 15, 1992, 47.

18. Aleksandr Lushchin, "You Joined as a Volunteer? The Estonian Army Is in the Formation Stage," Moscow *Nezavisimaya gazeta,* February 21, 1992, 3, in JPRS-UMA–92–010, March 18, 1992, 38; "Defense Forces to Be Established in Voru," Moscow BALTFAX, 1324 GMT, March 22, 1992, in FBIS-SOV–92–058, March 25, 1992, 86.

19. "Military Cooperation Agreed," Moscow BALTFAX, 1818 GMT, June 3, 1992, in FBIS-SOV–92–108, June 4, 1992, 12.

20. "Minister Discusses Baltic Defense Meeting," Riga Radio, 0900 GMT, June 3, 1992, in FBIS-SOV–92–110, June 8, 1992, 8.

21. "Draft Constitution Confirms 1940 Borders," Moscow BALTFAX, 2000 GMT, November 29, 1991, in FBIS-SOV–91–231, December 2, 1991, 35.

22. "Diplomatic Panorama," Moscow INTERFAX, 1159 GMT, May 7, 1992, in FBIS-SOV–92–089, May 7, 1992, 65; Mert Kubu, "Return of Territory near Narva, Petseri Demanded," Stockholm *Dagens nyheter,* May 3, 1992, C4, in FBIS-SOV–92–089, May 7, 1992, 65–66.

23. Yuriy Stroganov, "Russians in Estonia Are Running out of Patience," Moscow *Rossiyskaya gazeta,* June 20, 1992, 5, in FBIS-SOV–92–122, June 24, 1992, 83–84; Daniel Sneider, "Estonia Unruffled by Move to Suspend Troop Pullout," *Christian Science Monitor,* November 5, 1992, 8.

24. "I.M.F. to Aid 2 Baltic States," D2.

25. Aleksandr Cherepanov, "Recollections of the Naval Future," Moscow *Rossiya,* April 29, 1992, 5, in JPRS-UMA–92–022, June 17, 1992, 29–30.

26. M. Ziyeminsh, "Latvia. T. Jundzis: 'Of Course, I Served in the Soviet Army …,' " *Krasnaya zvezda,* November 30, 1991, 3, in FBIS-SOV–92–232, December 3, 1991, 56–57.

27. "Government Views Fate of Soviet Army Property," Riga Radio, 0530 GMT, December 5, 1991, in FBIS-SOV–91–235, December 6, 1991, 45.

28. Matti Huuhtanen, "Time to Go Home, Baltics Implore Ex-Soviet Troops," *Chicago Tribune,* June 24, 1992, A5.

29. "Further on Troop Withdrawal from Baltic States," Moscow Radio, 1110 GMT, May 29, 1992, in FBIS-SOV–92–105, June 1, 1992, 18.

30. John Hoagland, "The Empire Strides Back: Russia's Army in Retreat," *Washington Post,* June 21, 1992, C4.

31. "Language Tests for Government Employees Continue," Moscow BALTFAX, 0932, September 15, 1992, in FBIS-SOV–92–179, September 15, 1992, 52–53.

32. Galina Kuchina, "Parliament Rejects 1944 Land 'Annexation,' " Moscow TASS, 2234 GMT, January 22, 1992, in FBIS-SOV–92–015, January 23, 1992, 113.

33. Mikhail Pogorelyy, "West Concerned About Our Nuclear Reactor Safety," *Krasnaya zvezda,* July 22, 1992, 3, in FBIS-SOV–92–143, July 24, 1992, 8.

34. Andrey Zhdankin, "Secret Services," Moscow *Rossiyskaya gazeta,* July 11, 1992, 5, in FBIS-SOV–92–137, July 16, 1992, 45.

35. "Baltic Troop Withdrawal to Begin in 1994," Moscow BALTFAX, 1715 GMT, November 29, 1991, in FBIS-SOV–91–233, December 4, 1991, 36; K. Uspila, "Who Is Owner of Soviet Army's Property?" *Krasnaya zvezda,* December 4, 1991, 11, in FBIS-SOV–92–235, December 6, 1991, 46.

36. "Lithuania and Russia in Accord on Troop Pullout by Next August," *New York Times,* September 9, 1992, A10; "How Much of the Army of the Former USSR is in Lithuania?" Vilnius *Lietuvos rytas,* June 12, 1992, 1, in JPRS-UMA–92–028, July 29, 1992, 2.

37. Kazis Ustsila, "Results Issued on Army Pullout Referendum," Moscow TASS, 1458 GMT, June 15, 1992, in FBIS-SOV–92–116, June 16, 1992, 71; "Former Soviets' Ouster Is Backed by Lithuania," *New York Times,* June 16, 1992, A7.

38. "Landsbergis Says Troop Pullout Great Victory," Vilnius Radio, 2300 GMT, September 10, 1992, in FBIS-SOV–92–179, September 15, 1992, 56.

39. "Soviet Military Strength in Baltics Detailed," Vilnius Radio, 2130 GMT, August 13, 1991, in FBIS-SOV–91–158, August 15, 1991, 45.

40. "Yeltsin: Troops Will Leave Lithuania; '93 Pullout Deadline Valid, Report Says," *The Washington Post*, November 4, 1992, A46.

41. "The Army Is Not a Little Toy," Vilnius *Respublika*, January 23, 1992, 2, in JPRS-UMA–92–011, April 1, 1992, 70.

42. Y. Stroganov, "Fleet Personnel Discontented," *Pravda*, November 21, 1991, 6, in FBIS-SOV–91–228, November 21, 1991, 45; Sergey Gruk, "Lithuania Does Not Officially Lay Claim to Kaliningrad. Unofficially, the Lithuanian Ambassador to the United States Talks About Incorporation in the Future," *Izvestiya*, March 3, 1992, 4, in FBIS-SOV–92–043, March 4, 1992, 86.

43. "Problems over Polish Minority's Status Noted," Moscow INTERFAX, 1918 GMT, December 24, 1991, in FBIS-SOV–91–248, December 26, 1991, 36.

44. "Klaipeda Russians Call for Distribution of Arms," Vilnius Radio, 2300 GMT, September 12, 1992, in FBIS-SOV–92–179, September 15, 1992, 57.

45. Nikolay Lashkevich, "Lithuania Clarifies Borders," *Izvestiya*, January 20, 1992, 2, in FBIS-SOV–92–015, January 23, 1992, 28.

46. "Government Discusses Border Issues With Belarus," Moscow BALTFAX, 1521 GMT, September 20, 1992, in FBIS-SOV–92–184, September 22, 1992, 70.

Western Region

4

Western Region

The western region of the former Soviet Union best illustrates what happens when the strong authoritarian impulses that maintain the appearance of unity fade away. As the Pacific region of the Russian Federation looks to the east, Central Asia and Caucasus are drawn southward, and the Baltic states seek their natural affinity with Scandinavia and northern Europe, the western region is on the brink of abandoning the unique orientation and legacy of what had been the Soviet Union. Now that the countries of Eastern Europe are independent, the new states of the western region constitute the sole buffer protecting Russia's borders with the West.

Belarus

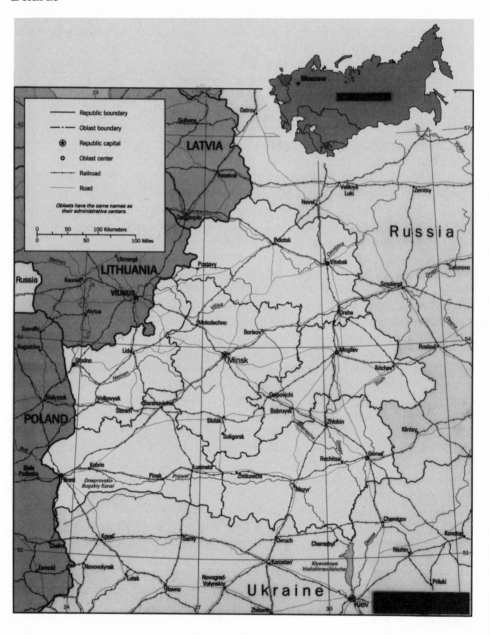

Belarus

BASIC DATA

Total Area: 80,154 square miles (207,600 square kilometers).

Population: 10.3 million. Some 78 percent are Belorussian, 13 percent are Russian, and 4 percent are Polish. The growth rate is 0.5 percent on an annual basis.

Religion: Russian Orthodox, Roman Catholic.

Official Name: Republic of Belarus.

Capital: Minsk, which is also the site of the main executive offices of the Commonwealth of Independent States.

Government:

- Executive Branch: Stanislav Shushkevich is chairman of the Supreme Soviet. The government is headed by a prime minister.
- Legislative Branch: Supreme Soviet.
- Judicial Branch: Supreme Court.

A draft constitution was published in August 1992 following a revision of the first draft, which was subjected to wide public discussion. It calls for a Sejm, or parliament, of 160 deputies and a president elected to a five-year term.

Economy: Until the breakup of the Soviet Union, almost 70 percent of its output was exported. Its economy is still closely integrated with those of its neighbors. Belarus produces food, machinery, and consumer goods.

History: The White Russians share a rich past as Eastern Slavs who, together with Russians and Ukrainians, created the original Russian state at Kiev in the ninth century. After conquest by the Mongols, they fell prey to Polish-Lithuanian rule until World War I, when the western half was ceded to Poland and the eastern half became the Soviet republic of Byelorussia. The 1939 Molotov-Ribbentrop Pact returned the territory to Stalin; following Germany's defeat, it was reoccupied. Stalin strongly discouraged the use of Belorussian, the area's native tongue, but efforts to revive it as the official language are under way.

THE ROAD TO INDEPENDENCE

Belarus declared its sovereignty on July 27, 1990, and its independence on August 25, 1991. One of four CIS nuclear powers, Belarus voluntarily passed all tactical nuclear weapons to Russia in early May 1992, two months before agreed upon. As a signatory of the May 23, 1992, Lisbon agreement, it promised to yield all strategic nuclear weapons to Russia by the year 2000, less those eliminated by the START and other arms control treaties.

Belarus has stated its intention to become a nonnuclear, neutral state. Prime Minister Vyacheslav Kebich traveled to China in January 1992, the first such visit by the head of a newly independent state of the former Soviet Union. Belarus has also supported the Helsinki Final Act, the Paris Charter for a New Europe, and other CSCE positions as vital "to our return to the family of European peoples." On April 8, 1992, the new state became the first Commonwealth member to sign the Paris Charter.[1]

Since Belarus was a founding member of the Commonwealth of Independent States, authorities in Minsk have repeatedly affirmed their commitment to the body. This has not prevented the republic from concluding bilateral agreements with CIS member states, much as Russia has done with the states of Central Asia. Belarus and Russia signed a comprehensive agreement detailing a host of issues in Minsk on June 26, 1992.[2]

Minsk has been somewhat more ambivalent with regard to its national currency. While acknowledging its presence within a common "ruble zone," in January 1992 it introduced coupons to serve as "interim currency" until a Belarusan currency is available. On May 25, a new "ruble" in denominations of 10, 50, and 75, was distributed as a parallel currency to the Russian ruble, with an exchange rate of 10 rubles per ruble.[3] Belarus has freed most prices, much as Moscow and Kiev did on January 2, 1992, and it is not in a strong position to support autarkic economic measures.

Because the republic is essentially landlocked, it reached a major agreement in March 1992 with Kaliningrad Oblast, the Russian Federation's isolated though strategic province on the Baltic southeast of Lithuania. According to the agreement, a highway will be built from the Belarusan city of Grodno to Kaliningrad via the Polish city of Suwalki. Belarusan goods will have direct access to an important Baltic port, and natural gas and other commodities will be exchanged in trade based upon the ruble. Going through Poland is a more direct route, and it avoids depending on Lithuania for transit rights and access to the Russian enclave.[4]

A matter of some sensitivity to the new state is the presence of substantial numbers of Russian armed forces on Belarusan soil. According to Defense Minister Col. Gen. Pavel Kozlovskiy, "there is one serviceman to every 43 members of the population in the republic."[5] This is the greatest concentration of military units and personnel of any state of Europe. For Belarus to become a nuclear free, neutral nation, a purely defensive doctrine will be required.[6]

To codify the continuing Russian presence, Belarus signed a Treaty on Cooperation in the Defense Sphere as a part of a comprehensive package of joint agreements. The bilateral accord defined the status of some 30,000 Russian forces of the estimated 130,000 Russian troops that will remain in Belarus.[7] Belarus has also become a participant in the Russian–Ukrainian joint stock corporation known as MAC, "the Big-Mac of the missile-building industry." This corporation will continue to build space defense missile components as it did for the Soviet military–industrial complex. Other defense plants in Belarus are also producing military equipment for Russia.[8]

Chairman of the Supreme Soviet Shushkevich has been consistent in proclaiming the need for Belarus to have its own armed forces. A parliamentary resolution set March 20, 1992, as the day a national military force would be created. The armed forces are expected to number between 90,000 and 100,000 and would consist primarily of units of the former Soviet army. Eventually, the army should be about 50,000 to 60,000 strong, once it is reconfigured and reorganized to serve national purposes. A Security Council coordinates military and defense policy.[9]

One of Belarus's main security dilemmas is the result of the April 26, 1986, Chernobyl disaster, which brought untold destruction and hardship to the small state—it was the primary recipient of the radioactivity. This—the greatest disaster in the republic's history—has raised the public's awareness of environmental issues.

SEPARATIST/TERRITORIAL DISPUTES

1. On February 24, 1992, Foreign Minister Pyotr Kravchenko informed a visiting European Community delegation that Minsk has a border claim against Lithuania that extends to Vilnius, thirty miles (forty-eight kilometers) away. The basis of this claim was not revealed, but Shushkevich, visiting Vilnius on March 26, 1992, described this assertion as a joke.[10]

2. On March 23, 1992, a border agreement between Lithuania and Belarus

resolved a pressing question. Vilnius wanted the border to be marked according to land use, since some farms have fields that extend into Belarusan territory. Minsk authorities, on the other hand, wanted to place the markers along the juridical boundary. The two states agreed that the markers will be placed along the legal border.[11] The total cost of this undertaking is estimated at 700 million rubles.[12]

3. There is a concern that Poles living in western Belarus may constitute an irredentist movement connected with the predominantly Polish-language Catholic churches in the region.[13]

4. Some 3 million Russians live in Belarus, constituting a sizeable minority of 13 percent of the republic's total population. President Stanislav Shushkevich has maintained that they do not constitute a threat, and he has refused to construct border posts to delineate the Russian–Belarus border.[14]

5. An estimated 290,000 Ukrainians also live in Belarus. They do not have access to Ukrainian schools, nor are Ukrainian-language programs transmitted on Belarusan television. Kiev's ambassador has called for the development of increased economic and cultural ties between the two new states as a means of furthering mutual understanding.[15]

Moldova

BASIC DATA

Total Area: 13,012 square miles (33,700 square kilometers). It was the second smallest union republic of the former Soviet Union.

Population: 4.5 million. Most of the republic's population (64 percent) is Moldovan, essentially ethnic Romanians. Ukrainians constitute 14 percent, and Russians 13 percent. The rate of growth is 0.7 percent. The language is very similar to Romanian.

Religion: Russian Orthodox, Ukrainian Uniate.

Official Name: Republic of Moldova.

Capital: Chisinau.

Government:

- Executive Branch: Mircea Snegur, incumbent president and sole candidate, was reelected to the presidency by popular vote on December 8, 1991. The government is headed by a prime minister.
- Legislative Branch: Supreme Soviet.
- Judicial Branch: Supreme Court.

Economy: Moldova's economy is focused on agriculture and food processing. Its currency—the lei—has been prepared for release, and its use as legal tender was approved in December 1992.

History: Since Moldova was a principality of the Russian empire in the seventeenth and eighteenth centuries, the people adopted the Cyrillic alphabet. The area between the Prut and Dniester rivers, known as Bessarabia,

Moldova

*Now Chişinău

was ceded to Russia in 1812, and it remained a part of that country until 1918 when it became part of Romania. In 1924, the Soviet regime created the Moldavian Autonomous Soviet Socialist Republic in the trans-Dniester region, east of the Dniester River.

The August 23, 1939, Molotov–Ribbentrop Pact changed the political geography of this area by ceding Bessarabia, northern Bukovina, and Herta to the Soviet Union; they were occupied by the Red Army on June 28, 1940. Bessarabia and trans-Dniester were incorporated into a new Moldavian Soviet Socialist Republic in 1940. Northern Bukovina, the neighboring Herta district, and the northernmost and southern parts of Bessarabia were merged into Ukraine under the terms of a 1947 peace treaty.

THE ROAD TO INDEPENDENCE

The Republic of Moldova proclaimed its sovereignty on June 23, 1990, and independence on August 27, 1991. Romanian was adopted as the state language, and the Latin script was reintroduced by order of Parliament on August 31, 1989. Its name was changed to the Republic of Moldova on May 23, 1991.

Since these signal events, Moldovan authorities have been fully occupied trying to maintain the new nation's sovereignty and integrity. An active insurgency in the trans-Dniester in the east, unrest among the ethnic Gagauz in the southwest, and continued tensions connected with the state's relationship with Romania have kept the small republic in turmoil.

In early 1992, Moldova's defense minister began to plan for the formation of a national army. In the first registration for the country's military draft, half of those registering requested alternative service rather than military duty. When the call-up took place in May 1992, 15,000 young men appeared. Eventually there will be an army of 20,000 men and 400,000 reservists. The Ministry of Defense is planning to create four motorized rifle brigades, an air defense brigade, a communications brigade, and a small air arm.[16]

When asked about the nature of the threat the small country faces, the deputy minister of defense observed, "Any Moldovan citizen can see very plainly that Romania cannot become our enemy. The same may be said of Ukraine. And Moldova has no borders with any other countries."[17] The Ministry of Defense is located in the ornate building that previously served as headquarters of Moscow's Southwestern Theater of Military Operations, from which strategic operations would be conducted against NATO. The new army expected to get most of its equipment from former Soviet units, particularly the 14th Army. This has become more problematic as combat in trans-Dniester has intensified.

Ties with Romania have been good and date from the formation of a unitary Romanian state on December 1, 1918. The parliaments of Romania and Moldova established a National Union Council in December 1991 with the mission of "speeding up the historic process of Romania's reunification." The council was open to all citizens of Bessarabia, northern Bukovina, Herta, and Romania.[18] This issue has led to heated discussions between those pressing for immediate reunification and those opposed to any formal ties with Bucharest.

Much of Moldova's recent history centers on the violent conflict in the trans-Dniester region. This has exacerbated domestic tensions, nearly bankrupted the new country, and led to direct involvement by Boris Yeltsin and the Russian army. On June 9, 1992, Prime Minister Valeriu Muravsky and most of his cabinet resigned, largely because of the ongoing conflict. President Snegur, who did not go to the Rio earth summit because of the fighting, asked the officials to remain for two more weeks, to permit a new government to be formed.[19] Despite the involvement of Russia and Ukraine, and appeals for UN intervention, the ceasefire that resulted has been tenuous.

SEPARATIST/DISSIDENT MOVEMENTS

1. The major source of conflict in present-day Moldova involves the heavily Russian-populated, Russian-speaking area on the left or eastern bank of the Dniester. This region, the only part of Moldova that has been under Soviet control since 1924, is home to approximately 600,000 people, of whom 400,000 are Russians and Ukrainians, and the remainder Moldovan. On September 2, 1990, the Dniester Moldavian Soviet Socialist Republic was proclaimed, a name later changed to the Dniester Republic. A parliament was elected in October 1990, and on December 1, 1991, former premier Igor Smirnov was chosen president in an election declared void by Moldovan officials.

Following presidential elections in Dniester, a system of parallel government began to appear, with police, military forces, and soviets representing both Moldova and Dniester coexisting. The Dniester Defense and Security Department is headed by Lt. Gen. Gennady Yakovlev, former commander of Moscow's 14th Army, based in Tiraspol. Yakovlev was expected to arrange the transfer of significant quantities of military equipment belonging to the former Soviet army to his new command.[20]

Increasing hostilities led the Dniester parliament to declare a state of emergency around Dubossary in March 1992. In response to increased deaths and destruction, President Snegur declared a Moldovan state of emergency on March 28, ordering the police and military forces "to liquidate and disarm the illegitimate armed formations" there. Amnesty was offered to belligerents who turned themselves in, and the dissidents were termed "terrorists."[21]

This was followed by reports that Russian soldiers belonging to units of the 14th Army had joined the Dniester insurgents, which was confirmed by a Russian spokesman, who said the soldiers had done so without authorization. Romania has been accused of providing military equipment to Moldova, and Russia has been similarly charged with supporting the separatists. Both sides wear Soviet army uniforms, with the Moldovan soldiers distinguished by Moldovan patches. Dniester soldiers have been joined by Ukrainian and Russian Cossacks, who have rallied to support fellow Slavs. The situation was inflamed by a statement from Russian Vice President Alexander Rutskoi, who said Russian troops would defend ethnic Russians throughout the former USSR.[22]

Fearing the situation was getting out of control, Boris Yeltsin took control of the 14th Army and held talks with Leonid Kravchuk, president of Ukraine, Moldova's President Snegur, and Romanian President Ion Iliescu at a Turkish Black Sea resort. A brief ceasefire was arranged but did not hold, and a UN fact-finding delegation was fired upon one week later. As many as one thousand people have died in the continuing hostilities.

Boris Yeltsin next met with President Snegur on July 4, 1992; they agreed that the Moldovan parliament would work out an arrangement giving the secessionists some form of autonomy. Then, on July 21, 1992, presidents Yeltsin and Snegur concluded an agreement that provided for a ceasefire and a safety corridor between opposing sides. It conveyed a special status for the breakaway region within Moldova and acknowledged the right of the Dniester peoples to self-determination "should the sovereign status of the Republic of Moldova change," a reference to its possible union with Romania at some future date. A Trilateral Control Commission based in Bendery and composed of Russian, Moldovan, and Dniester representatives was created to supervise the agreement.[23]

In the meantime, the Dniester Republic is continuing to acquire the vestiges of statehood, including armed forces and an independent banking system. This situation represents an attempt to keep at bay the multiple forces of disintegration rampant in the former Soviet Union. Only a person of the stature of Boris Yeltsin, an individual not without opposition in his own country, can contain the many disputes of the multiethnic peoples just emerging from a turbulent past, such as those living in trans-Dniestria.

2. Chisinau still claims areas of northern Bukovina, Herta, northern Bessarabia, and the southern Bessarabian regions along the Danube, which were incorporated into Ukraine following World War II.

3. The Gagauz, Turkic Christians who live in the southern portion of Moldova and number about 120,000, want to become an autonomous republic within Moldova. The Gagauz Republic, with its capital in Komrat, was declared in August 1990, but it has not been recognized by Moldovan authorities. Gagauz leaders seek greater autonomy over local affairs, and the republic's Supreme Soviet has acted to recognize the Dniester Republic. In presidential elections held on December 1, 1991, Stepan Topal was elected the republic's president.[24]

While the Moldovan leadership has expressed a willingness to grant the Gagauz peoples cultural and economic autonomy, Chisinau continues to resist granting further political autonomy to the self-proclaimed republic. On July 30, 1992, Topan declared that the Gagauz Republic exists: "It exists de facto, although the Moldovan Republic has not de jure recognized it."[25]

4. The possibility of reunification with Romania continues to perplex and seduce many in the new state. In mid-August 1992 the speaker of Moldova's parliament, Alexandru Mosnau, became the first official to declare openly that preparations for reunification were under way. The 1.5 million peoples who do not share the common Romanian heritage, particularly Russians and Ukrainians, can be expected to protest and resist this development.[26]

5. The parliament in Chisinau has not yet decided whether it will ratify the December 21, 1991, Alma-Ata agreement signed by President Snegur, thus permitting Moldova to become a full member of the CIS.

Ukraine

BASIC DATA

Total Area: 233,089 square miles (603,700 square kilometers).

Population: Fifty-two million, with an annual growth rate of 0.2 percent. Some 73 percent of the population is Ukrainian, 22 percent Russian, and the remainder Belorussian and Jewish. Eleven million Russians live in Ukraine, mostly in the east and south.

Religion: The Ukrainian Greek Catholic (Uniate) Church is primarily found in western Ukraine. This church recognizes the authority of the Roman Catholic pope but permits its clergy to marry and conducts Greek Orthodox rites. In 1991 the Russian Orthodox Church in Ukraine split into two parts: the existing church, subordinate to the patriarch in Moscow, and a Ukrainian Orthodox Church. Both compete with a third Orthodox faction, the independent Ukrainian Autocephalous Orthodox Church, which merged with elements of the Ukrainian Orthodox Church to form the Ukrainian Orthodox Church—Kiev Patriarchate on June 27, 1992. It is said to enjoy the support of Ukrainian officials.[27]

Official Name: Ukraine.

Capital: Kiev.

Government:

- Executive Branch: The head of state is President Leonid M. Kravchuk, elected to the new executive presidency on December 1, 1991. A cabinet

Ukraine

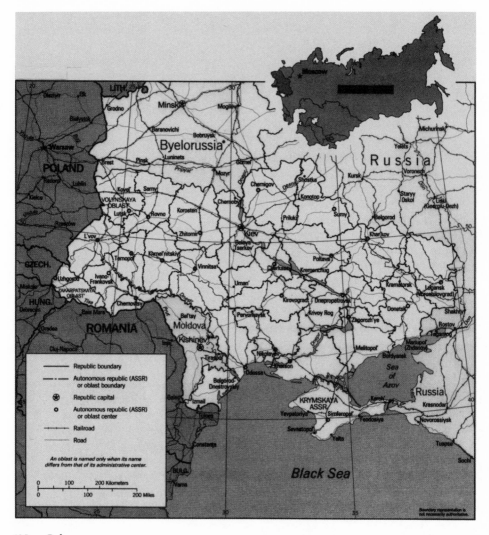

*Now Belarus
**Now Chişinău

of ministers coordinates the work of the government, which is headed by a prime minister.

- Legislative Branch: Supreme Council.
- Judicial Branch: Supreme Court.

A new constitution is to be adopted, and an advisory National Security Council makes recommendations to the president on national security issues. Kiev's decision in July 1992 to contribute a battalion of soldiers to the UN peacekeeping force at Sarajevo, Bosnia and Herzegovina (in the former Yugoslavia), represents a significant international commitment for the new state.

Kravchuk has appointed and installed a network of presidential representatives, called prefects, to serve as government administrators in most regions of the country. This is expected to be an interim measure to replace regional councils elected during the Communist era.

Tense ties have developed between Ukraine and Russia over a variety of issues. Most noteworthy has been the dispute over the ownership of the Crimea and the Black Sea Fleet. President Kravchuk is establishing a military force separate from Commonwealth forces. Ukrainian forces are to consist of a national guard of approximately 30,000 men as well as an army of up to 400,000.

Economy: Ukraine is the richest of the former Soviet republics. It is noted for its agricultural production and coal, primarily from the Donbass region of eastern Ukraine. Despite Ukraine's coal, its primary deficiency is energy—most of its oil, natural gas, and gasoline are furnished by other republics of the former Soviet Union. A major agreement for Iranian oil and natural gas, involving the construction of a three-tube, seven-billion-dollar pipeline through Azerbaijan, was concluded in February 1992.[28]

Ukraine has the second-largest defense industry in the former USSR, after Russia, with 700 factories and more than one million employees.[29] By October 1992, privatization had barely begun, with 96 percent of the economy still in state hands. Inflation was 30 percent per month, and Ukraine's interim voucher currency had fallen faster in value than the Russian ruble.[30] Plans have been made to issue privatization vouchers to all citizens in 1993, but much remains to be done before this takes place.

History: Christianity was introduced into Kievian Rus on the shores of the Dnieper River in 988. Ukraine has been torn between Poland to the west and Russia to the east. The March 1918 Treaty of Brest-Litovsk, along with the end of the Austro-Hungarian Empire later that year, brought a brief period of independence until 1919, when it was forcibly brought under the aegis of the new Soviet state.

Noteworthy in Ukrainian history was the enforced famine of 1932–1933, a deliberate policy of Stalin which resulted in the deaths of as many as five

million persons.[31] Terror, brutal Russification, and military occupation occurred both before and after the widespread devastation and loss brought
by World War II.

The most recent cataclysmic event in Ukraine's turbulent history was the
April 26, 1986, explosion of nuclear reactor no. 4 at Chernobyl. This was
the world's most serious nuclear power plant accident, endangering millions
of lives and causing widespread environmental devastation.

THE ROAD TO INDEPENDENCE

Stirrings for independence were felt throughout the Soviet era. In recent
years, Ukrainian nationalism has been particularly strong in western
Ukraine, where the Rukh pro-independence movement has its staunchest
following. The republic parliament declared its independence on August 24,
1991, in the aftermath of the failed coup attempt. In November 1991,
Ukraine assumed command of KGB border guards in the republic. Soviet
Interior Ministry troops were also taken over by Ukraine, to become part
of a national guard.[32]

The December 1, 1991, independence referendum precipitated the constitutional crisis in the former Soviet Union. Some 90 percent of voters
approved complete independence from the former Soviet Union, which
sealed the fate of the Soviet Union and led directly to the creation of the
Commonwealth of Independent States by Russia, Belarus, and Ukraine on
December 8.

A major issue was the control of the 4,000 nuclear weapons on Ukrainian
soil, some 15 percent of the Soviet total. They included 176 intercontinental
ballistic missiles carrying 1,240 nuclear warheads.[33] Soviet military units
being withdrawn from eastern Germany were reassigned in Ukraine until
early December 1991, when authorities in Moscow decided that they would
return to Russia.[34]

Another contentious problem is the ownership of the Black Sea Fleet,
largely based in the Crimea. This issue was addressed in direct talks between
President Yeltsin of Russia and President Kravchuk on June 23, 1992, when
the basic outlines of a compromise were agreed upon. Ukraine expects to
issue a national currency, the hryvnya, to end its monetary dependence on
Moscow.

UKRAINE AT THE CROSSROADS

Ukraine has historically been a borderland separating religions, peoples,
traditions, and cultures. It is the birthplace of Russia and its principal religion, and its lands have been contested by Mongols, Poles, Russians, Germans, and others. Today, Ukraine continues this tradition but with an
essential difference. The passing of the Soviet Union on December 25, 1991,

codified what had already occurred in the hearts and minds of Ukrainians living within and beyond its post–1945 borders: true independence.

The Red Army's 1919 subjugation of the nascent Ukrainian People's Republic started the nation's long and costly journey to free itself from the grip of Soviet power. That journey included the 1922 union treaty, Stalin's deliberate famine of 1932–1933, the "Great Terror" of 1936–1938, the brutalities of both Russians and Germans during World War II, the incarceration of hundreds of thousands of Ukrainians following the war, and years of deliberate Sovietization and occupation. The advent of the Gorbachev era and the approaching demise of the Soviet Union led to the July 16, 1991, declaration of sovereignty; the August 24, 1991, declaration of independence; the December 1, 1991, election of Leonid Kravchuk as president and the national referendum on independence; and, finally, the December 5, 1991, unanimous decision by parliament to annul the 1922 treaty.

Ukrainian efforts to assert autonomy and sovereignty must be seen in light of this recent history, which has compounded centuries of foreign conquest and subjugation. Indeed, Ukraine's deliberate journey to independence sounded the death knell of the Soviet Union. Leonid Kravchuk, after the December 1 referendum saw 90.3 percent of voters approve independence, noted: "A great historic event has occurred which I am confident will change not only the life of the Ukrainian people but the face of the world. The Soviet Union has disintegrated."[35] With this development, Mikhail Gorbachev knew by December 5 that the end was in sight: "I cannot visualize the union without the Ukraine."[36]

By December 8, 1991, two other republics joined Ukraine to form the Commonwealth of Independent States, and on December 21 they were joined by eight other former union republics. While Boris Yeltsin indisputably played a major role in these events, none could have occurred without Ukrainian participation. With 52 million people, the state has the second largest population of the former Soviet republics. Large numbers of its 11 million Russian inhabitants voted for independence, and many believe that Ukraine, of all fifteen new states, has the best chance for economic prosperity.

Persistent inflation, the lack of serious economic reform, and worsening economic conditions, however, led Parliament to dismiss Prime Minister Vitold Fokin's government on October 1, 1992. He was replaced by Leonid Kuchma, director of Uzhmash, said to be the world's largest rocket plant. Kuchma has promised to strengthen economic ties with both the CIS and Western states and to pursue a controlled shift to a market economy.[37]

IN SEARCH OF UKRAINIAN NATIONAL SECURITY POLICY

The future of the new Ukrainian state now stands at a critical point. As the key borderland republic of the former Soviet Union, the programs, policies, and institutions that evolve there not only will largely determine its future but also will have a great influence on what transpires in the other former Soviet republics, particularly Russia. The conundrum within which it now finds itself involves national security in the broadest, strategic sense of the term. As Ukraine proceeds in its quest for political autonomy and economic progress, five key factors will influence the security policies that evolve. In addition, all will serve to point the new state along a strategic course—either toward the future or back to the past.

1. *Military issues.* Because military might was a central policy of the Soviet era and was vital to the longevity of the Soviet state, it was to be expected that military affairs would dominate early Ukrainian-Soviet interaction.

Ukrainian assertiveness was demonstrated on October 22, 1991, when its parliament authorized the formation of a national army of 400,000 and a national guard of some 30,000 troops. This move occurred despite Mikhail Gorbachev's warning on the previous day that the "privatization" of military equipment and personnel was an unconstitutional and dangerous act. To Konstantin Morozov, the new defense minister, "the course of history cannot be changed. The Ukraine will have its own armed forces."[38]

On October 24, 1991, the Ukrainian parliament turned its attention to nuclear matters. It formally acknowledged Moscow's command of that portion of the Soviet nuclear arsenal based on Ukrainian soil, but it insisted on Kiev's right to control its use jointly.[39] This arsenal consisted of some 1,420 strategic warheads, carried by 176 ICBMs and 2,390 tactical warheads, along with 30 heavy bombers armed with cruise missiles. This would make Ukraine the third most powerful nuclear state after the United States and Russia.[40] On October 26, the country's parliament reaffirmed the principles contained in its July 16, 1991, sovereignty statement: it would not receive, produce, or acquire nuclear weaponry. Ukraine intended to become and remain a nonnuclear state.[41]

With the founding of the CIS on December 8, 1991, the disintegration of the Soviet Union was irretrievably set into motion. On December 12 it was announced that President Kravchuk had taken command of former union forces in the Kiev, Odessa, and Carpathian military districts as well as of the Black Sea Fleet.[42] The 1.5 million Soviet troops on Ukrainian soil, less those assigned to strategic deterrence missions, were now claimed by the new state.

Early in its formative stages, the Ukrainian parliament established firm control mechanisms for the new armed forces: the president as commander in chief, a Defense Council consisting of senior state and military officials, a defense minister, and a senior defense staff. A national army, air force, and navy were to be created from the Soviet forces then on Ukrainian territory and forces returning from Eastern Europe. The republic's status as a neutral and nonnuclear state was consistently maintained.[43]

It was also clear that many details would have to be resolved before an independent Ukrainian force could be a reality. First, the country's air defense was a part of the unified Soviet air defense network. Much would have to be done to provide an independent air defense that could distinguish friendly aircraft from nonfriendly intruders, monitor the airspace of a nation roughly the size of France, and supervise the more than three thousand aircraft operating in Ukrainian airspace on a daily basis.[44]

The newly created national guard was charged with defending constitutional rights and the nation's independence and sovereignty, protecting foreign embassies, conducting natural disaster relief efforts, and assisting the border guards. The first guard troops were sworn in on January 5, 1992, and training began four days later.[45] A National Security Service, based upon remnants of the KGB, was also created, with military counterintelligence, civil counterintelligence, and intelligence collection responsibilities.[46]

Leonid Kravchuk moved quickly to form a Ukrainian navy based upon existing units of the Black Sea Fleet. According to a general representing the Ukrainian Defense Ministry, "the position of Ukraine on the Black Sea Fleet is clear and understood. We believe that it is necessary to allocate to strategic forces only that portion of the fleet which accomplishes the appropriate missions. All remaining fleet assets must be transferred to the naval forces of Ukraine."[47]

Interest in the status of the fleet had been building since the aircraft carrier *Admiral Kuznetsov* passed through the Bosporus and Dardanelles on December 2, 1991. In mid-February 1992, six SU–24 bombers and crews were "hijacked" to Russia, in an apparent attempt to escape Ukraine's grasp. Nearly 400 ships, including thirty diesel submarines and sixty-five in reserve; 100,000 men; and 400 aircraft based at Tuapse in Russia, at Sevastopol, Odessa, and Balaklava in Ukraine, and at Poti in Georgia, form the Black Sea Fleet.[48] Ukraine claims more than 80 percent of the fleet that is considered nonstrategic in nature.[49]

Ukrainian President Kravchuk acted on April 5, 1992, to prevent further diversions by claiming actual ownership of the portion of the fleet based in Ukraine, leading Boris Yeltsin to claim the fleet as Russia's sole property. Further confrontation was averted by the two leaders on August 3, 1992, when they signed an agreement placing the Black Sea Fleet under joint jurisdiction for three years to permit time for both nations to decide on the final division of its assets.

The status of Ukraine's nuclear arsenal also provided the basis for disagreement with Moscow. Although Ukraine, Belarus, and Kazakhstan agreed to dispatch all tactical nuclear warheads to Russia by July 1, 1992, for eventual dismantling as part of the CIS Alma-Ata foundational agreement, Kravchuk suspended the transfer in March because he demanded guarantees that the weapons would be properly disposed of and their components protected. This halt resulted in a protocol between Russia and Ukraine on April 16, 1992, that detailed procedures for the weapons' control, neutralization, and destruction.

The strategic weapons problem was further addressed in May when Ukraine, Belarus, and Kazakhstan formally agreed that they would yield all nuclear arms by the year 2000 and ban them from their soil forever. The Lisbon agreement of May 23, 1992, was necessary for the United States and Russia to proceed to ratify and implement the 1991 START agreement on strategic weapons, as well as follow-on cuts agreed to at the June 1992 Washington summit. It would also leave Russia as the sole former Soviet nuclear state.[50]

In a statement to NATO, Ukrainian Foreign Minister Anatoliy Zlenko observed that this voluntary cession of nuclear arms had warranted the granting of guarantees by NATO and international bodies to protect Ukraine from any nuclear state. This issue of security guarantees received further resonance in mid-November, when Ukrainian leaders threatened to withhold parliamentary ratification of START, the Lisbon protocol, and the Nuclear Nonproliferation Treaty. Realizing that the nuclear materials in the strategic warheads are of great value, this threat implies that unspecified guarantees and payment of some kind will be necessary if Ukraine is to yield the strategic advantage that the materials represent. The new country's economic straits compound the emotions over this issue.[51]

This concern with security guarantees for a nonnuclear Ukraine does not appear unreasonable, given the legacy the new state inherited and the extent to which military imperatives ruled the former Soviet Union. Indeed, both Moscow and Washington have provided unspecified security guarantees to encourage Ukraine to ratify Start I, a requirement before Start II can take effect. The nuclear material in these weapons is estimated to be worth at least $1 billion,[52] and Ukraine may properly assert that it paid its fair share of the cost. To lose this asset is not as troublesome as gaining a long-term strategic liability: a nuclear-armed Russia with which Ukraine continues to have a host of disagreements.

2. *Social issues.* No nation's security is on a firm basis when its society is affected by serious fissures. For Ukrainians, these strains are familiar: the eastern and southern regions inhabited by large numbers of Russians with identifiable language and religious differences; western areas where Ukrainian nationalism is strong; and the Crimea, where conflict with Tatars claiming their ancestral homeland in a region heavily inhabited by Russians potentially destabilizes a situation already tense due to the controversy over the Black Sea Fleet.

Following the December 1, 1991, national election and independence referendum, many expected such tensions to surface openly. According to Roman Szporluk of Harvard University, "certain experts were expecting conflict—between western Ukraine and eastern Ukraine; between Ukraine and Russia; clashes with Jews, Poles. None of this took place."[53] Concern has also focused on the eastern and western diaspora of ethnic Ukrainians, including some seven million in Russia who lack Ukrainian schools or other cultural facilities.[54]

Societies that have undergone such trauma as in Ukraine will require years, if not generations, before coherence, national purpose, and civility can be restored. Patience, both domestic and international, is a primary prerequisite, yet social and other pressures often preclude this necessary healing process. The danger of unchecked nationalism in a number of virulent forms, including Rukh, the Ukrainian nationalist group, and the Republic Movement of Crimea, which advocates independence for the peninsula, persists. Security, in its domestic as well as its external variants, may continue to prove elusive.

3. *Economic problems.* Ukrainian national security is closely associated with economic stability and prosperity. While Ukraine produced 56 percent of the Soviet Union's corn, 25 percent of its wheat, 47 percent of its iron, and 23 percent of its coal, it was almost completely dependent on the USSR for natural gas, oil, and petroleum products.[55] Ukraine's abundant uranium deposits at Zheltyye Vody went into a large proportion of the Soviet Union's nuclear weapons.[56] The resulting economic interdependence served to limit national sovereignty.

Key to economic independence have been efforts to eliminate use of the ruble as the sole national currency. Soon after the formation of the CIS, Leonid Kravchuk expressed skepticism about the viability of a common "ruble zone" of commonwealth states: "The ruble zone can turn into a fiction. We could find ourselves in the ruble zone without any rubles."[57] While Ukraine made plans to issue its own currency, the hryvnya (based upon Canadian financing), ruble shortages occurred throughout the former Soviet Union.

In March 1992, the Ukrainian parliament approved a plan to divorce the nation from the ruble and its attendant problems: inflation, scarcity, and price instability. This program would effectively separate Ukraine from the economic structure of the ten other CIS states, which authorities in Kiev saw as an advantage, given the perilous state of the Russian economy. As an intermediate step, Ukraine has been using coupons for cash purchases of food and other basic necessities.[58]

In preparation for the introduction of the hryvnya, reusable coupons would serve as an interim currency, with the ruble reserved for trade with other former Soviet republics. Kravchuk refused to participate in the CIS common bank that was created at the October 9, 1992, summit at Bishkek, and he announced on Ukrainian television his intention for the country to develop on its own.[59] Ukraine has also asserted its right to pay its share of the former Soviet Union's external debt, which in turn would give it claim to 16.37 percent of the Soviet Union's assets.[60] The estimated eighty-one billion dollars owed by the former Soviet Union, Western banks have held, is still the collective responsibility of former member states.[61]

Economic issues will have a direct-bearing on the future of Ukraine as a viable nation-state. International aid is tied to significant monetary and fiscal reforms imposed by the IMF, and unless Kiev is cooperative in this regard,

Western assistance may be slow in arriving. Economic security is tightly intertwined within the fabric of national security, and much remains to be done before economic stability is achieved.

4. *Environmental challenges.* The fact that the world's most serious nuclear power plant disaster occurred in Ukraine has made environmental issues a top priority in any national security equation. The Chernobyl disaster of April 1986 is estimated to have cost between ten and twenty billion dollars.[62] The human cost in lives destroyed and disrupted, however, is incalculable.

Now the concern is that any Western investment in Ukraine and in other former Soviet republics may be jeopardized by another environmental disaster of Chernobyl proportions. As an energy importer, Ukraine depends upon nuclear power for 40 percent of its electricity.[63] Ukraine neither has the financial strength to rehabilitate inadequate nuclear plants nor alternative energy sources (beyond coal) to substitute for nuclear power.

Some sixteen Chernobyl-type graphite core reactors still operate in the former Soviet Union. The International Atomic Energy Agency views their safety as "a matter of great international concern." Many old-type reactors in operation "lack important safety features which are basic to similar pressurized water reactors in the West," including containment vessels to prevent accidental emissions.[64]

The Chernobyl disaster officially caused the deaths of thirty-one people. It sent clouds of radiation across Western Europe, Scandinavia, and the North Pole, and it resulted in a major reevaluation of the safety and utility of nuclear power. The long-term consequences to the citizens of Ukraine, and to their soil, water, and all living things, are yet to be fully realized. In May and August 1992, a series of fires in abandoned areas surrounding the Chernobyl power plant spread radiation contaminants to fields and settlements that had previously escaped the harmful effects.

A September 1992 study, produced with the first reliable statistics of the health effects to those exposed to the Chernobyl radiation, revealed a significant increase of thyroid cancer among children.[65] In addition, studies in August and September 1992 of the so-called sarcophagus of steel and concrete used to entomb the devastated reactor show that surface cracks and fissures are spreading, leading authorities to fear its collapse.[66]

Such developments explain to a large extent Ukraine's antipathy toward all things nuclear, despite its continued dependence on nuclear power. Public outrage over the Chernobyl disaster, industrial pollution, and food and water contamination suggest that environmental issues will remain central to any Ukrainian conception of national security for the foreseeable future.

5. *Political-strategic issues: the Crimea.* No single issue has evoked such emotion as the status of the former Crimean Autonomous Soviet Socialist Republic, considered a "bastion of Soviet-style communism."[67] Party *nomenklatura* and military matters have long dominated the peninsula, and its 2.4 million inhabitants were subject to Moscow's firm hand. When Nikita

Khrushchev gave the Crimea to Ukraine in 1954, in commemoration of three hundred years of Ukrainian-Russian friendship, this act was considered to be of little consequence because of the reality of Soviet rule and because the Crimea borders only Ukraine, from which it receives some 80 percent of its electrical power.[68]

The issue of the independence of Ukraine and disputes over the ownership of former Soviet forces and property—notably the Black Sea Fleet—were further inflamed by an independence proclamation by the Crimean Supreme Soviet. The Crimea had been a part of Russia since its incorporation by Catherine the Great in 1783, and the Ukraine Supreme Soviet reaffirmed the Crimea as a part of the Ukrainian state on February 12, 1991. On December 27, 1991, however, the Crimean Supreme Soviet voted to establish the Republic of the Crimea as an autonomous state with ill-defined powers. This act was followed, on April 29, 1992, by a Ukrainian law that established the Republic of Crimea as a sovereign and independent part of Ukraine.

Events did not stop at that point. Next, the Crimean Supreme Soviet passed an act proclaiming state independence on May 5. Previous grants of autonomous status within Ukraine were rejected, and a national referendum on independence was planned.[69] On May 6 the Supreme Soviet reversed its stand and changed the constitution to reflect its position as a component of the Ukrainian state.

The Russian parliament voted on May 21 to declare the 1954 cession of the Crimea to Ukraine void. This move was rejected by the Ukraine parliament, which on June 4, 1992, declared the issue "a direct interference into the domestic affairs of Ukraine because, in accordance with the current Constitution and the legislation of Ukraine, the Crimea is its autonomous part."[70] The Crimean Supreme Soviet's May 6 compromise, in which the peninsula reverted to Ukrainian control, nonetheless asserted broad powers for the Crimea.

Complicating the dispute is the Crimea's demographics. The region is heavily Russian, with some 1.6 million Russians, 600,000 Ukrainians, and about 200,000 Tatars, a Muslim people deported by Stalin in 1944 for their questionable loyalty.[71] The Tatars do not recognize the legitimacy of the Crimean Supreme Soviet, and with support from the Ukrainian nationalist group Rukh, they seek an autonomous Tatar state within Ukraine. Large numbers of Tatar peoples have emigrated to Crimea in recent months to reclaim the homeland their ancestors ruled from 1449 to 1783.

Ukraine President Kravchuk has encouraged the Tatar diaspora movement as a way of strengthening Ukraine's hold on this Russian-dominated region. In contrast, Moscow's support for the activist Republic Movement of Crimea is seen as a part of a larger Russian agenda to return the Crimea to Moscow's fold.[72] Beyond this, domestic political strains within a highly variegated Ukraine may shape political-strategic problems in a way that limits President Kravchuk's room to maneuver. According to Ukraine's parliamentary chairman, Ivan Plusch, Kravchuk believes "a leader should feel the nation and go with the nation."[73]

The Crimea contains two items that are of some interest to those following the legacy of the former Soviet Union. First, it is the site of a fully equipped backup landing site for the Buran space shuttle, which normally takes off and lands at the Baykonur cosmodrome in Kazakhstan.[74] Of more historical interest, however, is the state dacha known as Facility Zarya, where Mikhail and Raisa Gorbachev were held during the August 1991 attempted coup. Administered by the KGB's 9th Directorate, its title was passed to Ukraine on June 8, 1992.[75]

Neither Ukraine nor Russia has much to gain from a prolonged dispute over the Crimea. Given Ukraine's feeling of strategic vulnerability associated with its declared intention to be nonnuclear, conflict over the Crimea may mask other, more irreconcilable differences with Russia—typified by the armed separatist movement in Trans-Dniester—that may influence the strategic direction of Ukrainian defense policy. The new powers granted to the Republic of the Crimea by Ukraine were added to the Crimea's constitution on September 25, 1992. Residents are Ukrainian citizens, but the constitution provided for dual citizenship for those claiming Russian ties as well.[76]

Military issues, social issues, economic problems, environmental challenges, and political-strategic issues will prove decisive to the formulation of Ukraine's security policies. To a very large extent, how they play out in the future depends on the willingness of Russia and Ukraine to challenge or to compromise, as well as on the threat that each perceives to its national interests.

Kiev's relationship with Moscow will continue to be of decisive importance for the foreseeable future. There is a widely held belief that Ukraine has not been taken seriously in its quest for independence and sovereignty. According to one account, "Like most Ukrainians, Kravchuk says he believes his country has been overshadowed in relations with the West by its giant neighbor to the north, Russia, and its maverick president, Boris Yeltsin."[77] To Kravchuk, Moscow has "imperial ambitions" over former Soviet territories that could become more pronounced when Russia achieves a nuclear monopoly by the year 2000.[78]

This feeling of insecurity has propelled Ukraine to act decisively to form a national army. It is an insecurity derived not only from its relations with and perceptions of Moscow, but also from other former Soviet republics. Indeed, "The major political driving force behind Ukraine's positions is the widely held sense among nationalists that an army represents a central attribute of statehood, and that Ukraine must struggle against any Commonwealth command that could become the nucleus of another Moscow-centered power."[79]

Given the widely held skepticism regarding the Commonwealth of Independent States as both a political and a military instrument of statehood, Kiev is confronted with a Russia committed to creating a modern, highly mobile, rapid reaction type of army. In its final form, this army will number approximately 1.5 million, and it will be primarily professional, based upon personal contracts. This force is to be in place by the year 2000.[80]

At the conclusion of this program of military revitalization and realignment, Russia will emerge as the former USSR's sole nuclear power. Russia's pledge not to be the first to use nuclear weapons continues to guide its defense policy, and Defense Minister Pavel Grachev has said that these weapons "would be used only to ensure sufficient defense if there is a threat from the outside, a threat that cannot be met by political means and by conventional forces."[81]

Beyond this imponderable situation, the resurrection of a Russian army is central to restoring Russia as a great power. According to Vice President Rutskoi, "everybody should keep in mind the following, while restoring the Russian Army, we are restoring Great Russia."[82]

What, then, is the nature of the military threat confronting Russia, the largest and most powerful of the new states? To Defense Minister Grachev, this threat includes "the existence of powerful armed forces in some states, mobilization possibilities and a system of their deployment close to Russian borders as well as attempts at using political and economic pressure and military blackmail against Russia."[83] Ukraine, as Moscow's largest neighbor to the west, must ponder the significance of this statement.

Ukraine's defense conundrum is a renewed security dilemma with a historical twist. Should Kiev seek to build a large, modern army similar to the new Russian army, this action may be viewed as a threat to neighboring states, which in turn may find it necessary to replicate a similar military force. The security dilemma—the tendency of states seeking more security actually to achieve less due to countermoves by opposing states—may well apply. This phenomenon fueled the Cold War's arms race at an expense to U.S. taxpayers of $11 trillion; it also served to accelerate the Soviet collapse. Now it lies dormant at the feet of the new Eurasian nations of the former Soviet Union, which may fall into the same trap of buying less security at the expense of more arms, if allowed to proceed unchecked.

The historical dimension is the legacy inherited by all new Eurasian states of the former Soviet Union. This legacy has seen military investment consume at least 30 percent of the USSR's gross output and employ an estimated one-fifth of its work force. To have a model such as this as the template for the future could direct defense policy back in time, to large, expensive armed forces poised to defend the state and its perceived interests at virtually all costs.

The Ukrainian desire for security guarantees reflects this awareness that past patterns of military policy may reassert themselves in the post-Soviet states. The security dilemma will ensure that this costly, potentially dangerous situation does not produce greater security but, instead, will lead to social instability and economic dislocations that will do irretrievable harm to the new states. It is important at this significant moment to acknowledge that Kiev's commitment to democracy does not have to repeat past patterns of Soviet military threat and expenditure.

The West and international institutions bear a special responsibility to prevent the past from revisiting the future in the former Soviet Union. For Ukraine at this critical period, its military, social, economic, environmental, and political-strategic insecurities need not direct its national security policy down this familiar path.

SEPARATIST/DISSIDENT MOVEMENTS

1. Ukraine's four southern oblasts, heavily populated by ethnic Russians— Odessa, Kherson, Nikolayev, and Crimea—have discussed forming a new state in the Black Sea region called Novorus.[84] The likelihood of this development has declined as the status of the Crimea, a 1954 "gift" from Khrushchev in honor of three hundred years of Russian-Ukrainian friendship, has become increasingly contested.

2. The Crimea has been embroiled in a dispute between Ukraine and Russia that is complicated by Muslim Tatars who claim it as their ancestral homeland. Stalin expelled the Tatars from the Crimea in 1944 for alleged collaboration with the Nazis. Several raions in the Crimea populated by Ukrainians brought there after the Tatar expulsion have organized to oppose secession moves.[85] Tensions created by a growing number of Tatars who demand the seizure of their ancestral homelands from the current occupants are a serious source of potential conflict in the Crimea.

3. Romania seeks the return of its former territories of northern Bukovina and South Bessarabia, along with the regions of Herta and Khotin bordering Romania, which were lost to the Soviet Union in 1940. This move is supported by the Moldovan Popular Front as a necessary prerequisite to the unification of all former Romanian territories.[86]

4. The territory of western Poland known as eastern Galicia passed to Stalin in September 1939 as a result of the Molotov–Ribbentrop agreement, which divided Poland between Germany (in the west) and the Soviet Union (in the east). Incorporated into Ukraine, it was lost to Hitler following his June 22, 1941, attack on the Soviet Union—Operation Barbarossa—but was recaptured by the Red Army in 1945. Polish irredentist sentiments in this region are sometimes expressed.

5. Russians living in eastern Ukraine have formed an association in Kharkov to protect their rights and culture.[87]

NOTES

1. Andrey Pershin, Andrey Petrovskiy, and Vladimir Shishlin, "Presidential Bulletin," Moscow INTERFAX, 1525 GMT, June 12, 1992, in FBIS-SOV–92–115, June 15, 1992, 42; Andrey Shtorkh, "Republic Joins Paris Charter," Moscow ITAR-TASS, 1812 GMT, April 8, 1992, in FBIS-SOV–92–069, April 9, 1992, 52.

2. Pershin, Petrovskiy, and Shishlin, "Presidential Bulletin," 42.

3. "Banks to Cancel Coupons, Introduce Bank Notes," Moscow INTERFAX, 1921 GMT, May 18, 1992, in FBIS-SOV–92–097, May 19, 1992, 37; "Bank Chairman Announces Introduction of Currency," Moscow INTERFAX, 1446 GMT, May 24, 1992, in FBIS-SOV–92–104, May 29, 1992, 53.

4. "Belarus, Kaliningrad Reach Trade Agreement," Moscow Mayak Radio Network, 2200 GMT, March 23, 1992, in FBIS-SOV–92–058, March 25, 1992, 64.

5. Mikhail Shimanskiy, "What Army Will Belarus Have?" *Izvestiya,* September 17, 1992, 3, in FBIS-SOV–92–183, September 21, 1992, 47.

6. Ibid.

7. "Gaydar and Kebich Satisfied with Talks," *Izvestiya,* July 22, 1992, 2, in FBIS-SOV–92–141, July 22, 1992, 11.

8. Natalya Kalinichenko, "CIS Republics Establish the Big-Mac of Missile-Building Industry," Moscow *Kommersant,* March 11–18, 1992, 5, in JPRS-UMA–92–023, June 24, 1992, 46.

9. "National Army Discussed," Moscow Radio One Program, 1600 GMT, March 19, 1992, in FBIS-SOV–92–055, March 20, 1992, 72; "Shushkevich Establishes Security Council," Moscow INTERFAX, 1543 GMT, May 28, 1992, in FBIS-SOV–92–104, May 29, 1992, 53.

10. "Belarus Official Lays Claim to Lithuanian Border Lands," *New York Times,* February 25, 1992, A7; "Shushkevich Denies Territorial Claims," Vilnius Radio Network, 1100 GMT, March 26, 1992, in FBIS-SOV–92–062, March 31, 1992, 52.

11. "Novosti" newscast, Moscow Television First Program Network, 2100 GMT, March 23, 1992, in FBIS-SOV–92–058, March 25, 1992, 64.

12. Andrey Pershin, Andrey Petrovskiy, and Vladimir Shishlin, "Presidential Bulletin," Moscow INTERFAX, 1626 GMT, September 22, 1992, 40.

13. Staff Delegation, *Trip Report on Moscow, Georgia, Moldova and Belarus, June 25–July 4, 1992* (Washington: Commission on Security and Cooperation in Europe, August 1992), 2.

14. Maria Graczak, "Belarus—A Lot of Weapons, No Money," Moscow *Rossiya,* September 9–15, 1992, 7, in FBIS-SOV–92–183, September 21, 1992, 46.

15. "Ambassador to Belarus Comments on Relations," Kiev Radio, 0000 GMT, August 14, 1992, in FBIS-SOV–92–162, August 20, 1992, 38.

16. "May End up Without Soldiers," Moscow INTERFAX, 1635 GMT, February 26, 1992, in FBIS-SOV–92–039, February 27, 1992, 63; Yuriy Golotyuk, "Army Still Not Created but Generals Fight," Moscow *Megapolis Express,* April 22, 1992, 1, in JPRS-UMA–92–018, May 20, 1992, 45.

17. Golotyuk, "Army Still Not Created," 45.

18. "Council for Romanian Reunification Established," Bucharest ROMPRES, 1835 GMT, December 2, 1991, in FBIS-SOV–91–232, December 3, 1991, 75.

19. "Moldova Chief Quits over Regional Unrest," *New York Times,* June 10, 1992, A14.

20. "Dnestr Republic Claims Soviet Army Property," Moscow INTERFAX, 1520 GMT, December 4, 1991, in FBIS-SOV–91–234, December 5, 1991, 60.

21. "Moldova Imposes Emergency Rule and Orders Disarming of Militias," *New York Times,* March 29, 1992, A6.

22. "Moldova Imposes Emergency Rule," A6; Judith Gram, "U.N. Peace Mission in Moldova Is Thwarted by Separatist Fighting," *New York Times,* June 30, 1992, A3; Vincent Schodolski, "Russian Soldiers Fight in Moldova; Yeltsin on Spot," *Chicago Tribune,* June 23, 1992, A1.

23. "Agreement on Settlement of Dniester Region Conflict Ready for Signature," *Izvestiya,* July 22, 1992, 1, in FBIS-SOV–92–141, July 22, 1992, 10.

24. "Topal Elected President of Gagauz Republic," Moscow Radio Rossii Network, 2100 GMT, December 1, 1991, in FBIS-SOV–91–231, December 2, 1991, 54.

25. Jan Pergler and Jaromir Stetina, "The Gagauz Republic Exists," Prague *Lidove Noviny,* July 30, 1992, 1, 5, in FBIS-SOV–92–154, August 10, 1992, 58.

26. "Moldova Embraces Romania," *Wall Street Journal,* August 28, 1992, A4.

27. "Church," *Moscow News,* July 5–12, 1992, 2.

28. Sergey Tsikora, "Without Waiting for Tyumen Oil, the Ukraine Is Buying Iranian," *Izvestiya,* February 4, 1992, 1, in FBIS-SOV–92–024, February 5, 1992, 72–73.

29. Yuriy Kornev, "The Military–Industrial Complex in the Prism of Economics and Politics: On Conversion, On the Times, On Himself," Kiev *Pravda Ukrainy,* June 23, 1992, 2, in JPRS-UMA–92–033, September 2, 1992, 37.

30. "Ukraine: We Have a Plan," *The Economist,* October 3, 1992, 54–55; "The Old Comrades Club," *The Economist,* October 3, 1992, 19.

31. Robert Conquest, *The Harvest of Sorrow: Soviet Collectivization and the Terror-Famine* (New York: Oxford University Press, 1986), 306–30.

32. "Ukraine: The Big One," *The Economist,* November 23, 1991, 55.

33. William C. Potter, "Ukraine as a Nuclear Power," *Wall Street Journal,* December 4, 1991, A16.

34. "Withdrawal of Troops to Republic Stops," Moscow POSTFACTUM, 0254 GMT, December 7, 1991, in FBIS-SOV–91–239, December 12, 1991, 53.

35. Fred Hiatt, "Ukraine Vote Leaves Union Shattered," *Washington Post,* December 3, 1991, A1.

36. Chrystia Freeland, "Ukraine's Parliament Formalizes Independence," *Washington Post,* December 6, 1991, A48.

37. "Ukraine Selects Prime Minister," *Wall Street Journal,* October 14, 1992, A7.

38. Francis X. Clines, "Legislators Back Effort to Create a Ukrainian Army," *New York Times,* October 23, 1991, A1.

39. "Ukraine Wants Voice in Use of Atomic Arms," *New York Times,* October 25, 1991, A7.

40. Lyudmila Beletskaya and Aleksey Kucherenko, "Putting a Brave Face on It. Ukraine Still Has the Bomb," Moscow *Kommersant,* March 16–23, 1992, 22, in FBIS-SOV–92–057, March 24, 1992, 1.

41. "On the Nuclear-Free Status of the Ukraine," statement of the Ukraine Su-

preme Soviet, Kiev *Pravda Ukrainy,* October 26, 1991, 1, in JPRS-UMA–91–032, December 17, 1991, 19–20.

42. "Kravchuk Assumes Command of Armed Forces," Moscow TASS, 1806 GMT, December 12, 1991, in FBIS-SOV–91–240, December 13, 1991, 71.

43. Sergey Balykov, "Parliament Legislates Armed Forces Structure," Moscow TASS, 1834 GMT, December 13, 1991, in FBIS-SOV–91–241, December 16, 1991, 68.

44. Aleksandr Gorobets, "Look After Combat Readiness," Kiev *Pravda Ukrainy,* November 2, 1991, 2, in JPRS-UMA–91–032, December 17, 1991, 17–18.

45. S. Shevtsov, "May Common Sense Prevail," Moscow *Sovetskaya Rossiya,* January 24, 1992, 1, in FBIS-SOV–92–016, January 24, 1992, 84; "National Guard Creation Under Way," Moscow Radio Rossii Network, 1200 GMT, December 28, 1991, in FBIS-SOV–91–250, December 30, 1991, 50.

46. Lyudmila Mavrina, "National Security Service Leaders Meet Press," Moscow Radio Rossii Network, 0100 GMT, April 19, 1992, in FBIS-SOV–92–076, April 20, 1992, 44.

47. N. Zaika, "Leader of Group of Experts on the Ukrainian Defense Ministry Lays out the Position of His State on Strategic Forces," *Krasnaya zvezda,* February 6, 1992, 1, in JPRS-UMA–92–006, February 20, 1992, 15.

48. "Novosti" newscast, Moscow Television First Program Network, 2209 GMT, January 6, 1992, in FBIS-SOV–92–004, January 7, 1992, 60–61.

49. Gerald F. Seib and Natalia A. Feduschak, "Russia, Ukraine Will Go Head to Head over Military Issues at C.I.S. Conference," *Wall Street Journal,* March 20, 1992, A6.

50. Don Oberdorfer, "3 Ex-Soviet States to Give up A-Arms," *Washington Post,* May 24, 1992, A1.

51. Aleksey Trotsenko, "Ukraine Confirms Nonnuclear Status to NATO," Moscow ITAR-TASS, 2002 GMT, June 3, 1992, in FBIS-SOV–92–108, June 4, 1992, 4; Serge Schmemann, "Ukraine Asks Aid for Its Arms Curb," *New York Times,* November 13, 1992, A10.

52. Natalia A. Feduschak, "Ukraine Seeks to Get Control of Nuclear Arms," *Wall Street Journal,* March 26, 1992, A10.

53. James F. Clarity, "Free Ukraine's Nationalism: Will Pride Become Prejudice?" *New York Times,* February 12, 1992, A10.

54. Volodymyr Teteruk, "Let Us Gather the Holy Trinity," Kiev *Holos Ukrayiny,* January 22, 1992, 8, in FBIS-SOV–92–022, February 3, 1992, 67–68.

55. "Ukrainian Candidate to Pursue Independence," *Carlisle* (Pa.) *Sentinel,* November 30, 1991, A6.

56. Ihor Herashchenko, "A Non-Nuclear Ukraine: Pro and Con," Kiev *Narodna gazeta,* October 1991, 5, in JPRS-UMA–91–032, December 17, 1991, 18–19.

57. Francis X. Clines, "Joint Command Is Planned for Atom Arms," *New York Times,* December 31, 1991, A1.

58. "Ukraine's Parliament Approves Plan That Could End Nation's Use of Ruble," *Wall Street Journal,* March 25, 1992, A8.

59. Roman Solchanyk, "Ukrainian Position at CIS Summit," *RFE/RL Daily Report,* No. 196 (E-mail), October 12, 1992, 1.

60. "Ukraine to Limit Ruble Use," *Wall Street Journal,* June 1, 1992, A9; "Ukraine

to Pay Its Share of Soviet Debt on Its Own," *Wall Street Journal,* January 30, 1992, A8.

61. "Ukraine Clears Way for Loans," *Wall Street Journal,* March 16, 1992, A11.

62. Paul Lewis, "U.S. and Six Plan Nuclear Cleanup in Eastern Europe," *New York Times,* May 21, 1992, A1.

63. William Drozdiak, "Ukraine's Leader Says Russia Still Has 'Imperial Ambitions,' " *Washington Post,* June 18, 1992, A40.

64. Lewis, "U.S. and Six Plan Nuclear Cleanup," A14.

65. Gina Kolata, "A Cancer Legacy From Chernobyl," *New York Times,* September 3, 1992, A9.

66. "Chernobyl Unit in 'Horrible Condition'," Kiev Radio, 0000 GMT, August 12, 1992, in FBIS-SOV–92–157, August 13, 1992, 44; Nikolay Krupenik, "Cracks Discovered in Chernobyl Nuclear Plant," Moscow ITAR-TASS, 1345 GMT, September 17, 1992, in FBIS-SOV–92–183, September 21, 1992, 40.

67. "Ukraine: The Crimean Question," *The Economist,* January 11, 1992, 45–46.

68. Ibid.

69. "Referendum Planned for 2 Aug.," Moscow Mayak Radio Network, 1700 GMT, May 5, 1992, in FBIS-SOV–92–088, May 6, 1992, 45.

70. "Deputies Reject Russian Decisions on Crimea," Kiev Radio Ukraine, 0000 GMT, June 4, 1992, in FBIS-SOV–92–109, June 5, 1992, 69.

71. Mikhail Kochetkov and Yevgeniy Menkes, "[Kravchuk] Holds News Conference at UN," Moscow ITAR-TASS, 0718 GMT, May 12, 1992, in FBIS-SOV–92–092, May 12, 1992, 47.

72. Chrystia Freeland, "Crimea: Caught in the Middle," *Washington Post,* February 13, 1992, A33; Chrystyna Lapychak, "Ukraine Sees Crimean Move as Russian Ploy," *Christian Science Monitor,* May 26, 1992, 5.

73. Laurie Hays, "As He Builds a Nation, Ukraine Chief Becomes Thorn in Yeltsin's Side," *Wall Street Journal,* March 17, 1992, A10.

74. V. Savchenko, "Are 'Star Wars' in Store for Ukraine and Russia? It's a Complete Secret," Kiev *Nezavisimost,* September 5, 1992, 2, in JPRS-UMA–92–035, September 23, 1992, 10.

75. "Vesti" newscast, Moscow Television Network, 1600 GMT, August 26, 1992, in FBIS-SOV–92–168, August 28, 1992, 37.

76. Lev Ryabchikov, "Crimean Deputies Adopt Constitutional Changes," Moscow ITAR-TASS, 1909 GMT, September 25, 1992, in FBIS-SOV–92–189, September 29, 1992, 32.

77. Chrystyna Lapychak, "Ukrainian President to Seek Security Pact in First Visit to U.S.," *Christian Science Monitor,* May 1, 1992, 6.

78. Drozdiak, "Ukraine's Leader Says," A40.

79. Serge Schmemann, "Friction Rises as Ukraine and Russia Clash over Ex-Soviet Armed Forces," *New York Times,* March 5, 1992, A3.

80. Mikhail Shevtsov, "Outlines Reforms," Moscow ITAR-TASS, 1435 GMT, May 30, 1992, in FBIS-SOV–92–105, June 1, 1992, 26.

81. Daniel Sneider, "Turning Russia's Army into a Lean Machine," *Christian Science Monitor,* June 9, 1992, 7.

82. Ibid.

83. Roman Zadunaiskiy, "Grachev on Army's 'Sweeping Changes,' Threats,"

Moscow ITAR-TASS, 1417 GMT, June 1, 1992, in FBIS-SOV–92–106, June 2, 1992, 14.

84. "Oblasts Discuss Creation of 'Novorus' State," Moscow All-Union Radio Mayak Network, 0900 GMT, November 16, 1991, in FBIS-SOV–91–222, November 18, 1991, 65.

85. M. Zhukov, " 'Sovereign' Rayons of Autonomous Crimea," Kiev *Holos,* November 13, 1991, 3, in FBIS-SOV–91–234, December 5, 1991, 65.

86. "Romania Refuses to Recognize Independence," Moscow INTERFAX, 1650 GMT, November 29, 1991, in FBIS-SOV–91–231, December 2, 1991, 57.

87. "Association of Russians Formed in Kharov," Moscow All-Union Radio Mayak Network, 0200 GMT, December 27, 1992, in FBIS-SOV–92–252, December 31, 1992, 54.

The Caucasus

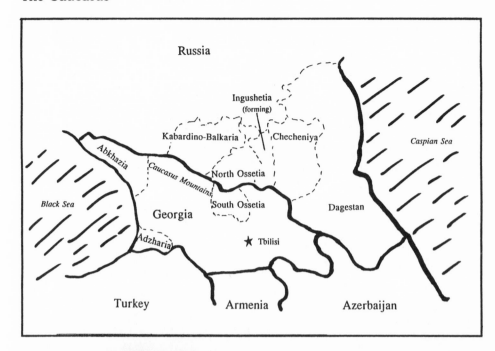

5

The Caucasus

The Caucasus, a territory slightly larger than the three Baltic republics, is divided into the Northern Caucasus and Transcaucasus regions. In the 1989 national census—the Soviet Union's last such count—more than 21.3 million people comprising 100 nationalities lived in the Caucasus.

As a result of more than 250 years of deliberate Russian conquest, the Northern Caucasus today is within the political jurisdiction of the Russian Federation. It consists of five autonomous republics—Chechen-Ingush, Dagestan, Kabardino-Balkar, Kalmuk, and North Ossetian—and two autonomous oblasts—Adyghei and Karachay-Cherkess. Most of these autonomous areas are in various states of turmoil associated with the dissolution of the Soviet Union. For details of their ongoing political transformation, see the chapter on the Russian Federation.

The Northern Caucasus is less than 1 percent of the area of the former Soviet Union, and it is less densely populated than the Transcaucasus. Many of its inhabitants are Muslim, notably the Chechens, Ingush, Balkar, and Dagestan peoples. Significantly, there is much overlap of populations, with more than one-fourth living outside their titular homelands. One of the major demographic shifts that have occurred since the 1989 Soviet census includes a decline of Russians or those designating themselves as Russian. This trend is even more significant in the Transcaucasus.[1]

The Transcaucasus comprises some 5.5 percent of the population of the former Soviet Union. This region has seen some dramatic changes since the 1989 census, one of them being a massive migration of ethnic populations. Azeris living in Armenia have returned to Azerbaijan; Armenians in Azerbaijan have moved to Armenia; and Slavic peoples have left the region in large numbers.[2]

This diaspora of peoples has been magnified by protracted and costly ethnic strife, in part the result of the manner in which the region was organized in the early Soviet period. Armenia, one of two Christian former union republics in the Transcaucasus, has been in prolonged conflict with Azerbaijan, a Shiite Muslim republic. Complicating matters are Azerbaijan's two ethnic enclaves: Nakhichevan autonomous republic, a Muslim region located in Armenia, and the Nagorno-Karabakh autonomous oblast, a region with a large Armenian population within Azerbaijan. Georgia, the second Christian republic, finds itself at odds with its three ethnic enclaves: the Abkhaz autonomous republic, Adzhar autonomous republic, and the South Ossetian autonomous oblast.

Russia has historically been in a prolonged state of war with the peoples of the Caucasus; some assert that the region's differences of religion, culture, and language have been further accentuated by a highly diverse climate and terrain.[3] Christianity reached the north shores of the Black Sea and eventually the Northern Caucasus by way of Greek settlements. This influence was isolated in the thirteenth century by Tatar-Mongol invasions that supported the Islamic faith introduced into the area in the seventh and eighth centuries. A later re-Christianization occurred by the nineteenth century, coincident with Russian conquests. This has led to a patchwork of religions of varying intensity and practice that persists to the present.[4]

Russia, under the rule of Peter the Great, moved to secure access to the southern seas following the seizure of Azov in 1695. Russia's campaigns in the Caucasus were aimed at Persia, and were won at great cost. Most notable was the 1790 capture of the legendary Mansur, who mounted the first Islamic holy war in the region against the Russians and is considered the father of Caucasian independence.[5]

With the fall of the tsar and eventually of the Provisional Government in Petrograd (now St. Petersburg), the three states of Azerbaijan, Armenia, and Georgia formed the Federal Republic of Transcaucasia on April 22, 1918; it lasted just over a month before each country proclaimed its separate independence. The republic of North Caucasus was created on May 11, 1918, with a view to merging with its southern neighbors to form a Caucasian Federation. The Red Army attacked each entity in turn, however. Despite a May 7, 1920, treaty acknowledging the sovereignty and independence of Georgia, the army seized it in early 1921. With the Caucasian governments in exile in Paris, the Soviets resumed earlier Russian efforts to subvert areas to the south, particularly Persia and Afghanistan.[6]

Because of the close ties between the Muslim minorities occupying Russia's Northern Caucasus autonomous republics and oblasts with events and peoples of the Transcaucasus, on September 8, 1992, Russian Foreign Minister Kozyrev proclaimed: "The Caucasus region is a traditional sphere of Russian interests, and we do not intend to abandon it."[7]

Georgia

BASIC DATA

Total Area: 26,911 square miles (69,700 square kilometers).

Population: 5.5 million. Some 70 percent are Georgian, 9 percent Armenian, and 5 percent Russian. The growth rate is 0.8 percent.

Religion: Georgian Orthodox, Russian Orthodox, Armenian Orthodox, Sunni Islam.

Official Name: Republic of Georgia.

Capital: Tbilisi.

Government:

- Executive Branch: Zviad Gamsakhurdia became the republic's first popularly elected president on May 26, 1991. After a prolonged armed struggle, he fled the capital in early January 1992. Since March 10, 1992, Eduard Shevardnadze headed the State Council, the supreme organ of legislative and state power, until national elections could be held. A consultative body, the Darbazi, advised the Council. The head of government is the prime minister, who presides over the council of ministers. In elections for a new parliament, which took place on October 11, 1992, Shevardnadze was chosen by 90 percent of voters for the post of Speaker of the Parliament. On November 6, 1992, he was elected head of state by Parliament and was considered a de facto president.
- Legislative Branch: Parliament.
- Judicial Branch: Supreme Court.

Georgia

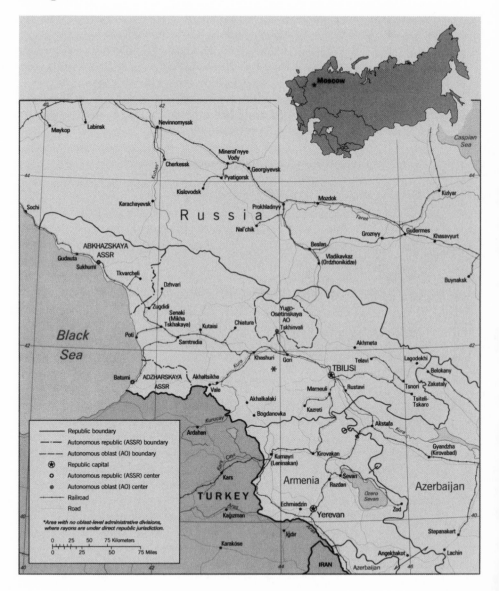

Legend:
- Republic boundary
- Autonomous republic (ASSR) boundary
- Autonomous oblast (AO) boundary
- ⊛ Republic capital
- ○ Autonomous republic (ASSR) center
- ⊚ Autonomous oblast (AO) center
- Railroad
- Road

*Area with no oblast-level administrative divisions, where rayons are under direct republic jurisdiction.

0 25 50 75 Kilometers
0 25 50 75 Miles

- A National Security and Defense Council coordinates national security policy.

Economy: The state has had a flourishing private sector, exporting agricultural products such as citrus, vegetables, and wine. Until recently, tourism was a popular business. Prolonged conflict with Gamsakhurdia forces and separatist movements in South Ossetia and Abkhazia, however, have devastated the Georgian economy. By September 1992 inflation had reached 50 percent a month, unemployment stood at 20 percent, rail connections with Moscow had been severed since August 12th, and industrial production had dropped by two thirds since 1990. State credits from Russia have sustained large defense plants such as the Sukhoi factory, which makes SU–25 and SU–27 jet fighters. Beyond this, there are concerns that a developing "culture of violence" is threatening an entire generation.[8]

History: Many nations merged to form the Georgian nationality, with its own distinct language and rich culture. A part of the Roman Empire later conquered by Mongols, it was fought over by Turks and Persians for three centuries until annexed by Russia in the early nineteenth century. Following the October Revolution, Georgia became independent except for its brief participation in the Federal Republic of Transcaucasia. In 1921 Moscow incorporated it by force into a Transcaucasian Republic, and in 1936 it became a union republic. Its most famous son of the Soviet era was Joseph Stalin, though it has given the world great writers and artists. Shota Rustaveli, a twelfth-century poet considered the father of the Georgian literary language, wrote *The Knight in the Panther's Skin,* considered the national epic.

THE ROAD TO INDEPENDENCE

Georgia announced its sovereignty on March 9, 1990. On April 9, 1991, it proclaimed its independence—a day specifically chosen in memory of "Bloody Sunday," April 9, 1989, when nineteen citizens were killed in the heart of Tbilisi by Soviet troops using sharpened shovels and lethal gas. Georgia has been torn by civil war since August 1991, when most of its national guard rebelled against President Gamsakhurdia. Much of the unrest was associated with what many saw as Gamsakhurdia's heavy-handedness and disregard of democratic principles. After severe fighting that destroyed much of central Tbilisi and its main street, Rustaveli Prospect, Gamsakhurdia fled with his armed supporters on January 13, 1992, leaving at least ninety dead.

Eduard Shevardnadze, who twice served as foreign minister for Mikhail Gorbachev and was called a traitor by Gamsakhurdia, offered on January 6, 1992, to assist the democratization process, promising to "help my people, my friends, and my colleagues, and, naturally, as my first duty, the democratic movement."[9] On March 7, 1992, Shevardnadze, who had served as republic Communist party leader in Tbilisi for thirteen years before joining Gorbachev's cabinet in Moscow, returned to Georgia for the first time since April 1989.

Shevardnadze's return was highly symbolic. As he entered the city he stopped to greet and receive the blessing of the patriarch of Georgia. He then visited the cemetery where those who died in April 1989, as well as those killed in the civil unrest leading to Gamsakhurdia's ouster, were buried. Finally, he paid his respects outside Government House on Rustaveli Prospect, where so much tragedy had occurred. Later he announced the creation of the Revival and Democracy Fund of Georgia, which he established to rebuild the ravaged country.[10]

On April 11, 1992, the Georgian State Council announced the formation of the republic armed forces, to be subordinate to the Defense Ministry. The military would consist of a twenty thousand-man army to be led by some of the more than one thousand career officers serving in the CIS forces. Also included were border forces, an air force, and a navy, based in part on the transfer of certain units and bases of the Black Sea Fleet already agreed upon in Moscow. The national guard will be merged into this new force.[11]

Support for the new government was demonstrated by the visit of U.S. Secretary of States James Baker on May 26, 1992, Georgia's national day. On this holiday, commemorating Georgia's independence from imperial Russia, Baker hailed his old friend Shevardnadze as a "courageous leader who is known and respected internationally," leading Georgia's foreign minister to proclaim that the visit ended Georgia's international isolation.[12] After a June 24, 1992, coup attempt, the most serious challenge to Shevardnadze since his return to Tbilisi, he remained undaunted: "Our determination to build a democratic and humane state, well ordered and highly organized, remains intact."[13]

Central to Georgia's future is the urgent task of resolving ongoing ethnic unrest to its west and north, as well as its role in the Commonwealth of Independent States. When the CIS was born on December 8 and 21, 1991, Georgia was embroiled in a virtual civil war centered on Government House, where President Gamsakhurdia was hiding. Shevardnadze has not been hopeful about the CIS's future. In April 1992, he said he was not optimistic about the organization, and indicated that it would be useless for Georgia to join such a disintegrating institution.[14] Georgia did join NATO's North Atlantic Consultative Council, and Georgia has sent observers to CIS meetings.

A protocol establishing formal diplomatic relations between Tbilisi and Moscow was concluded on July 2, 1992.

To maintain relations with the new Eurasian states, Chairman of the State Council Shevardnadze has advocated the continuation of bilateral ties, particularly with Russia. He has indicated that Georgia cannot exist without help from Moscow, and he has placed considerable importance to this relationship.[15] Georgia also joined the Black Sea Economic Council on June 25, 1992, along with Russia, Ukraine, Turkey, Greece, Romania, and other regional powers. Georgia hopes to introduce its own currency, the marchili, as soon as its economic situation stabilizes. The country's insurgencies, however, are receiving primary attention.

On the day of the national parliamentary elections, October 11, 1992, this reality forced Eduard Shevardnadze to admit that the challenges he faced were the most difficult of his life: "Here is a half-hungry people with limited resources, internal contradictions, a small state with a multinational composition, enormously complex geopolitics. Here the question is survival—survival."[16] When Shevardnadze was endorsed as speaker by an overwhelming majority vote, he was grateful: "I am ready to kneel before my people for their wisdom and endurance.... We have done what we promised. Our people have finally chosen the democratic path."[17]

Shevardnadze has been concerned that ethnic disputes will continue to paralyze the new states of the former USSR. He has supported CSCE intervention and the CSCE process by calling for a ceasefire and a halt to all ethnic disputes for a given period, such as five years. During this time no new separatist claims would be raised, talks concerning the juridical standing of contested regions would be deferred, and safety corridors would be formed to separate belligerents. This would sufficiently stabilize and defuse such conflicts by stating that the right to self-determination enshrined by the CSCE applies only within the boundaries of existing states. To change borders by referenda, he said, "would lead to a big war."[18]

SEPARATIST/DISSIDENT MOVEMENTS

1. The South Ossetian Autonomous Oblast, a constituent part of Georgia, has sought to join the North Ossetian autonomous republic, located to its north in the Russian Federation, as a united entity within Russia. The Ossetians are primarily Orthodox Christians who speak Russian and Ossetian in the north and Ossetian and Georgian in the south.

The South Ossetian Democratic Republic was established on September 20, 1990, but was declared illegal by authorities in Moscow. On December 21, 1991, the South Ossetian Supreme Soviet, which had already announced its intention to join Russia, declared its independence at a meeting in Tskhinvali.

Georgia, under the leadership of Zviad Gamsakhurdia, resisted all independence efforts, and the formation of a South Ossetian national guard led to armed confrontations with Georgian forces. Despite Gamsakhurdia's replacement by Eduard Shevardnadze, hostilities intensified in March and

April 1992; there were reports that Russian volunteers were aiding the Ossetian rebels and South Ossetia's newly formed national guard.

In the meantime, North Ossetia's parliament was considering a unilateral union with the south, abrogating the Federation Treaty and forming a new state called Alaniya.[19] Refugees, estimated to number 100,000 as early as December 1991, have been taxing life in North Ossetia.

North Ossetia closed the main military highway and gas pipeline into Georgia, an action welcomed on May 28, 1992, by Russian Vice President Aleksandr Rutskoi, who said, "The Georgian leaders must understand that the acts committed in South Ossetia will no longer go unpunished."[20] In Tskhinvali, South Ossetian leaders asked Russia for protection. As the death toll rose to exceed seven hundred, Boris Yeltsin and Eduard Shevardnadze arranged for a ceasefire to take effect on June 28, 1992. Yeltsin then departed for the Black Sea summit in Istanbul, leaving Rutskoi to arrange the details.

Based on this agreement, called the Dagomys accord, Russian, South Ossetian, and Georgian peacekeeping troops wearing UN-style blue helmets and armbands created a buffer zone between South Ossetia and Georgia on July 14, 1992. This raised hopes that the "Ossetian model" for resolving interethnic disputes could be used elsewhere, as in fact occurred in Trans-Dniester shortly thereafter. Over 1,000 people were killed during the three-year conflict; Georgia continues to hold that South Ossetia is a constituent part of Georgia, while most South Ossetians continue to advocate union with North Ossetia as a part of Russia.[21]

2. The Abkhaz, a Turkic people who speak their own distinct language and who are primarily Sunni Muslim, have been seeking independence from Georgia. They are based in the former Abkhaz Autonomous Soviet Socialist Republic in northwestern Georgia. Serious clashes between the Abkhaz, a group of 80,000 people who constitute a 17 percent minority in the republic, and Georgians, who constitute a 46 percent majority, led to a number of deaths in July 1989. Tensions have again risen, and an Abkhaz Council of National Unity, composed largely of Georgians, conducted acts of civil disobedience against Abkhaz authorities in May and June 1992, in the capital of Sukhumi.

On June 16, 1992, in an effort to defuse the tense situation, Georgia's defense minister organized a joint interethnic guard, composed of Georgian and Abkhaz forces, that will be subordinate to him.[22] The Abkhaz, who have long felt that their language, culture, and traditions were threatened by the Georgian majority, declared independence on July 23, 1992, and shortly afterwards kidnapped Georgian officials. Armed conflict ensued, with the Abkhaz aided by Confederation of Caucasian Peoples Muslim volunteers, which led to the deaths of at least three hundred persons. The secessionists are largely composed of supporters of former President Gam-sakhurdia who want the new Republic of Abkhazia to join the CIS as an independent state. In August, Russian troops evacuated Russian vacationers from Black Sea resorts at Sukhumi. A ceasefire arranged by Boris Yeltsin, Shevardnadze, and Abhkaz leaders on September 3 did not hold.

Reports that Russian forces were supporting the separatists led to strained Georgian–Russian ties, and the Supreme Soviet in Moscow passed a resolution on September 25 denouncing Georgian leaders. Yeltsin, at the CIS summit at Bishkek, declared on October 8 that "We simply cannot allow" an all-out conflict.[23] UN observers were sent to the scene following the Security Council's call for all parties to observe the ceasefire, which included the establishment of a buffer zone between warring sides. Peace talks followed in Moscow; the resulting accord has led to an uneasy truce, the success of which only time will tell.

3. In Georgia's second autonomous republic, Adzharia, located in the southwest, the ethnic Georgian but Sunni Muslim population has evinced separatist urges primarily out of a fear of assimilation. Former President Gamsakhurdia had threatened to end their autonomous status,[24] and the government in the capital of Batumi remains uncertain of the direction Georgian nationalism may take under the Shevardnadze regime. Georgia's conflict with Abkhazia, however, has solidified Adzhar opinion. The chairman of the autonomous republic's Supreme Soviet publicly supports Georgia's policy against the armed separatists.

4. The Confederation of Caucasian Peoples has sought to protect the interests of Caucasian minorities. Formed in November 1991, they have extended military assistance to support local peoples against Georgian and Russian hegemony in Kabardino-Balkaria and Abkhazia. Composed almost wholly of Sunni Muslims, the Confederation includes people from Kabardino-Balkaria, Dagestan, and Checheniya, and elsewhere.

Eduard Shevardnadze, on October 10, 1992, threatened to attack confederation leaders in the breakaway Republic of Checheniya—the location of Zviad Gamsakhurdia—in the Russian Federation: "If we have to conduct a war against certain forces in Russia, what can we do. If we all have to die, we will die. But we will not give away our land."[25]

5. Meskhetian Turks, Turkic Muslims who were deported en masse from southwestern Georgia to Central Asia by Stalin in 1944, wish to return to their ancestral homeland. Some 12,000 people were evacuated to the Krasnodar region of Russia during ethnic riots in the Fergana Valley of Uzbekistan in 1989. As many as 50,000 may return, and Shevardnadze has indicated his willingness to accommodate those wishing to settle in Georgia. Others plan to join fellow peoples in Turkey, a decision made possible by an agreement with Ankara.[26]

Armenia

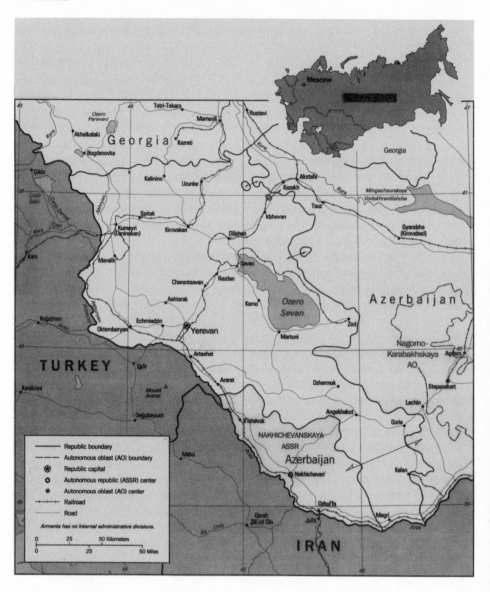

Republic boundary
Autonomous oblast (AO) boundary
Republic capital
Autonomous republic (ASSR) center
Autonomous oblast (AO) center
Railroad
Road

Armenia has no internal administrative divisions.

0   25   50 Kilometers
0   25   50 Miles

Armenia

BASIC DATA

Total Area: 11,506 square miles (some 29,800 square kilometers). It is the smallest of the new Eurasian states of the former Soviet Union.

Population: 3.4 million, of whom 93 percent are Armenian and 2 percent Russian. An out-migration of Azeris and Russians has increased the proportion of Armenians, making Armenia the most homogeneous of all former union republics. The annual rate of population growth is 0.8 percent.

Religion: Armenian Orthodox.

Capital: Yerevan.

Official Name: Republic of Armenia.

Government:

- Executive Branch: Levon Ter-Petrosyan became Armenia's first popularly elected president on November 11, 1991, following elections on October 16. Top executive authority is vested in a Supreme Council. Government is headed by a prime minister. The Council of Ministers coordinates governmental affairs, and issues of security are handled by the National Security Council.
- Legislative Branch: Supreme Soviet.
- Judicial Branch: Supreme Court.

Economy: Armenia, a producer of machinery and fruit, has had its economy crippled by a five-year confrontation with Azerbaijan over the status of the Nagorno-Karabakh Autonomous Oblast, a largely Armenian-populated enclave of 170,000 people within and a part of Azerbaijan. A blockade of energy and raw materials by Azerbaijan since the conflict began in February 1988 have brought untold hardships to Armenia, second only to the loss of life associated with the conflict and a devastating December 1988 earthquake, which killed 55,000 people. The energy shortage has caused Armenia to plan to restart its two VVER–440 pressurized water nuclear reactors. These first-generation Soviet reactors were taken out of service after the 1988 earthquake, after questions were raised about their safety.

History: Armenians are descended from ancient tribes, and their language is the oldest literary language in the former Soviet Union, dating to A.D. 406. In the nineteenth century this landlocked, mountainous country was caught in struggles between Russia and Turkey. In 1915, the massacre and deportation of Armenians in eastern Anatolia led to as many as 1.5 million deaths, an act that spurred anti-Turkish attacks around the world and has strained ties with Ankara up to the present time.

In May 1918, following the short-lived Transcaucasian Federal Republic that joined Armenia with Georgia and Azerbaijan, Armenia declared its independence. After a brief war with Azerbaijan over Karabakh and a war with Turkey that forced Yerevan to cede Nakhichevan, the Red Army entered the Caucasus and Armenia fell in November 1920. In March 1922, Armenia was joined with Georgia and Azerbaijan to form a Transcaucasian Republic, and in November the new republic formally became part of the Soviet Union, with Nakhichevan and Karabakh becoming part of Azerbaijan. In 1936 Armenia became a separate union republic.

THE ROAD TO INDEPENDENCE

Armenia declared its intent to become independent on August 23, 1990, and on September 23, 1991, it proclaimed its actual independence. It started forming national guard units soon thereafter, and in December its Supreme Soviet acted to restrict Armenian draftees to service in the Soviet army and border guards on the territory of the republic, except for those who volunteered to serve elsewhere. At the same time, the USSR Supreme Soviet declared unconstitutional the Armenian parliament's decision to make Nagorno-Karabakh an autonomous Armenian republic and Azerbaijan's decision abolishing the enclave's autonomy.[27]

Starting on November 4, 1991, the gas pipeline supplying 80 percent of Armenia's energy from Russia through Azerbaijan was closed. In the meantime, Levon Ter-Petrosyan was inaugurated as Armenia's president on November 11. Eleven days later, a helicopter carrying senior Azerbaijani officials and military officers was, by some accounts, shot down, disrupting Armenian-Azerbaijani negotiations to defuse the Nagorno-Karabakh crisis and inflaming tensions still further. A rail blockade restricted needed food and other supplies, compounding the harsh effects of the energy blockade.

By November 24, the situation was sufficiently grave for Armenia to request UN intervention.

As the crisis continued, Moscow, which was facing a political crisis of its own, threatened to withdraw its 2,400 Soviet peacekeeping troops from Nagorno-Karabakh. In January 1992 sixty people were killed in a single weekend, and in February CIS troops were finally ordered to leave by Marshal Shaposhnikov, in hopes of stemming the rising fatalities. Another costly attack on March 7, leaving two hundred people dead, followed the forced resignation of Azerbaijani President Ayaz Mutalibov over widespread Azeri unhappiness with the war's progress. Such intensified operations inspired Armenia to send conscripts to Georgia for military training, and on March 22, to start forming a national army that would eventually number between 30,000 and 35,000. Rumors that Turk and Iranian volunteers were assisting the Azeris fueled the crisis further.[28]

The Armenian economic crisis also continued unabated. On March 25, 1992, President Ter-Petrosyan declared an economic state of emergency based upon the continued energy, transportation, and communications blockade.[29] On the same date, Armenia's parliament approved the concept of a new national currency called the dram (composed of 100 lumas). Since then, Armenia has indicated that it prefers to remain in the ruble zone for the indefinite future.

In late March, a ceasefire negotiated by Iran gave way to further hostilities as Armenian forces went on the offensive. By June 9, 1992, the six-mile (almost ten-kilometer) corridor connecting Nagorno-Karabakh to Armenia had been opened, and most of the enclave was controlled by Armenian forces. This relative success came at a time when the government in the enclave's capital, Stepanakert, representing a self-proclaimed Republic of Nagorno-Karabakh, was torn between the radical Dashnak (Armenian Revolutionary Federation) controlling its parliament, and the more moderate Armenian National Movement, headed by President Ter-Petrosyan.[30]

On September 25, 1992, a ceasefire between Armenia and Azerbaijan came into effect. Negotiated by Russian Minister of Defense Grachev, it called for the exchange of prisoners, the resumption of rail ties, and the creation of a five-kilometer-wide buffer zone between warring sides. Observers from Russia, Georgia, Belarus, Ukraine, Kazakhstan, and the CSCE, when given permission by their governments, are to monitor the ceasefire, and they are also responsible for law enforcement in their sectors. The Lachin corridor connecting Nagorno-Karabakh with Armenia will eventually be opened when it is safe to do so.[31] Sporadic violations continue, and the situation remains volatile.

A second enclave affecting Armenia's progress to independence is Nakhichevan, an autonomous republic within the borders of Armenia but also a statutory part of Azerbaijan. Nakhichevan's history dates to 1500 B.C., and its capital is said to have been founded by Noah. A Russian possession since 1828, it fell into Soviet hands, like the rest of the Caucasus, through conquest by the Red Army.

The Treaty of Kars, signed by Armenia, Georgia, Azerbaijan, and Turkey on October 13, 1921, is sometimes used as the authority by which Turkey serves as Nakhichevan's guarantor. Article 5 places Nakhichevan under Azerbaijan's protection, but it grants no special rights to Turkey.[32] The enclave's current status was codified in 1924. Its population of approximately 320,000, largely Azeri Turkic peoples who are Shiite Muslims, is bounded by Turkey and Iran to the south and surrounded on three sides by Christian Armenia, with which it has been involved in active hostilities since Yerevan's fortunes improved in the war in Nagorno-Karabakh.

Geydar Aliyev, former Soviet Politburo member who claimed he left Moscow in 1987 when he learned of Gorbachev's sympathies for Armenia, is chairman of the Supreme Mejlis (council) of Nakhichevan. Aliyev has said that Armenia wants to conquer Nakhichevan. The enclave's primary route to Azerbaijan, a rail line through Armenian territory, has been severed as a part of the Azeri rail blockade of Yerevan. Aliyev has often stated that Turkey is committed to come to his aid according to the Treaty of Kars, which he renewed in a March 1992 visit to Ankara. Turkey acknowledged Aliyev's loyalty by agreeing in March 1992 to loan Nakhichevan $100 million to finance a bridge over the Araks River and to establish air and rail links between Turkey and the enclave.[33]

On May 28, 1992, a bridge 12 meters (almost 40 feet) wide and 286 meters (944 feet) long connecting Nakhichevan with Turkey, the Bridge of Hope, was opened. It makes it possible for the populations of Turkey and the Turkic peoples residing in Nakhichevan to visit each other freely for the first time in seventy years. Turkish Prime Minister Suleyman Demirel presided at the ceremonies and then opened the Turkish Bank in the enclave's capital and largest city, Nakhichevan, where he said, "Your 60 million brothers in Turkey are with you under all conditions; I want you to know that." On December 26, 1992, a second bridge crossing the Araks River was inaugurated. It connected the enclave with Iran, which promised to supply badly needed natural gas and electricity.[34]

Armenia's Ministry of Defense formed its first regiment in June 1992, and other units based on the former Soviet army formations are being planned. A signatory to the May 15, 1992, Collective Security Treaty at the CIS summit at Tashkent, Armenia believes it can provide for its defense more economically through an alliance with the other new CIS states.[35] A bilateral agreement with Russia, signed in September 1992, provides the legal basis for the stationing of Russian troops in Armenia.

SEPARATIST/DISSIDENT MOVEMENTS

1. The Nagorno-Karabakh conflict has continued for more than five years and has cost at least 3,000 lives. Until recent events in Yugoslavia, it had

caused the largest flow of refugees since World War II as members of the two ethnic groups fled to their respective titular homelands. On January 3, 1993, presidents Bush and Yeltsin called for a cessation of hostilities in a joint statement that reflected their concern with the continued bloodshed. With both the Christian Armenians and Muslim Azeris accusing Russian forces of participating in the struggle, and efforts by Turkey, the United Nations, the CSCE, Iran, and others to mediate the crisis, this struggle of people and history is a microcosm of similar, nearly intractible conflicts to be found virtually throughout the entire former Soviet Union. This crisis continues to serve as the catalytic issue by which Slavs and Europeans, Turkic and Persian peoples, Christians and Muslims may part ways.

2. The situation in Nakhichevan remains tense due to shortages of food and fuel as well as sporadic skirmishes and artillery fire along the enclave's border with Armenia. Geydar Aliyev's close ties with Turkey are a stabilizing force, and he has also appealed for aid from Iran. Following serious attacks in May 1992, there were concerns that the war over Nagorno-Karabakh would spread to Nakhichevan and possibly to northern Turkey. Armenia continues to assert that it has no territorial ambitions concerning Nakhichevan, and ties with Baku have become strained due to Aliyev's concerns over what he sees as efforts by Azerbaijan's ruling Popular Front to interfere in his republic's internal affairs. The situation remains dangerous.

3. Ties between Armenia and Turkey are correct, but in the background there are strains associated with areas of northern Turkey that were formerly part of greater Armenia. President Ter-Petrosyan has said that Armenia does not have any land claims against its neighbors and that borders cannot be changed. Armenia and Turkey do not have diplomatic relations.

Azerbaijan

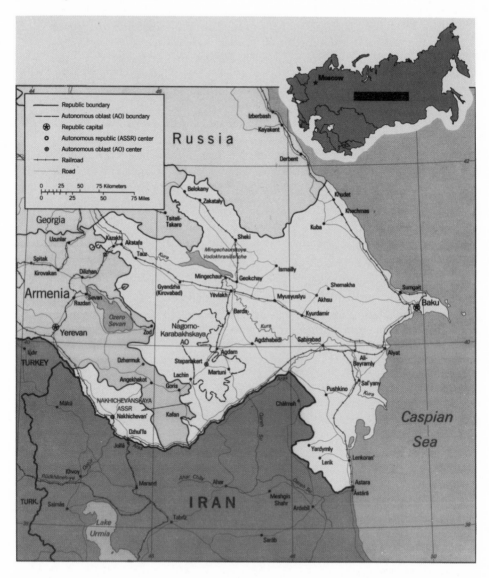

Azerbaijan

BASIC DATA

Total Area: 33,436 square miles (86,600 square kilometers).

Population: 7.5 million. About 83 percent are Azeri, a Turkic people; 6 percent are Russian, and 6 percent are Armenian. There has been an outflow of Russians, and nearly all Armenians are concentrated in the autonomous oblast of Nagorno-Karabakh. Population growth is 1.6 percent annually.

Religion: Shiite Islam, Armenian Orthodox, Russian Orthodox.

Official Name: Azerbaijani Republic.

Capital: Baku.

Government:

- Executive Branch: Abulfaz Elchibey, chairman of the anti-communist Popular Front, became president on June 16, 1992, following the country's first multicandidate election on June 7. A prime minister is the senior government officer, and a Defense Council is responsible for defense policy.
- Legislative Branch: National Assembly.
- Judicial Branch: Supreme Court.

Elchibey, in an August 23, 1992, national address, said that Azerbaijan's most difficult problem is the war over Nagorno-Karabakh. Beyond this, he listed the nation's greatest challenges as forming a strong and capable army, adopting a new national currency, and speeding up plans for a market economy. He emphasized that Azerbaijan prefers to deal with all other countries on a bilateral rather than a multilateral basis, and that he will give priority to ties with Russia, Ukraine, Iran, and Turkey.[36] In late December 1992, a parliamentary decision to reinstate Turkish as the official language led to riots in Baku.

Economy: Azerbaijan is a producer of oil and gas, as well as of cotton and other agricultural crops. The war over the status of Nagorno-Karabakh, as well as hostilities in the Nakhichevan Autonomous Republic in Armenia—a constituent part of Azerbaijan—have destroyed much of the nation's economy. No significant privatization has taken place, although Western oil companies have actively sought to exploit the new country's extensive oil reserves. Introduction of a new currency, the manat, took place in August 1992, but it has met with mixed success. Azerbaijan became one of the first of the former Soviet republics to attend the Islamic Economic Cooperation Organization (ECO) Session of February 16, 1992, at its summit meeting in Tehran. It formally joined the ECO in November 1992.

History: The area, inhabited since the eight century B.C., has been ruled by Persians, Arabs, and Mongols, who gave it their language and religion. Russian involvement was solidified by 1828 when the Treaty of Turkmanchi gave Russia control of the Nakhichevan and Yerevan khanates and set the border of Azerbaijan at the Araks River. This effectively divided the Azeri peoples.

Following a brief period of independence and participation in the Transcaucasian Federal Republic after the collapse of the monarchy in St. Petersburg, Red Army units seized Baku on April 28, 1920, and formed the Azerbaijan Soviet Socialist Republic. This was merged with the Armenian and Georgian republics in 1922 to create the Transcaucasian Soviet Socialist Republic. In 1936 all three became separate union republics. Nagorno-Karabakh was made an autonomous province of Azerbaijan in July 1923, and Nakhichevan was formed in February 1924 as an autonomous republic belonging to Azerbaijan.

THE ROAD TO INDEPENDENCE

Azerbaijan declared its sovereignty on September 23, 1989, and its independence on August 30, 1991. Prior to this time, an outbreak of hostilities between Azeris and ethnic Armenians in the city of Sumgait, north of Baku, on February 28, 1988, triggered ethnic strife throughout the country, leading to a large-scale transmigration of peoples and an ongoing war centered on Armenian–Azerbaijani border areas and the enclave of Nagorno-Karabakh, where 85 percent of the 170,000 inhabitants are Armenian.

Political instability centered on the frustrations associated with the inconclusive fighting, punctuated by horrors of war such as mutilations, body snatching (in a predominantly Islamic country in which the treatment of the dead and a proper Islamic burial are important), and atrocities against women and children, has characterized this country's path to independence.

Much of this legacy belongs to Ayaz Mutalibov, first secretary of the Azerbaijani Communist party, who was elected president by the republic's Supreme Soviet in May 1990. Following the August 1991 abortive coup in Moscow, Mutalibov resigned his party position and ran without opposition in the first popular election for president on September 8. He won the election, which was disputed by the Popular Front, a nationalist group that increasingly opposed the government.[37]

As the struggle with Armenia dragged on and increasingly focused on Nagorno-Karabakh, it became apparent that the republic required a more effective military force. On October 10, 1991, the national legislature, then called the Supreme Soviet, voted to create an army of approximately 35,000, starting with Azeris serving in the Soviet army and, later, naval units from the Caspian Sea Flotilla. This was to be coordinated by the Defense Council, which intended to establish an air force and border guards as well. Weeks after the creation of the Commonwealth of Independent States, Azerbaijan, along with Ukraine and Moldova, announced its intention to maintain an army independent of the CIS structure.[38]

As the war continued, the deaths of hundreds of Azeris at the Nagorno-Karabakh village of Khojaly on February 25–26, 1992, led to widespread outrage over the ineffectiveness of the Baku government in prosecuting the conflict. Violent supporters of the opposition Popular Front demanded the ouster of President Mutalibov, who resigned on March 6. The Front installed a caretaker government until a new government could be elected on June 7, but political paralysis ensued and there were further reversals on the battlefield.

On the evening of May 14 the Communist-dominated Azerbaijani parliament voted to restore Mutalibov, who promptly declared a state of emergency and canceled the planned elections. Riots by armed supporters of the Popular Front took place, and the parliament, presidential palace, and television station were seized; Mutalibov fled within twenty-four hours. After three days of armed confrontation, the parliament voted to dissolve and to pass power to a coalitional National Council dominated by Popular Front members. The Council vowed to hold the June 7 elections and to win the Nagorno-Karabakh conflict.[39]

On June 7, 1992, the elections took place in all areas except Nagorno-Karabakh. The elevation of Abulfaz Elchibey to the presidency has been termed the "Velvet Revolution" because of the relatively peaceful manner in which it was conducted and because of Elchibey's commitment to democracy, human rights, and the rule of law.[40] While Elchibey is also seen as the person most likely to win Nagorno-Karabakh, his election gives new impetus to peace efforts by the CSCE, Turkey, Saudi Arabia, and others.

Elchibey's election also has cast Iran and Turkey in new roles, with Ankara assuming the favored position. Iran offered, in a December 1991 visit by Foreign Minister Ali Akhbar Velayati, to build a new rail link to connect Azerbaijan with Nakhichevan via Iran. He also promised to open an Iranian bank in Baku, to establish an air route and reopen the Astara-Tabriz-Jolfa highway, and to support Azerbaijan's membership in the Economic Co-operation Organization. In an April 1992 agreement, Iran promised to build a three-tube pipeline for shipping Iranian natural gas to Ukraine through Azerbaijan.[41] In August, however, Baku sent eighty students to Turkish military schools for a five-year officers' training program, at Turkey's expense.[42]

Negative rumblings in relations with Iran have also been heard, primarily associated with the twenty-three million Azeri people in Iran whom Tehran has sought to assimilate at the expense of their Azerbaijani culture. In addition, Iran's peacemaking efforts have been viewed by many as an attempt "to help Armenia, not Azerbaijan."[43]

Moscow has also received its share of the blame. Azerbaijan's prime minister accused Russia of providing arms for Armenia in a March 1992 television interview. In April, Baku's defense minister said CIS troops have been used in a policy of "terror and violence and military aggression against Azerbaijan," in an effort to "drive the Azerbaijan Republic into the CIS at all costs."[44]

The charge against the CIS is the most significant for Azerbaijan, since Ayaz Mutalibov signed the December 21, 1991, foundational document at Alma-Ata but the country's parliament never ratified it. Baku has been reluctant to join CIS military structures, and the Popular Front has vowed to quit the Commonwealth and to pursue ties with other nations by means of bilateral agreements and relationships. Azerbaijan's parliament voted on October 7, 1992, to abstain from CIS membership, but it is expected to continue to send observers to CIS meetings and to cooperate in areas of mutual interest.

SEPARATIST/TERRITORIAL DISPUTES

1. Iran has reason to be concerned that the Elchibey regime may assert ties with ethnic Azeris residing in northern Iran. "Iran insists on erasing Azerbaijani culture from their life, does not want to recognize their nationality, insists on calling them Persians, and prevents them from speaking or learning their mother tongue," according to Azerbaijan's information minister in February 1992.[45] For the future, irredentist impulses may impinge upon friendly relations between the two neighboring states, despite their religious affinity.

2. Nagorno-Karabakh will continue to be the former Soviet Union's major political-military-ethnic and religious incendiary. According to Paul Goble of the Carnegie Endowment for International Peace, "More than any other

problem in the post-Soviet space, the fighting in and around Nagorno-Karabakh threatens to expand and to involve not only regional powers but more distant countries as well."[46] Goble has proposed a creative plan for swapping territory between Armenia and Azerbaijan to eliminate the ethnic enclaves that are currently the focus of so much hostility.[47] A major offensive by Azerbaijan in late September 1992 killed at least five hundred people in one week. This led Russian Defense Minister Grachev to propose talks in Moscow, leading to an agreement to implement a comprehensive ceasefire on September 25. Unfortunately, hostilities have continued.

3. The status of Azerbaijan's participation in the Commonwealth of Independent States is a critical bellwether of that organization's future. This situation has been aggravated by Nagorno-Karabakh's request to join the CIS as an independent state on December 12, 1991. Much depends on the political accumen of Boris Yeltsin in finding some acceptable formula by which to resolve the Nagorno-Karabakh and Nakhichevan dilemmas and in providing substance to the CIS framework so that the doubts about its viability and usefulness may be more firmly resolved.

4. Relations with Dagestan, a Russian autonomous republic north of Azerbaijan, have been strained due to the presence of Azeris (primarily Shiite Muslims) who live there, refugees from the conflict in Nagorno-Karabakh, and Lezgins who are Sunni Muslims living on both sides of the common border. One group has proposed the creation of a Republic of Lezgistan, which would include Lezgins living in northern Azerbaijan and Dagestan. Parliamentary talks have been held between Azerbaijan and Dagestan to address this issue and other common problems.[48]

NOTES

1. Paul B. Henze, "The Demography of the Caucasus According to 1989 Soviet Census Data," *Central Asian Survey* 10, no. 1/2 (1991):155–59.

2. Ibid.

3. Haidar Bammate, "The Caucasus and the Russian Revolution (from a Political Viewpoint)," *Central Asian Survey* 10, no. 4 (1991):2–6.

4. Michel Tarran, "The Orthodox Mission in the North Caucasus—End of the 18th–Beginning of the 19th Century," *Central Asian Survey* 10, no. 1/2 (1991):103–05.

5. Nart, "The Life of Mansur, Great Independence Fighter of the Caucasian Mountain People," *Central Asian Survey* 10, no. 1/2 (1991):89–91.

6. Bammate, "The Caucasus," 2–27.

7. "Andrey Kozyrev: 'The Caucasus Region Has Strategic Significance for Russia'," Moscow *Rossiyskiye vesti*, September 8, 1992, 1, in FBIS-SOV–92–176, September 10, 1992.

8. Steven Erlanger, "Beyond Georgia's Strife, an Economy That Is Coming Apart," *New York Times*, September 22, 1992, A8.

9. "Novosti" newscast, Moscow Television First Program Network, 1600 GMT, January 6, 1992, in FBIS-SOV–92–004, January 7, 1992, 82.

10. Igor Gbritishvili and Albert Kochetkov, "Met by Military Council," Moscow TASS, 1156 GMT, March 7, 1992, and "Sees Patriarch," Moscow TASS, 1825 GMT, March 7, 1992, in FBIS-SOV–92–046, March 9, 1992, 56.

11. "State Council Resolves to Form Armed Forces," Moscow INTERFAX, 1509 GMT, April 11, 1992, in FBIS-SOV–92–071, April 13, 1992, 65; "Defense Ministry Details Armed Forces Plans," Moscow Radio Rossii Network, 0100 GMT, April 19, 1992, in FBIS-SOV–92–076, April 20, 1992, 63.

12. Barbara Crossette, "Baker Visits Georgia to Give a Boost to Shevardnadze," *New York Times*, May 26, 1992, A7.

13. Serge Schmemann, "A Day's Work in Georgia: Shevardnadze Dodges a Coup and Ends a War," *New York Times*, June 25, 1992, A3.

14. Sergey Gorbunov, "Shevardnadze Not Optimistic over CIS' Future," Moscow ITAR-TASS, 1223 GMT, April 8, 1992, in FBIS-SOV–92–069, April 9, 1992, 66; "More on CIS Membership," Moscow Radio One Network, 1800 GMT, April 22, 1992, in FBIS-SOV–92–079, April 23, 1992, 53.

15. "Novosti" newscast, Moscow Television First Program Network, 1400 GMT, April 14, 1992, in FBIS-SOV–92–073, April 15, 1992, 63; Aleksandr Semyonov, "Bilateral Ties Preferred to CIS Membership," Moscow ITAR-TASS, 1304 GMT, April 22, 1992, in FBIS-SOV–92–079, April 23, 1992, 53.

16. Serge Schmemann, "Shevardnadze, a Bit Daunted, Awaits a Mandate," *New York Times*, October 12, 1992, A7.

17. Serge Schmemann, "Shevardnadze Wins in Georgia; Hard Tasks Loom," *New York Times* October 13, 1992, A13.

18. Commission on Security and Cooperation in Europe, *Staff Delegation Trip Report on Moscow, Georgia, Moldova and Belarus, June 25–July 4, 1992* (Washington, D.C.: U.S. Government Printing Office, August 1992), 11–12.

19. Igor Terekhov, "Vladikavkaz Demands That Moscow Send Troops into South

Ossetia and Threatens to Leave Russian Federation," *Nezavisimaya gazeta,* May 29, 1992, 3, in FBIS-SOV–92–108, June 4, 1992, 57–58.

20. "Rutskoy Urges 'Return Measures' Against Georgia," Moscow INTERFAX, 1400 GMT, May 28, 1992, in FBIS-SOV–92–105, June 1, 1992, 36.

21. Radan Haluzik, "We Liked the Party's Ideas," Prague *Respekt,* September 21–27, 1992, in FBIS-SOV–92–189, September 29, 1992, 51–52.

22. N. Kandiashvili, "Vesti" newscast, 1900 GMT, June 16, 1992, in FBIS-SOV–92–117, June 17, 1992, 68.

23. Vanora Bennett, "Georgian Forces on 'Red Alert' as Civilians Flee City," *Washington Post,* October 9, 1992, A32.

24. Elizabeth Fuller, "Georgia's Adzhar Crisis," *RFE/RL Report on the USSR,* August 9, 1991, 8–13.

25. "Georgia May Dispatch Troops Into Russia," *Harrisburg* (Pa.) *Sunday Patriot-News,* October 11, 1992, A16.

26. "Presidential Bulletin," Moscow INTERFAX, 1750 GMT, May 20, 1992, in FBIS-SOV–92–099, May 21, 1992, 99; "Turkey Agrees to Resettle 50,000 Meskhetian Turks," Moscow POSTFACTUM, 1648 GMT, April 28, 1992, in FBIS-SOV–92–083, April 29, 1992, 68–69; "Agreement Allows Meskheti Turks to Return Home," Moscow POSTFACTUM, 2051 GMT, March 30, 1992, in FBIS-SOV–92–064, April 2, 1992, 85–86.

27. "Pulse of the Day," *Pravda,* December 3, 1991, 1, in FBIS-SOV–91–233, December 4, 1991, 72; "Azerbaijani, Armenian Decisions Ruled Illegal," Moscow INTERFAX, 2143 GMT, December 1, 1991, in FBIS-SOV–91–233, December 4, 1991, 17.

28. "Armenia Calls for National Army," *Carlisle* (Pa.) *Sentinel,* February 28, 1992, A5; "Turkish Group's Role in Azerbaijan Reported," Yerevan Armenpres, 1215 GMT, April 1, 1992, and "Turks, Iranians Said Fighting for Azerbaijan," Yerevan Radio, 1500 GMT, April 1, 1992, in FBIS-SOV–92–064, April 2, 1992, 81; "Cadets Begin Military Training in Georgia," Yerevan Radio, 1500 GMT, February 27, 1992, in FBIS-SOV–92–041, March 2, 1992, 63.

29. Sergey Bablumyan, "Armenia: Emergency Situation May Develop into Economic State of Emergency," *Izvestiya,* March 25, 1992, 1, and "President Declares Economic State of Emergency," Moscow Radio Rossii Network, 0200 GMT, March 26, 1992, in FBIS-SOV–92–059, March 26, 1992, 71.

30. Daniel Sneider, "Armenians Are Divided over Talks on Hard-Won, Disputed Enclave," *Christian Science Monitor,* June 17, 1992, 3.

31. "Protocol for Azerbaijan–Armenian Cease-Fire," Moscow ITAR-TASS, 1110 GMT, September 26, 1992, in FBIS-SOV–92–188, September 28, 1992, 4–5.

32. Igor Belyayev, "The Treaty of Kars Is Not Open to Capricious Interpretation, and 'Twisting' It Is Quite Dangerous," *Literaturnaya gazeta,* June 3, 1992, 9, in FBIS-SOV–92–110, June 8, 1992, 5.

33. Irfan Ulku, "Nakhichevan's Aliyev Interviewed on Turkey," Istanbul *Turkiye,* March 26, 1992, 13, in FBIS-SOV–92–061, March 30, 1992, 48–49; "Aliyev Comments on Border Adjustment Issue," Ankara *Turkish Daily News,* March 25, 1992, 5, in FBIS-SOV–92–061, March 30, 1992, 49.

34. "Turkish Prime Minister Visits Nakhichevan," Ankara TRT Television Network, 1900 GMT, May 28, 1992, in FBIS-SOV–92–104, May 29, 1992, 71; "Second

Bridge Connecting Iran, Nakhichevan Opens," Baku *TURAN*, 1309 GMT, December 28, 1992, in FBIS-SOV–92–251, December 30, 1992, 54.

35. A. Dokuchayev, "National Armies: The View From Within," *Krasnaya zvezda*, June 11, 1992, 2, in JPRS-UMA–92–023, June 24, 1992, 39–40.

36. "President Elchibey Addresses Nation 23 August," Baku *Turan,* 1100 GMT, August 24, 1992, in FBIS-SOV–92–164, August 24, 1992, 53.

37. Elizabeth Fuller, "The Azerbaijani Presidential Election: A One-Horse Race," *RFE/RF Report on the USSR,* September 13, 1991, 12–14.

38. A. Guseynov, "We Believe That This Is an Essential Thing," Baku *Molodezh Azerbaydzhana,* October 5, 1991, 2, in JPRS-UMA–91–031, December 12, 1991, 12; Thomas Goltz, "Azerbaijanis Move to Create Army," *Washington Post,* October 11, 1991, A23.

39. "Azerbaijani Communists Yield to Nationalists," *New York Times,* May 20, 1992, A12; "Rioters in Azerbaijan Take over Parliament," *New York Times,* May 16, 1992, A4; Justin Burke, "Azeri Nationalists Promise Election, Renewed Battle over Karabakh," *Christian Science Monitor,* May 18, 1992, 1.

40. "Deputy Prime Minister Gives News Conference," Moscow Radio Rossii Network, 1000 GMT, June 17, 1992, in FBIS-SOV–92–117, June 17, 1992, 63–64.

41. "Commentary Noted Improved Iranian Relations," Baku Radio, 1200 GMT, December 3, 1991, in FBIS-SOV–91–235, December 6, 1991, 82–83; "Iran to Help Build Rail Link," Moscow TASS, 0831 GMT, December 4, 1991, in FBIS-SOV–91–234, December 5, 1991, 68–69; "Iran, Azerbaijan to Join Gas Pipeline Project," Kiev Radio, 1300 GMT, April 28, 1992, in FBIS-SOV–92–084, April 30, 1992, 47–48.

42. "80 Military Students Sent to Turkey for Training," Baku ASSA-IRADA, 1214 GMT, August 25, 1992, in FBIS-SOV–92–166, August 26, 1992, 51.

43. "Azerbaijan: Caspian Cauldron," *The Economist,* June 13, 1992, 55; "Azerbaijan Information Minister Tells Al-Sharq al-Awsat: We Reject Political Domination and Do Not Seek Tutelage of Other Empires," London *Al-Sharq al-Awsat,* February 1, 1992, 2, in FBIS-SOV–92–025, February 6, 1992, 75.

44. "Insight into the World Program," Ankara TRT Television, 2140 GMT, March 16, 1992, in FBIS-SOV–92–052, March 17, 1992, 75; "Russia Accused of Aggression by Azeris," Baku *Bakinskiy rabochiy,* April 16, 1992, 1, in JPRS-UMA–92–018, May 20, 1992, 25–26.

45. "Azerbaijan Information Minister," 75.

46. "Lessons from Central Asia—Nagorno Karabakh and Afghanistan Considered," *United States Institute of Peace Journal 5* (June 1992):1.

47. Vladimir Yemelyanenko, "Karabakh: Peace Based On a U.S. Formula?" *Moscow News,* September 27–October 4, 1992, 4.

48. " 'Tension' Observed in Ties With Dagestan," Moscow Radio Rossii Network, 1600 GMT, July 12, 1992, in FBIS-SOV–92–134, July 13, 1992, 76.

6

Central Asia

The four Central Asian republics—Uzbekistan, Kyrgyzstan, Tajikistan, and Turkmenistan—and Kazakhstan are the homes of over 55 million Muslim peoples who constitute the Asian heart of the former Soviet Union. Kazakhstan is usually included in this area because its inhabitants are predominantly Muslim and its southern regions were part of imperial Russia's district of Turkestan. Ringed in the south by the Pamir Mountains and Tien Shan Mountains, and stretching from the Caspian Sea in the west to the Altai and Sayan mountains in the east, this area of vast arid deserts and mountain highlands is now the site of a "great game" for political influence such as even Kipling could not have imagined.

The breakup of the USSR renewed the competition between Turkey and Iran, successors of the Ottoman and Persian empires, for the hearts and minds of kindred peoples to the north. Envisioning a secular Islamic pan-Turkic empire tied to Ankara or a fundamentalist Islamic union linked to Tehran, outside actors such as Saudi Arabia, Pakistan, Russia, and the United States are now confronted with a resurgence of diplomatic activity that promises to remake the essence and determine the future direction of Eurasia.

Connected to this contest is Azerbaijan to the west, home to seven million Turkic Azeri peoples who speak Azeri (similar to Turkish) and who are Shiite Muslims. Some 320,000 Azeris live in the Armenian enclave of Nakhichevan, an administrative reponsibility of Azerbaijan. Until the fall of the Soviet Union, the Soviet Azeris were cut off from some twenty-three million Farsi-speaking Azeris living to the south in Iran.

Within Central Asia, most residents are Turkic except in Kazakhstan, which has a significant Russian population, and Tajikistan, whose citizens are Persian. Despite this ethnic tie, nearly all peoples are Sunni Muslims and speak versions of Turkish. As a result, links with either Iran or Turkey

Central Asia

through ethnicity, language, or religion are present but not predominant. A number of countries have a stake in whether the region gravitates toward secular, pro-Western Turkey or radical, fundamentalist Iran. Russia, for one, has significant economic and defense ties with these countries, particularly with nuclear-armed Kazakhstan.

China is concerned that the 8.2 million Muslims in the Xinjiang-Uigur Autonomous Region, 63 percent of its population, may become restless and seek to renew links with fellow Uigurs and Kazakhs in Kazakhstan and Krygyzstan. Memories of 1933 and 1949 attempts to form an East Turkestan republic there have been fanned by the separatist Islamic Party of East Turkestan. Fears that the three to seven million Tajiks in northern Afghanistan may seek to establish a Greater Tajikistan are also destabilizing.[1]

Dreams of renewing the ancient greatness of Samarkand as the center of Asia are tied to this religious reawakening. Samarkand was the major crossroads for the Silk Road to China and for the spice route to India and the gold trek to Siberia. It was also a center of Islamic learning. Though much has changed in modern Uzbekistan, this legacy of greatness has not been forgotten.[2]

Iran seeks to establish an arch of fundamentalist states to shield itself and its faith from foreign encroachments. Asserting that Ankara is acting on America's behalf to "buy the Muslims of Central Asia,"[3] Tehran's involvement has spurred religious ferment in the region. The 160 mosques in Central Asia in 1989 have increased to more than 5,000 in 1992, and the number of Islamic seminaries (*medressehs*) has risen from one to nine. Most agree that nationalism takes precedence over religion, but the possibility that the two may combine presents a potent challenge to regional leaders.[4]

Central Asian states have extended tenuous links to Islamic organizations. In December 1991, Azerbaijan joined the Organization of the Islamic Conference at its meeting in Dakar, Senegal. Kazakhstan sent representatives, and it is anticipated that all six Muslim states of the former Soviet Union will eventually join. Participation in the haj (the pilgrimage to Mecca), reverence for the holy places of Mecca and Medina, and the feeling that all Muslims belong to the *umma* (community of believers) will bring all Muslims together, regardless of their differences.[5]

The possibility of an Islamic common market was addressed at a February 16–17, 1992, session of the Economic Cooperation Organization formed by Pakistan, Iran, and Turkey. Azerbaijan, Uzbekistan, and Turkmenistan sought to join the organization, while Kazakhstan, Kyrgyzstan, and Tajikistan were represented by observers at the ECO's Tehran session.[6] All were accepted into formal membership on November 28, 1992.

Differences of a practical nature among the Central Asian republics were the subject of an April 22, 1992, summit meeting at Bishkek, capital of Kyrgyzstan. Termed a meeting of "heads of state of post-communist Asia,"[7] the session endorsed the Turkish model of the secular state. Askar Akayev, president of Kyrgyzstan, described Turkey as "the morning star that shows the Turkic republics the way." This focus on democratic practices and market economies led Tajikistan's chief clergyman to urge Tajiks to look upon Turkey as their example for the future.[8]

In the summit's final declaration the heads of state agreed to observe international treaties on disarmament and human rights and to call for regular meetings of area leaders. Nursultan Nazarbayev, president of Kazakhstan, proposed that all countries of Central Asia conclude a common defense treaty, with a view toward forming a defense union with Russia. Such a treaty would enable the new states to form armies consistent with their means and with the CIS's purpose.[9] This agreement in fact did occur at the May 15 CIS summit at Tashkent.

Another expression of common interests was the meeting of the heads of state of Turkmenistan, Kazakhstan, Krygyzstan, Uzbekistan, and Iran, as well as the prime ministers of Turkey and Pakistan, at Ashkhabad on May 9–10, 1992. The meeting was held to discuss regional issues, particularly those relating to economic development and cooperation. The six agreements signed reflected an expansion of economic ties, particularly air and sea services; the construction of highways and pipelines; and agreement to build a trans-Asian rail line linking Iran with the Central Asian rail network.[10]

The Ashkhabad session also provided a useful insight into the expectations and future plans of the non-CIS participants. Iranian President Hashemi Rafsanjani, heading a delegation numbering over one hundred, admitted that his country is engaged in a rivalry with Turkey for influence in the region. Prime Minister Demirel of Turkey was more circumspect in his remarks. When asked whether Turkey is competing with Tehran in the Central Asian republics, Demirel replied that Turkey sought only peace. He observed that the ancient silk route between Beijing and France must be reestablished and that Turkey would assist in the building of pipelines to deliver Asian oil and gas to Europe.[11]

Despite Demirel's reluctance to address Turkey's interest in the region more directly, it is clear that Central Asia will play a large role in Turkish policy. Prior to the Ashkhabad summit, Turkish President Turgut Ozal was the first head of state to make official visits to the new states; he was followed by Prime Minister Demirel, who promised substantial economic and political assistance. Turkey has formed a ministry to deal exclusively with the new Muslim states, has offered six thousand scholarships for study in Turkey, is training twenty-nine diplomats from the six states, and is using satellites to broadcast news and culture eighty-nine hours a week to an estimated fifty-seven million Turkish-speaking people.[12] Pluralist Turkey has also offered $1.1 billion in credits and assistance in converting Central Asian alphabets from Cyrillic to the Latin script.[13]

In an attempt to foster regional cooperation, which did not include Turkey, in October 1992 Iran organized and convened in Tehran what was termed the Caspian Sea Association. Russia, Kazakhstan, Turkmenistan, and Azerbaijan sent representatives, and the group pledged to work to study the Caspian Sea, its environment, biological resources, and ports and facilities; and to conduct further scientific research. Iranian President Rafsanjani observed that the area's extensive oil and gas reserves are exported worldwide and that "a guarantee of the world's receipt of these reserves depends on our cooperation."[14]

Saudi Arabia also has provided significant assistance to the six new predominantly Muslim states. In February 1992 the foreign minister of Saudi Arabia, which is the site of the two Islamic holy cities, offered to furnish one million Korans and to finance the expenses of Islamic pilgrims from the new countries for two pilgrimage seasons.[15] Saudi Arabia provided some $2.5 billion in loans and direct aid prior to the Soviet Union's collapse. According to a Saudi official in October 1991, "For 70 years, those people were cut off from religion. We will send preachers en masse and they are Sunnis and they will calm the people down"—in contrast with "revolutionary themes" emanating from Iran.[16]

Iran has tried to increase its influence in the area by offering scholarships and conducting an extensive public relations program using visiting official delegations. Although somewhat at a disadvantage among the predominantly Turkic peoples who adhere to the Sunni path of Islam, Tehran has been active behind the scenes. Iran's model of a theocratic state has thus far been less appealing, given its distinctive cultural, linguistic, and religious character.

All this has placed Moscow in a quandary, in which the prospect of a prolonged "great game" is not inviting. Some 11 million ethnic Russians live in Central Asia, and 20 million Muslims (of the 55 million Muslims who live in the former Soviet Union) live in Russia. With enough ethnic troubles within Russia at the present time, the possibility of further destabilization along its southern borders is disturbing. In Moscow's favor, according to one Foreign Ministry expert, is that many economic ties with Russia remain intact and that the Russian language is still used for communication between ethnic groups. However, the danger of the new states "falling prey to other geopolitical interests" persists.[17]

Moscow's decline of influence is considered by some to be a bitter harvest of Soviet policy in the region. The backlash in the Islamic world following the 1979 Soviet invasion of Afghanistan and a not-so-subtle message of Soviet domination and control caused the Soviet Union to be seen as an imperialist power. The values of Islam have in some cases caused Muslims to feel superior to their non-Muslim neighbors, and the efforts of Iran since the January 1979 fall of the shah have emphasized this point.[18] Finally, Central Asian unrest that occurred from 1989 to 1990 in Dushanbe, the

Fergana Valley, Novyi Uzen', Ashkhabad, Osh, and elsewhere has been seen as the result of deliberate manipulation by Moscow and its republic officials to stem rising nationalism.[19]

Disturbances in Tajikistan, which led to the overthrow of President Rakhmon Nabiyev in early September 1992, have been widely blamed on "outside forces," particularly Islamic fundamentalists entering the country from Afghanistan. This development poses a threat to all Central Asian states, leading Uzbekistan's president, Islam Karimov, to assert: "Central Asia must not be allowed to be a new seat of tension and a target of geopolitical gambles."[20]

The continued rivalry of Turkey and Iran comes at a time of great unease and uncertainty. For now, posits a scholar at Moscow's Institute of Oriental Studies, "most Central Asian societies are deeply secular, and for them the Turkish model is the most attractive." To the chief of Azerbaijan's Moscow mission, "Our priorities in foreign policy are those countries which have achieved political and economic development, and we like the Turkish example of turning all heads to the West."[21] This orientation, in part, was responsible for an agreement by the Central Asian states, at a January 1993 summit meeting in Tashkent, to create a common market and to cooperate to save the Aral Sea.

This changing Central Asian dynamic has motivated the United States to become the first country to establish formal diplomatic relations with all fifteen new Eurasian states. Secretary of State James Baker has been concerned about Iranian moves in particular: "It's one of the reasons we think it's important that we, ourselves, have contact and dialogue with these former republics." Asian specialist Graham E. Fuller has put the issue in perspective: "There is now a struggle for the soul of Central Asia—and Turkey, Iran, Saudi Arabia, Pakistan and the United States will all play a part.... We are present at the creation again."[22]

Professor Firuz Kazemzadeh of Yale University has captured the essence of the current challenge for Washington: "Conducting relations with Central Asia will not be easy. Yet the United States stands at a propitious moment for influencing the future of that remote and very significant part of the world."[23] Should the United States and the West fail to act, the results may be truly unpredictable. According to Uzbek political observer Jabar Abduvakhid, director of the Tashkent Institute of Oriental Studies, "If the West waits until tomorrow or the day after to get involved, it may be too late."[24]

Kazakhstan

BASIC DATA

Total Area: 1,048,000 square miles (2,717,300 square kilometers). Kazakhstan is the second largest of the new nations after Russia.

Population: 17.1 million. Kazakhs constitute 40 percent, Russians 38 percent, Slavs 7 percent, and Germans 6 percent (47 percent of the former Soviet Union's two million Germans). The growth rate is 1.2 percent.

Religion: Sunni Islam, Russian Orthodox.

Official Name: Republic of Kazakhstan ("stan" means "land of").

Capital: Alma-Ata.

Government:

- Executive Branch: Nursultan A. Nazarbayev became the sovereign republic's first elected president on December 1, 1991. The cabinet of Ministers is the top government body.
- Legislative Branch: Supreme Soviet.
- Judicial Branch: Supreme Court.

In December 1991, President Nazarbayev appointed governors to represent him in the fifteen regions of the republic, in order to strengthen local authority. In January 1992 the system of soviets, a key instrument of Communist rule, was abolished, and bodies of self-government were established in their place. Plans to adopt a new constitution are under way, but it has been complicated by the issue of which of the country's languages should be considered official.

The republic's Semipalatinsk test range was one of two primary nuclear

Kazakhstan

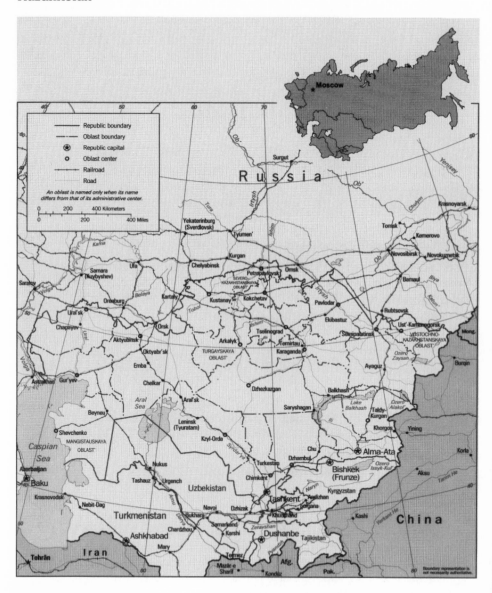

testing grounds of the former Soviet Union. Kazakhstan is the only Central Asian republic to possess nuclear weapons. President Nazarbayev has pledged that no nuclear tests will take place; Semipalatinsk will become a science center. "The Kazakh people have gone through hundreds of tragedies similar to that of Hiroshima," he announced in late November 1991. "Therefore the closure of the testing ground is the implementation of the people's will."[25] Kazakhstan is also home of the Baykonur cosmodrome, from which space launches are conducted.

Economy: Kazakhstan produces energy, fuel, chemicals, and food. It produces one-fifth of all coal mined in the former USSR, and its Tengiz oil deposits are among the five largest in the world, with an estimated 2.2 billion tons of oil.[26] It is the richest of the Central Asian republics, which generally lag behind the Slavic republics.

Agriculture has been the source of livelihood for 75 percent of those of working age. Its role in the national economy was solidified by Khrushchev's 1953 Virgin Lands project, designed to mobilize and modernize agriculture. Kazakstan, along with other arable regions of the Soviet Union, was considerably affected politically, culturally, and economically.[27]

President Nazarbayev has sought to preserve the ruble zone, and he has been an active supporter of CIS multilateral institutions, including the common bank adopted at the October 9, 1992, Bishkek summit. While Kazakhstan has more than fifty enterprises of the former Soviet military–industrial complex on its soil,[28] Nazarbayev is intent on developing the private market: "I now remain true to my convictions, that there can be no political independence, or complete independence, as some put it, without economic independence."[29]

History: The Kazakhs are a mixture of largely nomadic Turkic and Mongol peoples. Russian rule was imposed on the region in 1731. Islam, which had become established in the seventh to ninth centuries, was firmly in place by the nineteenth century, encouraged by Russian authorities who saw it as a unifying influence. Following the Russian Revolution, a small independence movement was quashed by the Red Army in 1919. By 1920, Kazakhstan was an autonomous republic, and in 1936 it was elevated to the status of a full republic. The republic dropped "Soviet Socialist" from its title on December 10, 1991, by order of its Supreme Soviet.

THE ROAD TO INDEPENDENCE

The Kazakh Republic declared its sovereignty on October 26, 1990, and its independence on December 16, 1991. Nursultan Nazarbayev, chairman of the Kazakh Council of Ministers since March 1984, party leader since June 1989, and elected to the new post of president by the republic's Supreme Soviet on April 24, 1990, has been instrumental in the prominence Kazakhstan has achieved. Since declaring sovereignty, he has acted resolutely to assert Kazakh interests while maintaining a harmonious relationship with Moscow. His position was strengthened considerably when he ran unopposed in the first direct election for president on December 1, 1991, winning 99 percent of the vote.[30]

Nazarbayev worked quickly to assert Kazakh independence, noting in January 1992 that "we do not have a lot of time. Within two years, there'll be fresh stagnation, and then big social unrest, unless positive and very radical change can happen."[31] Consequently, he has worked to keep the formerly Communist-dominated economy operating, despite a 40 percent drop in production, and to maintain peace with the 6 million Russians in Kazakhstan and 850,000 Kazakhs in Russia.[32] He has also encouraged respect for the multinational character of his country, preferring that its citizens be called Kazakhstanis to distinguish them from those of Kazakh nationality.

To better ensure the republic's independence, a republican guard directly subordinate to the president was established in March 1992. Designed to act as a special military force with the mission of protecting the sovereignty and constitutional rights of Kazakhstan's citizens, it is expected to number 2,500 by 1993.[33] The Armed Forces of the Republic of Kazakhstan were formed on May 8, 1992, one day after Boris Yeltsin announced the creation of a Russian army. According to President Nazarbayev, this move was initiated "by the necessity of implementing a single state policy in the defense sphere and by other states' forming their own armed forces."[34]

The president serves as the commander in chief, and the forces are composed of units of the former Soviet army stationed on Kazakh soil. A Ministry of Defense was created on May 8. By initial indications, the army would number around fifty thousand, and the navy would include units currently in the Caspian Sea Flotilla. Finding enough Kazakh citizens to serve as officers has been an obstacle. Despite these developments, authorities in Alma-Ata have insisted that agreements concerning the CIS armed forces would be strictly observed.[35]

Some of the initial problems with which the new state had to deal concerned the two major former Soviet Ministry of Defense facilities based in Kazakhstan: the Semipalatinsk nuclear test range and the Baykonur cosmodrome. President Nazarbayev acted quickly to stop nuclear testing, asserting that Kazakhstan was second only to Japan in the extent it has suffered from atomic energy. Secret nuclear explosions conducted for forty years were the source of Kazakhstan's opposition to weapons of mass destruction. In April 1992 Nazarbayev noted that his country was a "temporary nuclear power."[36] He hoped that his nuclear neighbors—China, India, and Pakistan—would follow the same policy.[37]

Fundamental to Kazakhstan's nonnuclear position was the May 15, 1992, CIS collective security pact signed by Kazakhstan, Russia, and four other

Commonwealth members at Tashkent. This agreement provided the new state with a nuclear umbrella and according to Nazarbayev, "Russia is now Kazakhstan's military and political ally. [T]he matter of providing Kazakh territory for the purpose of common defense and deployment of nuclear missiles will be decided on mutually advantageous terms."[38] During his Washington visit four days later, Nazarbayev reiterated his pledge to make Kazakhstan nonnuclear and codified it by signing the START protocol at Lisbon on May 23.

Semipalatinsk was closed in early 1991, and on May 15, 1992, portions of it were converted into the country's national nuclear center and atomic energy agency. They will employ nuclear scientists to monitor radiation and protect the environment. Nazarbayev also acted to close the uranium mines at Shalgi and Tasbulak and to reduce the amount of uranium mined on the Caspian Sea island of Mangyshlak.[39] In September 1992, Kazakhstan declassified and released data on its uranium reserves to the International Atomic Energy Agency, to include their geological characteristics and value.[40] (For a further discussion of strategic facilities on Kazakh soil, see Chapter 7.)

The abuse of the environment is a continuing issue in Kazakhstan. In February 1992 the state's parliament declared the Aral Sea an "ecological disaster zone." In the Caspian Sea and the Volga estuary, which contain 90 percent of the world's sturgeon, caviar production has declined by two-thirds since 1977, due to pesticides and overfishing. The republic has also suffered from the increased salinization of arable land due to salts deposited by irrigation waters.[41] Environmental matters are on the Kazakh political agenda, but pressing economic and political issues have received primary attention.

To further stabilize the situation, Kazakhstan signed a memorandum of mutual understanding with Iran in late 1991. It provides for expanded trade, direct air links, student exchanges, and consulates in the respective capitals, and it includes a rail net that would connect Iranian railroads running from the Persian Gulf with the former Soviet rail system throughout Central Asia as far as the Pacific.[42] This trans-Asia rail link was further codified at the May 9–10 summit of Asian states held at Ashkhabad. Direct highway links connecting Alma-Ata and Tehran were inaugurated on September 10, 1992.[43]

A similar agreement was signed with Turkey in April 1992, when Prime Minister Demirel visited Alma-Ata. Both sides agreed to hold yearly summit meetings, as Uzbekistan and Kyrgyzstan had already agreed to do, and to establish airline service. In a later agreement Ankara offered Alma-Ata a wide range of educational assistance, including Turkish high schools in Kazakhstan.[44]

Another major agreement was that concluded with Russia on May 25, 1992. Signed by the states' presidents, the Agreement of Friendship, Cooperation, and Mutual Assistance Between Russia and Kazakhstan was praised by Yeltsin as an example that other CIS members should emulate. It pledged that the common border will "remain transparent," it synchronizes a number of reforms and common policies, particularly the joint use of the Baykonur cosmodrome,[45] and it codifies Moscow's assistance to Alma-Ata in forming the Kazakhstan armed forces.[46] Such bilateral treaties between Russia and other CIS member states are expected to clarify policies and provide further detail to CIS agreements already concluded.

Fears persist that Kazakhstan may become unstable. On June 17, 1992, some five thousand protesters marched through the streets of Alma-Ata, demanding the resignation of the republic's former Communist leaders. The ruling Socialist Party of Kazakhstan was created from the former Communist party. Other parties exist—notably the People's Congress of Kazakhstan, connected to the environmental, antinuclear Nevada-Semipalatinsk movement—and a proposed new constitution would institutionalize political pluralism. In the meantime, calls for a coalition government and an exodus of Russians and Germans could place new pressures on the fledgling government.

SEPARATIST/DISSIDENT MOVEMENTS

1. There are no known territorial disputes of significance. The northern border with Russia is largely unmarked, and joint meetings have been held to discuss its demarcation.

2. Kazakhstan, together with Russia, Kyrgyzstan, and Tajikistan, have held meetings with China to resolve questions regarding the demarcation of their borders. The opening of rail links between Urumchi, capital of China's Xinjiang-Uigur Autonomous Region, and Alma-Ata on June 23, 1992, will shorten the route to the Pacific by some 3,000 kilometers and will greatly increase cross-border trade.[47] It will also lead to greater contacts among the Uigur peoples on both sides of the border, the largest non-Chinese minority in China, and with Kazakhs living in China. In the past, China has sought to discourage such contacts.

3. Like the rest of the Central Asian republics, Kazakhstan's threat of future dissidence depends on finding a satisfactory formula whereby all segments of society may participate in government at all levels.

Uzbekistan

BASIC DATA

Total Area: 173,591 square miles (447,400 square kilometers).

Population: 22 million: 71 percent are Uzbek, 8 percent Russian, and 5 percent Tajik. It is the third largest new Eurasian state in population after Russia and Ukraine, growing at 2.4 percent annually.

Religion: Sunni Islam, Russian Orthodox.

Official Name: Republic of Uzbekistan.

Capital: Tashkent.

Government:

- Executive Branch: Islam Karimov was elected president on December 29, 1991. A prime minister runs the government (the post of vice president was eliminated in January 1992).
- Legislative Branch: Majlis.
- Judicial Branch: Supreme Court.

In November 1991, the ruling Communist party reestablished itself as the People's Democratic Party of Uzbekistan. It is headed by President Karimov. A new constitution was adopted on November 9, 1992. It changed the name of the legislative body to Majlis (parliament). The Uzbek language is being gradually adopted for official purposes.

In January 1992 serious disturbances occurred in Tashkent over price increases, causing at least six deaths and hundreds of injuries.

Economy: Cotton (both raw and fabricated) is a major product. Land devoted to cotton cultivation will decline by an estimated 55 percent by the

Uzbekistan

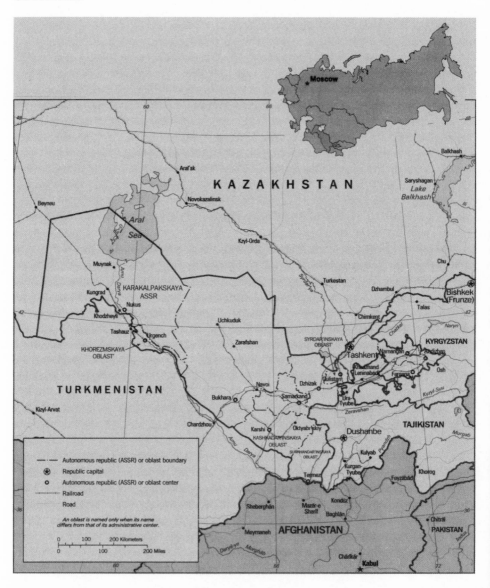

year 2000; as of 1992, Uzbekistan produces 1.45 million tons of cotton fiber yearly.[48] Cotton monoculture, high birth rates, and serious environmental difficulties have made the republic vulnerable to unrest. It joined the Islamic Economic Cooperation Organization at its February 1992 meeting in Tehran and the International Monetary Fund in September 1992. Although Uzbekistan has printed its own currency, the soum, it continues to support and participate in the ruble zone.

History: The Mongol conquest in the thirteenth century served to establish ties between Central Asia and Russia for the first time. Apparently named after Khan Uzbek (1282–1342), who converted the Golden Horde to Islam, Uzbekistan was basically a grouping of Turkic tribes. In the fourteenth century Tamerlane administered his empire of conquest from Samarkand, which was then one of the world's greatest cities and a center of Islamic culture. In the nineteenth century Russians colonized the region, which included an emirate at Bukhara and khanates based in Khiva and Khokand. After the Bolshevik Revolution, the area became the Autonomous Republic of Turkestan; in 1924 its borders were redrawn and it was named the Uzbek Soviet Socialist Republic. A number of peoples, including 200,000 Koreans, were forcibly moved to the republic by Stalin.

THE ROAD TO INDEPENDENCE

Islam Karimov, who had been the head of Uzbekistan's Communist party, was elected president by the republic's Supreme Soviet in March 1990. He was popularly elected to that position in December 1991, in a move designed to enhance his legitimacy. The republic declared its sovereignty on June 20, 1990, and its independence on August 21, 1991.

Despite these developments, Uzbekistan is considered a state in transition, its popular national consciousness incomplete. This fact, to Donald S. Carlisle, means that it is unlikely the country will be and act truly independent. Visions of reviving a Greater Turkestan may prove equally elusive.[49]

The 5 percent of the population who are Tajik—Persian peoples who speak Farsi—follow the Sunni path of Islam. President Karimov seeks to emulate the Turkish example of a secular state, but he has been challenged by a resurgent Islamic Renaissance Party set upon establishing an Islamic republic. An opposition party named Birlik (unity) was founded in 1989. A later offshoot, a party named Erk (freedom), like Birlik, seeks a multiparty democracy.

According to a senior government minister, neither the government nor the opposition believes the republic will become fertile soil for Islamic fundamentalism, which has only 2,000 to 3,000 adherents in the Fergana Valley. Nevertheless, one Birlik leader is convinced that only the rapid democratization of the country's politics will stem the spread of Islamic radicalism, which could be explosive if it remains unopposed.[50] President Karimov, who has initiated a program to educate Uzbek youth about the dangers of Islamic fundamentalism, proclaimed, "Our country is a most quiet country in Central Asia. I can positively declare that Islamic fundamentalism cannot take root in our country."[51]

An Uzbek national guard was created in January 1992, and by July it numbered 1,000 members. A Ministry of Defense was formed in July 1992, and a draft has been conducted for regular and alternative service in the Uzbek armed forces. According to President Karimov, the army will ultimately number around 25,000 to 30,000. On August 18, 1992, a protocol was signed with Kyrgyzstan that provided for cooperation in military matters.[52] Uzbekistan is a signatory to the CIS Collective Security Treaty, which provides for a common defense if attacked.

The environmental disaster of the shrinking Aral Sea has affected Uzbekistan as much as Kazakhstan. The lake is shrinking at the rate of thirty centimeters (twelve inches) yearly, and to restore it to its 1960 level would require a halt of water usage for three decades. Of the 7.6 million hectares (19 million acres) of irrigated land in the basin catchment area, 4.3 million hectares (10.75 million acres) are in Uzbekistan. The current and future shortage of water for the area's growing population means that there will be water disputes among regional nations for the indefinite future.[53]

The use of the Aral Sea's scarce water primarily for Uzbekistan's cotton crop has polluted and salinated area rivers, affected the weather negatively, and impoverished and sickened millions of people. Starting with Stalinist planners in the early 1950s, "They decided that the sea was not necessary ... that the value of the cotton would be greater than the loss of fish." This has led to illnesses of epidemic proportions, with "pesticides and heavy metals in mothers' breast milk." As a result, infant mortality is close to one hundred per thousand live births, ten times the U.S. figure. This calamity is beyond the scope of a single state to resolve, and the country that caused it is gone.[54]

At the present time, President Karimov and other Uzbek leaders see their futures tied to Moscow and the CIS. On May 30, 1992, Karimov and Russian President Boris Yeltsin signed a treaty of friendship and cooperation to provide the basis for the two countries' extensive interaction. Speaking in the Great Kremlin Palace, Yeltsin noted that such bilateral treaties strengthen the CIS structure and "provide a useful incentive to enriching mutual links between the states of the CIS."[55]

Under the terms of the treaty, both parties will coordinate policies on reform measures and will deal with one another on a priority basis. Yeltsin specifically stated that the Russians living in Uzbekistan should greet the treaty with assurance and hope. It was clear that the issue of cotton supplies for Russia constituted a key economic aspect of the agreement.[56]

Uzbekistan has been reaching out to the world, far beyond its limited orbit during the Soviet era. On September 1, 1992, it became a full member of the Non-Aligned Movement, bringing that organization to 108 principally Third World members.[57] President Karimov has denied that Islamic fundamentalism will dominate the country. Instead, he has continued to support a secular, market-oriented state, one with close ties to Russia: "The Russian people will choose their path—they have chosen it already—and they will travel down it. I am convinced that we will always be by their side."[58]

SEPARATIST/DISSIDENT MOVEMENTS

1. The Islamic Renaissance Party seeks to establish an Islamic republic. Although the party is banned, its support is said to be growing, particularly among those frustrated by the continued presence and influence of the ex-Communist elite.

2. As in other Central Asian countries, opening the political process to a broad spectrum of groups and interests may be Uzbekistan's greatest challenge. Two major opposition groups, Erk and Birlik, decided to adopt joint policies in July 1992 to combat what they term "political terrorism" conducted by the "totalitarian regime" in Tashkent. Birlik has been accused of engaging in illegal activities, and on January 19, 1993, it was suspended by the country's Supreme Court.[59]

3. The continuing environmental and health crisis associated with the Aral Sea and its tributaries will affect regional relationships for the foreseeable future.

4. Social stability and economic progress are also affected by Uzbekistan's success in abandoning its cotton monoculture in favor of more diversified agriculture and mixed industry. The increased cultivation of illegal drugs, however, is a growing problem.

5. Continuing armed unrest in nearby Tajikistan has alarmed authorities in Tashkent, particularly since Uzbeks comprise 24 percent of Tajikistan's population.

Kyrgyzstan

Names and boundary representation are not necessarily authoritative.

International boundary
Oblast boundary (approximate)
★ National capital
⊛ Oblast center
Railroad
Road

Information on the 1990 reorganization of administrative divisions is incomplete. It is not clear whether the administrative center of Issyk-Kul'skaya Oblast' is Issyk-Kul' or Prhoval'sk. An oblast is named only when its name differs from that of its administrative center.

0   50   100   150 Kilometers
0   50   100   150 Miles

Lambert Conformal Conic Projection, SP 47N/82N

Kyrgyzstan

BASIC DATA

Total Area: 76,641 square miles (198,500 square kilometers).

Population: 4.4 million, with an annual growth rate of 2 percent. Kyrgyz constitute 52 percent of the total, Russians 21 percent, and Uzbeks 13 percent. This reflects an out-migration of Russians and European peoples and a high Kyrgyz birth rate, currently 1.9 percent annually.

Religion: Sunni Islam, Russian Orthodox.

Official Name: Republic of Kyrgyzstan.

Capital: Bishkek.

Government:

- Executive Branch: Askar Akayev was elected the republic's first president by the Supreme Soviet on October 28, 1990; on October 13, 1991, he became the republic's first popularly elected president. He is the only Central Asian leader who had not served as a top Communist party official. Since February 11, 1992, Akayev has been both head of state and head of government, with the prime minister serving as deputy head of government.
- Legislative Branch: Supreme Soviet.
- Judicial Branch: Supreme Court.

The republic changed its name from the Kirghiz Soviet Socialist Republic to the Socialist Republic of Kyrgyzstan on October 26, 1990, and dropped "Socialist" after the failed August 1991 coup. A draft constitution, which establishes the legal basis for private property, is being circulated for possible adoption.

Economy: The republic produces cotton and other agricultural goods. It is expected to maintain close economic ties with Russia, which accounts for some 70 percent of Kyrgyzstan's external economic activity. There is considerable support for forming a regional market with the other Central Asian republics.[60] On July 4, 1992, the country's parliament adopted an 18-month program for economic reform that is to effect the transition to a private market economy. If it fails, Akayev has reportedly said that he and his government will resign.[61] The country plans to remain in the ruble zone for the foreseeable future.

History: The Kyrgyz are a Turkic people first recorded in the eighth century. They were conquered by other Turkic peoples and, in the thirteenth century, by the Mongols. Primarily nomadic herdsmen, they had converted to Islam by the mid-seventeenth century and came under Russian control in 1876. The area was conquered by the Red Army by 1922; after several designations, it became an autonomous republic in 1926 and a union republic in 1936. Russians have traditionally held leadership posts.

THE ROAD TO INDEPENDENCE

The republic declared sovereignty on December 12, 1990, the last republic of the former USSR to do so. It declared independence on August 31, 1991, following the failed coup attempt in Moscow. Boris Yeltsin visited Bishkek on his first trip as Russia's president, an honor many attribute to Akayev's staunch resistance to local military, party, and KGB leaders who supported the coup. The movement toward democracy has been termed the "silk revolution" by President Akayev. Because the republic raised only onefourth of its income from taxes and depended on Moscow for the remainder, Yeltsin's continued assistance is necessary.[62]

Kyrgyzstan is a multiethnic republic. Its fragility was revealed in June 1990 when 300 people were killed near Osh, an Uzbek-dominated city of 220,000 on the Kyrgyzstan-Uzbekistan border that sits astride an ancient silk route. Various theories account for the fighting—including deliberate intent. Kyrgyz schools have been built where only Uzbek schools existed, the Kyrgyz grip on political life there has been broken, and more housing for both groups has been made available.[63]

In March 1992 President Akayev met in Bishkek with the press services of the former Soviet republics, following erroneous reports that ethnic Russians were being asked to leave the republic He attacked the press as unnecessarily Russocentric, and he declared the former Soviet Union was still a single information area where there would be no advantage in taking issues out of context to serve narrow interests. Akayev called for all regions of the former USSR to be covered equally. He stated that as a result of Russocentricity, an information vacuum had evolved that had ignored what he termed "Kyrgyzstan's special mentality. History has arranged for us to be an amazing amalgam of the Asian and the European: in our thinking, in our emotional makeup, in our behavior."[64]

Bishkek has been actively privatizing farmland, and other economic initiatives directed toward establishing a market economy are seen as central to the republic's independence. President Akayev, however, sees continued dependence on the Commonwealth of Independent States as imperative: "We need time; we need five or ten years before we will be ready on a competitive basis and as worthy, equal partners to join the Western or the Eastern economic community. Debating it soberly, I simply consider that in the nineties—in this decade—we are fated to be in the Commonwealth."[65]

To better solidify his state's position, Akayev created a national guard on December 1, 1991, and assumed control of all military units stationed in the republic as of June 1, 1992. This move was necessitated by Russia's decision not to pay for forces stationed beyond its borders. Servicemen were to be paid from republic funds, and a State Committee on Defense was to supervise the preparation of doctrine and military regulations. Kyrgyzstan would be forced to reduce its forces substantially, and eventually to place combat units on reserve status.[66] Moves to create a national army were soon forthcoming, however. In July 1992, the government announced that the former Soviet 8th Motorized Infantry Division, which had been recently transferred to the jurisdiction of Kyrgyzstan, would be the foundation for a Kyrgyz national army. On September 10, 1992, the new country contributed troops to a multinational CIS effort to seal off Tajikistan's border with Afghanistan.[67]

Akayev has also reiterated an antinuclear policy, despite the fact that the first Soviet atomic and thermonuclear bombs contained Kyrgyz uranium. He has said that Kyrgyzstan will sell uranium according to International Atomic Energy Agency rules, and that the republic contains neither nuclear weapons nor weapons components.[68]

To maintain Kyrgyzstan's international position, it has been necessary for President Akayev to establish ties with all major states affecting his country's interests. He visited China in May 1992 and discussed border and trade issues. More substantial ties have been established with Turkey, including an April 1992 visit to Bishkek by Prime Minister Demirel, who proclaimed: "What we want to see in all these Moslem republics is peace, security and welfare. It is only natural that Turkey wants close cooperation with them."[69] At a ceremony during the visit, Demirel was more effusive: "Turks living in an area expanding from the Adriatic Sea to the China Sea have awakened and become active. Continue to fly the Turkic flag in this beautiful country."[70]

President Akayev feels particularly close to Turkey: "Kyrgyz and Turkish people are brother nations. They are bound together by blood, language and religion."[71] Since Turkey was the first country to open an embassy in Bishkek and has provided substantial financial and educational assistance, Akayev has said that "Turkey will be the locomotive for all Central Asian countries."[72]

In the first year of Krygyzstan's independence, President Akayev has asserted that the country's ties with the other new states of the former Soviet Union have proven to be particularly important. Speaking on August 31, 1992, in honor of Kyrgyzstan's first anniversary of independence, Akayev condemned the old system: "Socialism proved powerless economically and failed to give freedom to the people, paralyzing their ability to act independently, making them incapable of any business enterprise, and giving rise to parasitical psychology among them." Maintaining ethnic peace, particularly among the country's Russian, Uzbek, and Kyrgyz peoples, is especially important.[73]

In this process, Akayev has not neglected a more immediate patron and neighbor: Russia. On June 10, 1992, he signed a treaty of friendship, cooperation, and mutual assistance with Boris Yeltsin, who noted at the signing ceremony that the August coup had provided an opportunity to demonstrate their faithfulness as allies. Yeltsin listed his accomplishments since assuming the presidency as including civil peace among Russia's 130 nationalities and minorities, and the transition from Communist ideology and an administrative economy, all without "Yugoslav-style bloodletting." Particularly noteworthy in this agreement, he noted, was specific protection for the minority Russian population in Kyrgyzstan.[74]

The treaty with Russia, the second such treaty (the first was a similar agreement with Kazakhstan on May 25), also calls upon the signatories to cooperate in their mutual defense, to support joint CIS strategic forces, and to develop joint defense policies. A separate military agreement signed by military officials provides for the exchange of personnel, military data, and weapons.[75] It is believed that such agreements permit the stationing of both Russian and CIS forces on the sovereign territory of signatory states.

Clearly, a small, diverse country like Kyrgyzstan, located between China to the south and east, Kazakhstan to the north, and Persian-peopled Tajikistan to the southwest, and penetrated by an extension of densely populated Uzbekistan to the west, faces a difficult path in the days ahead. President Akayev has vowed that Islamic fundamentalism will not take root: "There is no basis in Kyrgyzstan for fundamentalism, our people are not contaminated with it, we have never had religious confrontation. . . . We are against religious interference in government of the state."[76] For Kyrgyzstan, which some consider to have the least fundamentalist influence, the latter may yet pose a serious challenge.

SEPARATIST/DISSIDENT MOVEMENTS

1. Approximately 210,000 Turkish people currently live in Kyrgyzstan; they are descended from the half-million Ottoman soldiers captured by Russia and brought to the area as prisoners of war. Some 30,000 of these expatriates wish to return to Turkey.[77]

2. Kyrgyzstan has twelve disputed land claims with China along their common border, which Bishkek seeks to resolve.[78] A "Free Uigurstan" Party, formed in Bishkek in July 1992 by a group of Uigurs living in Kyrgyzstan, seeks to form a State of Uigurstan in China's Xinjiang-Uighur Autonomous Region.[79] This will not endear China to the new state.

3. There are disputed border areas on the northwest border with Tajikistan, particularly in the vicinity of the cities of Badken and Isfara. This is near the junction with Uzbekistan, where the border is awkwardly configured.[80] Armed conflict has occurred over this issue in the past, and no resolution is in sight.

4. A particularly sensitive situation exists along the easternmost border with Uzbekistan, where certain groups are advocating the return of the Uzbek-dominated Kyrgyz cities of Osh, Uzgen, Dzhalal-Abad, and Karavan to Tashkent.[81]

5. Along Bishkek's northern border with Kazakhstan, there are border disputes and disturbances between Alma-Ata's Dzhambul Oblast and Bishkek's Talas Oblast.[82]

6. Ethnic Germans residing in Kyrgyzstan have sought greater protection and autonomy, leading President Akayev in early 1992 to designate Sokuluk and Chu as German national districts.[83] While this special act may satisfy one minority, it may lead others to seek special status.

7. Ethnic Russians feel threatened by growing Kyrgyz nationalist sentiments.

Tajikistan

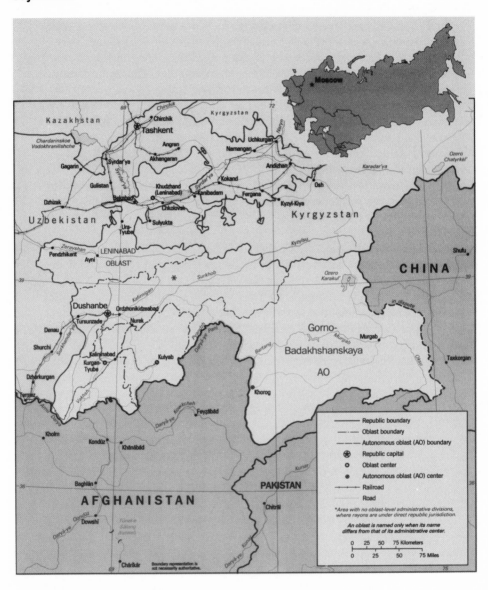

Tajikistan

BASIC DATA

Total Area: 55,251 square miles (143,100 square kilometers). It is the smallest of the Central Asian republics.

Population: 5.7 million, composed of 62 percent Tajiks, 24 percent Uzbeks, and 8 percent Russians. The population is increasing at an annual rate of 3 percent, the highest birth rate of the 15 new Eurasian states. Tajiks are Persian peoples who speak Tajik, similar to Farsi.

Religion: Sunni Islam, Russian Orthodox.

Official Name: Republic of Tajikistan.

Capital: Dushanbe.

Government:

- Executive Branch: Rakhmon Nabiyev, former Communist party first secretary, was elected president on November 24, 1991, in the republic's first popular presidential election, but he was forced to resign on September 7, 1992, by an armed coalition of democratic and Islamic forces. Akbarsho Iskandarov, chairman of the Supreme Soviet, was acting president until November 10, when the coalition government resigned amidst renewed conflict in Dushanbe. Nabiyev forces, supported by former Communists and others, continued to fight, and Russian intervention was necessary to restore order. The pro-Communists gained the upper hand, and on November 19 Imomali Rakhmonov was elected chairman of the Supreme Soviet. The government is headed by a prime minister.

- Legislative Branch: Until the September 7 crisis, the National Majlis (Assembly) confirmed all acts of the Supreme Soviet. The Supreme Soviet amended the constitution on November 27, 1992, to end the presidential form of government and institute a parliamentary republic.
- Judicial Branch: Supreme Court.

Economy: Tajikistan produces agricultural products, principally cotton, fruit, and vegetable oil. Plans were under way to introduce a national currency until the government collapsed following President Nabiyev's ouster. Tajikistan is generally considered to be the poorest component of the former Soviet Union.

History: The Tajiks are pre-Turkic peoples who are divided into two major groups, the lowland Tajiks and the mountain (Pamir) Tajiks. Waves of Turkic invaders and settlers affected the region but, unlike the Turks and Mongols, the Tajiks were not nomadic. By the late nineteenth century, northern Tajikistan was governed by Russia and southern Tajikistan by the emir of Bukhara. With the October Revolution, northern Tajikistan was incorporated into the Turkestan autonomous republic, formed in 1918. Dushanbe was captured by the Red Army in 1921, and the area was under Soviet control by 1925. The Tajik Autonomous Soviet Socialist Republic was created in 1924 as a part of the Uzbek Republic. By October 1929, it became a union republic and acquired Khodzhent Okrug from the Uzbek Republic.[84]

THE ROAD TO INDEPENDENCE

Tajikistan represents the best example of the conflict for power between political and religious forces in the absence of democratic traditions. The drama began ten days after the collapse of the August 1991 coup, when anticommunist demonstrators forced President Nabiyev from office and replaced him with reform leader Kadriddin Aslonov, who banned the Communist party and seized its property. Dushanbe's mayor supervised the destruction of the massive Lenin monument in the city's central square, to the delight of crowds, who spat and danced on its remnants.[85] The republic declared its independence on September 9, 1991, an act consistent with its declaration of sovereignty on August 24, 1990.

The Communists struck back on September 23, 1991, when the party's majority in the Supreme Soviet forced Aslonov out of office and arrested and held Mayor Maksud Ikramov of Dushanbe for trial. Former president and party chief Nabiyev was reinstated and made interim president until national elections in October. All Lenin statues were ordered to be guarded.[86]

In the unrest that followed, Islamic religious leaders asserted their presence by opposing Communist rule. The head of the Kazyat, the Muslim organization in Tajikistan, in November 1991 ruled out the creation of an Islamic state, but the Islamic Revival Party proclaimed that it would act to oppose the ruling Communists.

Protests returned to Dushanbe with the March 22, 1992, rearrest of Mayor Ikramov on charges of corruption, which he termed "an act of political terrorism."[87] Demonstrators demanded Ikramov's release, the dissolution of the Communist-dominated Supreme Soviet, and a referendum on a new draft constitution. Nabiyev threatened to employ "Los Angeles-style force" with a newly created national guard.[88]

The protests continued on and off until the night of May 5, when Tajik security forces opened fire on pro-democracy demonstrators and others seeking an Islamic state, killing at least fourteen. Nabiyev declared a state of emergency, but in the ensuing confrontation the presidential guard refused to fire on the people and sided with the opposition.[89]

This led President Nabiyev to sign a protocol with opposition leaders pledging to form a "national reconciliation government," to refrain from using force, to permit religious freedom within the context of a secular state and freedom of speech for individuals and the media, to recognize all political movements and organizations, and to create a representative national assembly, the Majlis, to govern the country. A draft constitution was later circulated for comment by the citizenry.[90] A small 1,000-man national guard was organized on August 18, 1992, as the country struggled to organize its own armed forces.[91]

The government of national reconciliation never received widespread support, and opposition groups in the country's northwest and southwest—Leninabad and Kulyab—refused to follow its directives. The assassination of the country's chief prosecutor on August 24 further destabilized the situation. As people of Tajik ethnicity—both Islamic fundamentalists and Nabiyev supporters—continued to come across the border from Afghanistan, bearing Soviet-supplied arms left over from the Afghanistan war, authorities in Moscow became alarmed. A group of military officers led by Marshal Shaposhnikov and representing the CIS, Russia, Kazakhstan, and Kyrgyzstan surveyed the situation in Tajikistan at the request of President Nabiyev. Shaposhnikov signed a protocol requesting the deployment of CIS forces, which began to arrive to seal the border and restore order.

Following at least two thousand deaths and the resignation of the coalition government on November 10, 1992, the situation continued to be highly volatile. As a signatory of the May 15, 1992, Tashkent Collective Security Treaty, Tajikistan has reason to expect military support from its allies. A bilateral treaty with Russia, initialed on July 21, 1992, also concerns military cooperation between the two countries, and a separate treaty provided for Moscow's control of border troops in Tajikistan.[92] However, the fear of unrest spreading to other Central Asian republics and the new factor of Islamic fundamentalism, despite denials from its adherents, led to an exodus of Russians and others who are anxious about further conflict.

Matters took a turn for the worse on November 19, 1992, when Imomali Rakhmonov, a hard-line Communist from Kulyab Oblast, was elected chairman of the country's Supreme Soviet. Despite the resistance of pro-democracy groups and Islamic fundamentalists inspired by members of the Islamic Renaissance Party, pro-Communist People's Front forces first controlled Dushanbe and then extended control to the countryside. Some 380,000 persons were displaced by the fighting, and 110,000 Tajiks sought refuge across the Amu Darya River in Afghanistan. Since April, an estimated 20,000 people had been killed in the unrest. The new regime instituted criminal proceedings against opponents; summary executions reportedly took place in Dushanbe; and People's Front forces were converted into a new Tajik army. On January 7, 1993, Rakhmonov ordered a state of emergency for the Dushanbe region in an effort to consolidate power.[93]

For Iran, this development constitutes a setback. While Iran's Shiism is cause for concern for most Tajiks, Tehran has made serious efforts to increase its influence. Iran's foreign minister visited Dushanbe in early December 1991, signing agreements that included opening consulates in the respective capitals, cultural cooperation, rail links, and an exchange of students and teachers. On January 9, 1992, Iran became the first foreign government to establish an embassy in Tajikistan.[94] A more immediate neighbor state to the south, Afghanistan—home to a large Tajik population—has received much attention from Dushanbe. At the same time, Turkey, a Sunni Islamic country like Tajikistan, is considered important to the nation's future, as is neighboring Pakistan.

A commodity of international interest is Tajikistan's uranium deposits, an asset shared by Turkmenistan and Uzbekistan. Tajikistan took over a Soviet enrichment plant in December 1991. President Nabiyev has said, "Tajikistan has never sold and will never sell uranium to other important countries."[95]

SEPARATIST/DISSIDENT MOVEMENTS

1. Until recent events, the Islamic Renaissance Party was the republic's largest party. It opposes Tajikistan's cooperation with the other former Soviet republics except for economic purposes. The party seeks to create an Islamic state based upon traditional Islamic values; this objective has now become more remote.

2. Unrest continues in Kulyab Oblast and in Vakhsh and Bakhtar raions of Kurghanteppa Oblast, in southwest Tajikistan. The Islamic Renaissance Party had as many as 30,000 members organized down to the village level,[96] aided by the large number of Tajiks living in Uzbekistan.

3. Many Uzbeks live in Leninabad Oblast in north Tajikistan, and many Tajiks live in Uzbekistan's Fergana Valley. This is viewed as a source of potential strife, and parts of their common border are contested.

4. The Gorno-Badakhshan Autonomous Oblast declared itself the Gorno-Badakhshan Autonomous Republic in December 1991, by a decision of the oblast soviet. Located in eastern Tajikistan, it will remain in the republic but expects more independence in its policies.[97]

5. Tajikistan is an active producer of opium poppies, and the element supporting its cultivation can be expected to continue to resist government efforts to stem this practice.

Turkmenistan

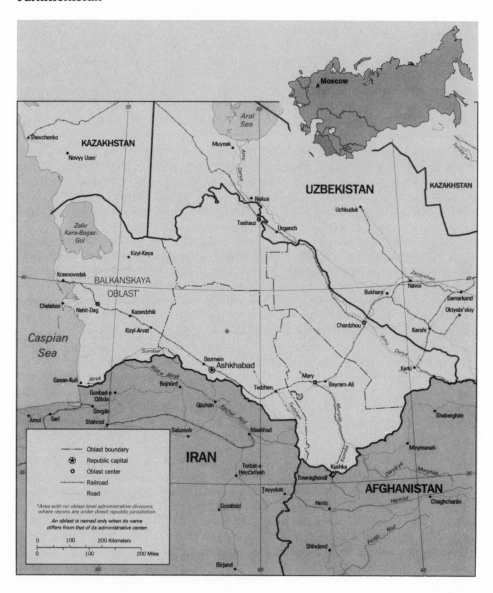

Turkmenistan

BASIC DATA

Total Area: 188,455 square miles (488,100 square kilometers).

Population: 3.8 million, of whom 72 percent are Turkmen, 9 percent are Uzbek, and 9 percent are Russian. The growth rate is 2.4 percent annually.

Religion: Sunni Islam, Russian Orthodox.

Official Name: Turkmenistan.

Capital: Ashkhabad.

Government:

- Executive Branch: Saparmurad Niyazov, Communist party first secretary and chairman of the republic's Supreme Soviet, became the first popularly elected president on October 27, 1990. He was the sole candidate for the office in the June 21, 1992, elections, which he won.
- Legislative Branch: Majlis (parliament), part of a larger Khalk Maslakhatiy (people's council), the supreme authority; it alone can change the constitution, hold referenda, alter the state's borders, and ratify treaties. It meets once a year.[98]
- Judicial Branch: Supreme Court and Supreme Economic Court.

The republic declared its independence as a democratic state on October 27, 1991, but the Communist party has maintained its grip on the power structures in this, the most conservative republic of the Commonwealth. Alexander Dodonov, second secretary of the republic's Communist party, declared in December 1991, "It's the nature of the Turkmen character. We like stability. There's real love for Lenin here."[99]

A new constitution was adopted on May 18, 1992, that emphasized human rights and political pluralism, and declared private ownership to be the basis of the republic's economy. It also strengthened the office of the president by giving it enhanced powers similar to a Western-type executive presidency. A National Security Committee coordinates security matters for the republic.

Economy: The republic possesses abundant oil and natural gas and is a major producer of cotton.

History: An infusion of Turkic tribes in the fifth and sixth centuries changed Turkmenistan from a Persian-speaking to a Turkic-speaking region; Islam soon followed. After centuries of various conquests, Russia gained ascendancy in 1881. A limit to Russian expansionism was achieved in 1895 when a joint Anglo-Russian Boundary Commission delimited the border with Afghanistan. This separated many Turkmen tribes from kinsmen to the south. After the Bolshevik Revolution, the formation of the Turkestan autonomous republic in 1918 led to an anti-Soviet revolt in Ashkhabad, but it returned to Soviet control by 1920. It became a Soviet Socialist Republic in October 1924.[100]

THE ROAD TO INDEPENDENCE

The republic declared its sovereignty on August 22, 1990, and independence on October 27, 1991, now a national holiday. On January 28, 1992, Niyazov established a Ministry of Defense responsible for civil defense, a national guard, and internal troops. Turkmenistan also signed the May 15, 1992, Collective Security Treaty at the CIS Tashkent summit. On June 8, 1992, a novel approach to the republic's defense was arrived at with the conclusion of a Russian-Turkmen military accord.

According to the agreement, Russian forces in Turkmenistan and Turkmen forces created from existing former Soviet military units in the republic will be under joint command. Conscription and training will be a joint responsibility; housing, medical services, and other support will be provided by Turkmenistan. Russia will handle financial matters, logistics, and military matériel, at least for a transition period. Turkmen President Niyazov saw this solution as optimal: "Both Turkmenistan and Russia need these forces today, and they should constitute a single defensive border for our states. This agreement is entirely in accordance with the Turkmen people's interests."[101]

President Niyazov, perhaps with an eye toward his southern neighbors, Iran and Afghanistan, was certain this solution would solve his republic's pressing need for defense forces: "This army is not targeted at anyone, it will only resolve defense tasks and protect both Russia and Turkmenistan.

If this happens, the age-old dream of our people—to live in friendship and cooperation with Russia—will come true."[102]

The protocol signed in June constituted a key part of a Russian–Turkmenistan Treaty of Friendship and Cooperation that Boris Yeltsin signed during a July 31, 1992, summit meeting with President Niyazov in Moscow. It tied the border republic directly to Russia's defense and defense needs, much as similar treaties Moscow had concluded with other Central Asian states. According to a press report, "the outline of a Eurasian community is appearing before our very eyes."[103]

Further Russian–Turkmenistan cooperation was embodied in an August 27, 1992, border cooperation agreement signed in Moscow. It placed all border units under joint control to permit time for Turkmenistan to create its own border forces. According to President Niyazov, "ensuring the security of the Turkmen border is becoming a component part of the security doctrine of Russia."[104]

The country's foreign policy is to a large extent mandated by the need for economic development. Turkmenistan's decision to join the Economic Cooperation Organization, founded by Turkey, Iran, and Pakistan, was made for reasons similar to those of the other Central Asian and Muslim states that joined: Azerbaijan and Uzbekistan. The resulting construction of railroads, highways, air links, and pipelines will directly improve life for all Turkmen. To Foreign Minister Avdy Kuliyev, this does not imply an ideological bias: "We do not intend to elevate anyone's ideology to the rank of a state ideology, not even the Islamic one, which has roots in our country. We have been in the thrall of ideological dogmas once before, and we see perfectly well what came of that."[105]

Relations with Iran are good, and by April 1992 a number of border-crossing points had been opened to facilitate mutual trade. Following an earlier visit by Iran's foreign minister, both countries agreed to open consulates in their respective capitals, and a number of agreements for cultural exchanges, transportation, and communications were concluded. A visit by President Hashemi Rafsanjani to Ashkhabad on May 11, 1992, led to the conclusion of a treaty of friendship and other agreements, including one for the construction of a rail line between the two countries. This follows an April agreement to build a gas pipeline from Turkmenistan to Iran, Turkey, and Europe, thus avoiding existing routes through Ukraine.[106]

A number of significant agreements were concluded with Turkey during President Niyazov's December 1991 visit to Ankara, including joint enterprises in transportation, communications, and energy. The decision by Ashkhabad to convert from the Cyrillic to the Latin alphabet will also warrant assistance from Turkey.[107] Turkmenistan's foreign minister, however, has declared that his country will follow a policy of equidistance between Ankara and Tehran, and that ethnic Turkmen who live in both countries will be considered citizens of those states.[108]

SEPARATIST/DISSIDENT MOVEMENTS

1. Turkmenistan is a victim of the Aral Sea ecological disaster. Its citizens in Tashauz Oblast, some 800,000 people, "drink the worst water in the world"; an average of three persons in each family are ill, and four of every five women and children are anemic.[109] Unless this situation is remedied, conflict over water and land rights, as well as claims for large amounts of humanitarian assistance by all affected citizens, are likely.

2. Citizens of southern Turkmenistan are concerned that the planned construction by a Russian enterprise of a nuclear energy station in northern Iran, some fifty kilometers (thirty-one miles) from the international border and in an area of active seismological movements, threatens their future health and safety.[110]

3. The unrest in Tajikistan and continuing concerns over the rise of Islamic fundamentalism in Central Asia have driven the leaders of Turkmenistan to seek assistance from Russia. Whether this can stem the tide of social change in this large republic bordering Iran and Afghanistan remains to be seen.

NOTES

1. Igor Rotar, "Central Asia: Moscow Plays Waiting Game and Risks Missing Out," *Nezavisimaya gazeta*, May 29, 1992, 1, 3, in FBIS-SOV–92–108, June 4, 1992, 13–14.

2. Craig Forman, "Moslems Seek Theocracy in the U.S.S.R.," *Wall Street Journal*, October 9, 1991, A12.

3. "Iran: Mosque as Carapace," *The Economist*, February 29, 1992, 44.

4. "Soviet Central Asia: The Next Islamic Revolution," *The Economist*, September 21, 1991, 58–59.

5. "Islam: Weak at the Top," *The Economist*, December 31–January 3, 1992, 42.

6. Aydyn Mekhtiyev, "Integration, Tehran Summit Meeting: States of the Former USSR Take Part for First Time," Moscow *Nezavisimaya gazeta*, February 18, 1992, 1, 3, in FBIS-USR–92–029, February 18, 1992, 26–27.

7. "Choosing Partners," *The Economist*, April 25, 1992, 34.

8. Ibid.

9. "Final Resolution Issued," Moscow POSTFACTUM, 1627 GMT, April 23, 1992, in FBIS-SOV–92–080, April 24, 1992, 7–8.

10. Beshim Perengliyev, "More on Joint Statement," Moscow ITAR-TASS, 1921 GMT, May 10, 1992, in FBIS-SOV–92–092, May 12, 1992, 10; K. Babayev and K. Bordyyev, "Novosti" newscast, Moscow Ostankino Television First Program Network, 1400 GMT, May 25, 1992, in FBIS-SOV–92–104, May 29, 1992, 9.

11. "Iranian President Admits 'Rivalry' with Turkey," Moscow POSTFACTUM, 1622 GMT, May 9, 1992, 6, in FBIS-SOV–92–092, May 12, 1992, 6; "Turkey's Demirel Denies Competing with Iran," Ankara Turkiye Radyolari Network, 2000 GMT, May 9, 1992, in FBIS-SOV–92–092, May 12, 1992, 7.

12. Chris Hedges, "Turkey Is to Broadcast to 6 Ex-Soviet Lands," *New York Times*, April 12, 1992, A12; Sergey Fyoktistov, "Central Asian Diplomats to Train in Turkey," Moscow ITAR-TASS, 1214 GMT, June 16, 1992, in FBIS-SOV–92–119, June 19, 1992, 9.

13. "The Front-Line Friend," *The Economist*, September 12, 1992, 18.

14. "Caspian Sea Organization Holds Session 4 October: President Meets With Delegates," Tehran Voice of the Islamic Republic of Iran First Program Network, 1030 GMT, October 4, 1992, in FBIS-NES–92–193, October 5, 1992, 50.

15. "Establish Relations," Riyadh SPA, 1231 GMT, February 21, 1992, in FBIS-SOV–92–037, February 25, 1992, 71–72.

16. Patrick E. Tyler, "Saudi Arabia Pledges $1 Billion to Soviet Union," *New York Times*, October 9, 1991, A9.

17. " 'Expert' Views Islamic Trend in Central Asia," Moscow Radio World Service, 1710 GMT, May 9, 1992, in FBIS-SOV–92–092, May 12, 1992, 24–25.

18. Alexandre Bennigsen and Marie Broxup, *The Islamic Threat to the Soviet State* (London: Croom Helm, 1983), 112–16.

19. Yaacov Ro'i, "Central Asian Riots and Disturbances, 1989–1990: Causes and Context," *Central Asian Survey* 10, no. 3 (1991):21–54.

20. Margaret Shapiro, "Spread of Ethnic Wars Feared in Ex-U.S.S.R.," *The Washington Post*, September 9, 1992, A25.

21. Peter Ford, "Turkish and Iranian Power Plays in Central Asia Have Moscow on Edge," *Christian Science Monitor,* February 7, 1992, 1, 4.

22. Thomas L. Friedman, "U.S. to Counter Iran in Central Asia," *New York Times,* February 6, 1992, A3.

23. Barbara Crossette, "U.S. Remains Moscowcentric on Once-Soviet Asia," *New York Times,* May 31, 1992, A16.

24. John Kohan, "Five New Nations Ask: Who Are We?" *Time,* April 27, 1992, 46.

25. A. Ladin, "Nazarbayev: Army Must Be Helped," *Krasnaya zvezda,* November 23, 1991, 2, in FBIS-SOV–91–228, November 26, 1991, 88.

26. Daniel Sneider, "U.S. Firm's Offer Stirs Controversy in C. Asia State," *Christian Science Monitor,* April 24, 1992, 1.

27. Martha Brill Olcott, *The Kazakhs,* Studies of Nationalities in the USSR, ed. Wayne S. Vucinich (Stanford, Calif.: Hoover Institution Press, 1987), 224–36.

28. "Trade and Investment," Moscow INTERFAX, 1818 GMT, August 20, 1992, in FBIS-SOV–92–163, August 21, 1992, 67.

29. "Nazarbayev on Current Issues," Moscow Ostankino Television First Program Network, 1115 GMT, September 6, 1992, in FBIS-SOV–92–174, September 8, 1992, 40,

30. Gennadiy Kulagin, "Further on Remarks," Moscow TASS, 1324 GMT, December 2, 1991, in FBIS-SOV–91–232, December 3, 1991, 90.

31. Francis X. Clines, "Kazakhs Seek a Level Capitalist Road," *New York Times,* January 27, 1992, A9.

32. Ibid.

33. I. Khobotova, "The Republic Guard," Alma-Ata *Kazakhstanskaya pravda,* August 27, 1992, 2, in JPRS-UMA–92–035, September 23, 1992, 45.

34. Vladimir Akimov, "Presidential Decree Creates Armed Forces," Moscow ITAR-TASS, 1309 GMT, May 8, 1992, in FBIS-SOV–92–090, May 8, 1992, 56.

35. Ibid.; "Presidential Bulletin," Moscow INTERFAX, 1921 GMT, May 8, 1992, in FBIS-SOV–92–092, May 12, 1992, 54; Baqtiyar Yerimbet, "How Many Officers Do the Kazakhs Have? What Means Do We Have to Increase Their Numbers?" Alma-Ata *Yegemendi qazaqstan,* February 14, 1992, 3, in JPRS-UMA–92–018, May 20, 1992, 35.

36. Daniel Sneider, "Kazakhstan to Accept Phaseout of Nuclear Arms," *Christian Science Monitor,* May 19, 1992, 3; Alexandr Peslyak, "Vesti" newscast, Moscow Russian Television Network, 1600 GMT, May 24, 1992, 3, in FBIS-SOV–92–101, May 26, 1992, 3.

37. V. Smelov, "Commonwealth States Broaden Contacts with Outside World," *Krasnaya zvezda,* February 21, 1992, 3, in FBIS-SOV–92–037, February 25, 1992, 3.

38. Sneider, "Kazakhstan to Accept Phaseout," 3.

39. "Nazarbayev Establishes Atomic Energy Agency," Moscow INTERFAX, 1234 GMT, May 16, 1992, in FBIS-SOV–92–096, May 18, 1992, 2; Vladimir Ganzha, "Uranium Mining, Production Activity Declines," Moscow TASS, 1521 GMT, December 2, 1991, in FBIS-SOV–91–233, December 4, 1991, 81.

40. "IAEA Membership Bid Spurs Information Release," Alma-Ata Kazakh Radio Network, 0800 GMT, September 9, 1992, in FBIS-SOV–92–177, September 11, 1992, 40.

41. "Aral Sea Declared 'Ecological Disaster Zone,' " Moscow Radio One Network, 1600 GMT, February 4, 1992, in FBIS-SOV–92–025, February 6, 1992, 66; Michael Dobbs, "The Coming Caviar Crisis," *Washington Post,* May 30, 1992, A1; "Salt of the Earth," *The Economist,* June 27, 1992, 34.

42. A. Ladin, *Krasnaya zvezda,* November 30, 1991, 2, in FBIS-SOV–91–232, December 3, 1991, 90.

43. "Ceremony Marks Opening of Road to Tehran," Tehran IRNA, 1446 GMT, September 10, 1992, in FBIS-SOV–92–177, September 11, 1992, 40.

44. "Educational Protocol Signed with Turkey," Alma-Ata Kazakh Radio Network, 1500 GMT, March 20, 1992, in FBIS-SOV–92–064, April 2, 1992, 76; "Turkic Republics Summit Discussed," Ankara Anatolia, 1425 GMT, April 29, 1992, in FBIS-SOV–92–084, April 30, 1992, 55.

45. Andrey Pershin, Andrey Petrovskiy, and Vladimir Shishlin, "Presidential Bulletin," Moscow INTERFAX, 2059 GMT, May 26, 1992, in FBIS-SOV–92–108, June 4, 1992, 30; Ivan Ivanov, "Treaty Signed," ITAR-TASS, 1645 GMT, May 25, 1992, in FBIS-SOV–92–101, May 26, 1992, 14.

46. A. Ladin, "National Armies—A View Inside: In a 'Shanyrak' Tent, Outlining Kazakhstan's Armed Forces," *Krasnaya zvezda,* July 2, 1992, 2, in JPRS-UMA–92–026, July 15, 1992, 37.

47. A. Nugmanova and V. Zhilyakov, "Novosti" newscast, Moscow Ostankino Television First Program Network, 0500 GMT, June 23, 1992, in FBIS-SOV–92–124, June 26, 1992, 81–82.

48. Steven Erlanger, "Uzbeks, Free of Soviets, Dethrone Czar Cotton," *New York Times,* June 20, 1992, A4.

49. Donald S. Carlisle, "Uzbekistan and the Uzbeks," *Problems of Communism,* September–October 1991, 23–44.

50. "Will Uzbekistan Become Islamic Republic?" *Rossiyskaya gazeta,* March 28, 1992, 3, in FBIS-SOV–92–064, April 2, 1992, 80.

51. O Chung-sok, "Uzbek President Interviewed on ROK Visit," Seoul *Choson ilbo,* June 15, 1992, 5, in FBIS-SOV–92–117, June 17, 1992, 55–56.

52. Semen Novoprudskiy, "Uzbekistan: 'Alternative' Servicemen Will become Conductors," Moscow *Nezavisimaya gazeta,* July 14, 1992, 3, in JPRS-UMA–92–031, August 20, 1992, 33–34; "By Telegraph Line: A Protocol of Intent Has Been Signed on the Interaction of the Military of Kyrgyzia and Uzbekistan," *Krasnaya zvezda,* August 18, 1992, 1, in JPRS-UMA–92–035, September 23, 1992, 21.

53. "A Way of Life Evaporates," *The Economist,* September 21, 1991, 59.

54. James Rupert, "A Death in the Desert: Soviet Plan Kills a Sea," *Washington Post,* June 20, 1992, A1; A16.

55. "Attends Signing Ceremony," Moscow Mayak Radio Network, 1215 GMT, May 30, 1992, in FBIS-SOV–92–105, June 1, 1992, 15.

56. Ibid.; Gennadiy Talalayev, "Comments on New Treaty," Moscow ITAR-TASS, 1728 GMT, May 30, 1992, in FBIS-SOV–92–105, June 1, 1992, 15–16.

57. Valery Fedortsov, "Nonaligned Movement Admits Uzbekistan as Member," Moscow ITAR-TASS, 1628 GMT, September 1, 1992, in FBIS-SOV–92–171, September 2, 1992, 47.

58. "Excerpt of News Conference Statement by President Islam Abduganiyevich Karimov in Tashkent on 31 August," Moscow Mayak Radio Network, 0630 GMT, September 1, 1992, in FBIS-SOV–92–171, September 2, 1992, 46.

59. "Opposition Groups Agree on Joint Actions," Moscow INTERFAX, 1215 GMT, July 5, 1992, in FBIS-SOV–92–133, July 10, 1992, 86; "Uzbek Supreme Court Suspends Birlik," *RFE/RL Daily Report* No. 12 (E-mail), January 20, 1993, 3.

60. Bermet Malikova, "Nation & Society," Moscow INTERFAX, 1348 GMT, November 15, 1991, in FBIS-SOV–91–222, November 18, 1991, 74.

61. "Plan for Radical Economic Reform Adopted," Moscow INTERFAX, 1459 GMT, July 4, 1992, in FBIS-SOV–92–133, July 10, 1992, 81.

62. "The Silk Revolution," *The Economist*, October 19, 1991, 57.

63. Justin Burke, "Once a Soviet Flash Point, Fragile Ethnic Peace Comes to Kirghizia," *Christian Science Monitor*, December 5, 1991, 4.

64. "Kyrgyzstan President Advocates Keeping Single Information Area," *Izvestiya*, March 23, 1992, 3, in FBIS-SOV–92–058, March 25, 1992, 68–69.

65. Vladimir Fedorov, "Utro" program, Moscow Central Television First Program and Orbita Networks, 1800 GMT, May 21, 1992, in FBIS-SOV–92–105, June 1, 1992, 54.

66. "Defense Committee Assumes Control," Moscow Radio Rossii Network, 0900 GMT, June 1, 1992, in FBIS-SOV–92–105, June 1, 1992, 54; Albert Bogdanov, "Vice President on Troops Reduction," Moscow ITAR-TASS, 1446 GMT, June 1, 1992, in FBIS-SOV–92–106, June 2, 1992, 33; "Further Reportage on Control of Troops," Moscow INTERFAX, 1838 GMT, June 1, 1992, in FBIS-SOV–92–106, June 2, 1992, 33.

67. Albert Bogdanov, "Kyrgyzstan Begins Creating National Army," Moscow ITAR-TASS, 0738 GMT, July 3, 1992, in FBIS-SOV–92–129, July 6, 1992, 74; "CIS Border Troops Arrive Upon Leadership Request," Moscow ITAR-TASS, 1037 GMT, September 10, 1992, in FBIS-SOV–92–176, September 10, 1992, 48.

68. Nikolay Paklin, "Kyrgyzstan Offers Uranium for Export," *Izvestiya*, March 20, 1992, 1, in FBIS-SOV–92–058, March 25, 1992, 3.

69. "Officials Hold News Conference," Ankara Anatolia, 1635 GMT, April 28, 1992, in FBIS-SOV–92–083, April 29, 1992, 57.

70. "Investment Agreement Signed," Ankara Anatolia, 1715 GMT, April 28, 1992, in FBIS-SOV–92–083, April 29, 1992, 57.

71. Aleksandr Chelyshev, "Akayev on 'Promising Prospects,' " Moscow TASS, 1659 GMT, December 25, 1991, in FBIS-SOV–91–249, December 27, 1991, 68.

72. "Turkey Seen as 'Locomotive' for Central Asia," Ankara TRT Television Network, 1600 GMT, May 31, 1992, in FBIS-SOV–92–110, June 8, 1992, 56.

73. Andrey Pershin, Andrey Petrovskiy, and Vladimir Shishlin, "Presidential Bulletin," Moscow INTERFAX, 1643 GMT, August 31, 1992, in FBIS-SOV–92–170, September 1, 1992, 44.

74. "Yeltsin on Accomplishments," Moscow INTERFAX, 1833 GMT, June 10, 1992, in FBIS-SOV–92–113, June 11, 1992, 16.

75. "Military Agreement Signed with Kyrgyzstan," Moscow Radio Rossii Network, 0000 GMT, June 14, 1992, in FBIS-SOV–92–115, June 15, 1992, 12–13.

76. Paklin, "Kyrgyzstan Offers Uranium," 3.

77. " 'Ottoman Turks' Promised Help," Ankara TRT Television Network, 1800 GMT, March 3, 1992, in FBIS-SOV–92–043, March 4, 1992, 72.

78. Aleksandr Knyazev, "President Takes Control of Troops on Territory,"

Moscow Radio Rossii Network, 1900 GMT, May 30, 1992, in FBIS-SOV–92–105, June 1, 1992, 53.

79. "NEGA Reports: Krygyzstan," Moscow *Nezavismaya gazeta*, July 29, 1992, 3, in FBIS-SOV–92–147, July 30, 1992, 49.

80. Knyazev, "President Takes Control," 53.

81. Ibid.; "District Seeks Referendum on Link to Uzbekistan," Moscow INTERFAX, 1305 GMT, May 10, 1992, in FBIS-SOV–92–092, May 12, 1992, 56.

82. Knyazev, "President Takes Control," 53.

83. "State Legalizes Status of German Districts," Moscow INTERFAX, 1407 GMT, March 17, 1992, in FBIS-SOV–92–053, March 18, 1992, 66.

84. Shirin Akiner, *Islamic Peoples of the Soviet Union* (Boston: Kegan Paul International, 1983), 302–04.

85. James Rupert, "Soviet Asian Communists Strike Back," *Washington Post*, September 24, 1991, A1.

86. Ibid.

87. " 'Unauthorized' Rally Continues," Moscow INTERFAX, 1624 GMT, March 28, 1992, in FBIS-SOV–92–061, March 30, 1992, 40.

88. Walter Ruby, "Tajik President Creates Guard to Crush Protests," *Christian Science Monitor*, May 6, 1992, 3.

89. "Long Standoff Turns Violent in Tajikistan Capital," *New York Times*, May 7, 1992, A14; U. Babakhanov and A. Ganelin, "Attempt at Analysis: Will There Be a Square of the Victorious Opposition in Dushanbe?" *Komsomolskaya pravda*, May 22, 1992, 1, in FBIS-SOV–92–106, June 2, 1992, 34.

90. "Reconciliation Government Announced," Dushanbe Radio, 1015 GMT, May 7, 1992, in FBIS-SOV–92–089, May 7, 1992, 53–54; "Constitution Previewed; Presidential Powers Eyed," Moscow INTERFAX, 1721 GMT, June 3, 1992, in FBIS-SOV–92–109, June 5, 1992, 81.

91. "On the National Guard of the Republic of Tajikistan," Dushanbe, *Narodnaya gazeta*, June 19, 1992, 2, in JPRS-UMA–92–028, July 29, 1992, 29.

92. "Bilateral Ties Treaty Initialed," Moscow Radio Rossii Network, 1900 GMT, July 21, 1992, in FBIS-SOV–92–141, July 22, 1992, 72; "Agreement Reached on Border Troops," Moscow Radio Rossii Network, 0500 GMT, July 22, 1992, in FBIS-SOV–92–141, July 22, 1992, 72.

93. Edward A. Gargan, "Refugees Fleeing Tajik Civil Strife," *New York Times*, January 14, 1993; "Presidium Issues Decree on Armed Forces," Dushanbe Radio, 1700 GMT, December 19, 1992, in FBIS-SOV–92–245, December 21, 1992, 73; Bess Brown, "State of Emergency in Dushanbe," *RFE/RL Daily Report*, No. 4 (E-mail), January 8, 1993, 2.

94. "Iranian Foreign Minister Arrives for Visit," Moscow Radio Rossii Network, 1000 GMT, December 1, 1991, in FBIS-SOV–91–233, December 4, 1991, 85.

95. "Republic Takes Control of Uranium Plant," Moscow INTERFAX, 1338 GMT, December 29, 1991, in FBIS-SOV–91–251, December 31, 1991, 69; Thomas L. Friedman, "Tajikistan Agrees to Curbs on Arms," *New York Times*, February 14, 1992, A7.

96. "Central Asia: Where Strange Things Happen," *The Economist*, September 12, 1992, 36.

97. "Gorno-Badakhshan Autonomous Republic Formed," Moscow Radio Rossii

Network, 1800 GMT, December 17, 1991, in FBIS-SOV–91–243, December 18, 1991, 74–75.

98. "New Constitution Gives President Wider Powers," Moscow POSTFAC-TUM, 1416 GMT, May 18, 1992, in FBIS-SOV–92–097, May 19, 1992, 45.

99. "Amid Calm and Gratitude for Soviet System, the Love of Lenin Lingers on in Turkmenia," *Christian Science Monitor,* December 5, 1991, 5.

100. Akiner, *Islamic Peoples,* 314–17.

101. Vladimir Kuleshov, "Joint Turkmen–Russian Forces To Be Set Up," *Izvestiya,* June 10, 1992, 1, in FBIS-SOV–92–114, June 12, 1992, 15.

102. O. Falichev, "Russia May Become Guarantor of Security in Central Asia," *Krasnaya zvezda,* June 10, 1992, 1, in FBIS-SOV–92–113, June 11, 1992, 73.

103. Vadim Perfilyev, "Novosti" newscast, Moscow Ostankino Television First Program Network, 1700 GMT, July 31, 1992, in FBIS-SOV–92–151, August 5, 1992, 31.

104. Andrey Pershin, Andrey Petrovskiy, and Vladimir Shishlin, "Presidential Bulletin," Moscow INTERFAX, 1646 GMT, August 31, 1992, in FBIS-SOV–92–173, September 4, 1992, 46.

105. Mikhayl Volkov, "Reliable Bridge to Foreign Parts," *Pravda,* February 25, 1992, 3, in FBIS-SOV–92–039, February 27, 1992, 72.

106. "Friendship Agreement Signed," Tehran Radio, 1930 GMT, May 11, 1992, in FBIS-SOV–92–093, May 13, 1992, 72–73; "Deputy Premier on Benefits Deal with Iran," Moscow INTERFAX, 1649 GMT, April 16, 1992, in FBIS-SOV–92–075, April 17, 1992, 63.

107. Nur Batur, "Wealthy Businessman Even Needs a Few Cents," Istanbul *Milliyet,* March 2, 1992, 7, in FBIS-SOV–92–047, March 10, 1992, 47–48.

108. "Foreign Minister on Central Asian Relations," Moscow TASS, 0108 GMT, December 25, 1991, in FBIS-SOV–92–002, January 3, 1992, 66.

109. "Damage, Suffering Described," Moscow Domestic Service, 1900 GMT, November 17, 1990, in FBIS-SOV–90–229, November 29, 1990, 103–04.

110. Igor Zhukov, "Nuclear Electric Power Station: Long Echo of Chernobyl—Russian Atomic Energy Industry Workers Ready to Build AES for Iran," *Nezavisimaya gazeta,* April 25, 1992, 6, in FBIS-SOV–92–081, April 27, 1992, 62–63.

7

The Debris of the Former Soviet Union

THE DEBRIS OF SYSTEMIC TRANSFORMATION

The passing of the Soviet Union in the evening hours of December 25, 1991, left in its wake shattered lives, ruined organizations, and incongruous events that only time can heal. Central to the drama was Mikhail Gorbachev, who in his farewell interview declared: "A burning stream of events is now passing over me, passing over all of us, scorching us more and more."[1]

Gorbachev noted that the Soviet Union's administrative boundaries between republics and autonomous entities were of no import, yet they must now be converted from administrative borders to state borders. This, he observed, was a dangerous and potentially contentious turn of events. He pleaded for the Commonwealth's success: "For God's sake let it be successful. . . . Something viable must emerge." The danger was not from the army but from the street, where the dissatisfied might be egged on by "political prostitutes and speculators."[2]

Gorbachev was disappointed by the progress achieved thus far: "I could see that we had been advancing slogans for two years, while 100 kilometers from Moscow all was quiet."[3] The Nineteenth Party Conference of June 1988 was the first serious effort to separate the state's legislative, judicial, and executive powers and restore the party to a purely political role. "Political pluralism," Gorbachev noted, "was still to come."[4]

This decision led to a confrontation with the *nomenklatura*—entrenched party leaders—as well as with state structures, the military-industrial complex, and those adhering to old values and the old system. Gorbachev said he was the target of colossal attacks and criticism, yet he persisted in replacing local party committees and secretaries three times and eventually held free elections. Gorbachev said he knew conservatives and their military-industrial allies would make a strike, which is why he continued to hold the top party position and kept his opponents nearby, within sight.[5]

The hard-liners, alert for an opportunity to act against Gorbachev, moved on August 19, 1991, the eve of the signing of the new Union Treaty:

> But they procrastinated too, also afraid that the people would not follow them, and they waited for the people's discontent. But suddenly there was the Union Treaty. Hope of stabilizing the country, in which they would no longer find a place for themselves. Look! Chairs had already been lined up in the Kremlin, with the republics in alphabetical order and each one's banner at the back, and here was the president's table. The president made a speech— that's it, I had already confirmed the procedure. . . . The typeface had been chosen for the treaty, and everything had been decided. And they saw that the last moment had come.[6]

Gorbachev was not sanguine about the outcome had they acted earlier. Just twelve or eighteen months prior to the August attempt it would have succeeded, he declared.[7]

Two great dangers now threatened the country's survival: its disintegration and questions of citizenship. Both revolved around the seventy-five million people who live outside their native territories and whose interests must be accommodated by newly established borders and travel procedures.[8]

On the evening of December 25 President Gorbachev addressed the nation in a live television address. Stating his disagreement with the decision to split the USSR into its component parts as codified by the December 21, 1991, Alma-Ata Commonwealth of Independent States accord, he proceeded to place the blame for the Soviet Union's ills squarely on the party-bureaucratic elite: "Society was being throttled in the jaws of the command and bureaucratic system. It was impossible to live like that any longer." Citing the need for radical change, he continued: "Even today I am convinced of the historical correctness of the democratic reforms begun in the spring of 1985."[9]

He then called upon all citizens, as heirs of a great civilization, to realize the rebirth of a new life:

> With all my soul, I wish to thank those who during these years stood alongside me in a just and good cause. Some mistakes could probably have been avoided, much could have been done better, but I am sure that sooner or later our shared efforts will achieve results. Our peoples will live in a flourishing and democratic society. I wish every one of you the best.[10]

Thus began the most dramatic and profound political transformation of the twentieth century, one distinguished from the excesses of the October Revolution by its grace, civility, and democratic aspirations. Nascent free enterprise arose to create the globe's largest flea market, which even saw the rumored sale of Lenin's body attract bids ranging up to $1 billion.[11] TASS, the Moscow-based news agency, reported in February 1992 that Russia had offered Israel its ultrasleek MiG–29 fighter aircraft in a dollars-only transaction. Anticipating at least one purchase—by the Mossad intelligence service for technical analysis—this was a radical departure from past Soviet sales to the region, which were made only to Arab states.[12]

Elements of the KGB came forward to confess their transgressions and to take credit, if any, for the failure of the coup attempt. The commander of the Alpha (brigade A) antiterrorist group of the KGB's Seventh Directorate was personally ordered by KGB Chairman Vladimir Kryuchkov to seize and arrest Boris Yeltsin, then at the Russian White House (parliament building). According to Maj. Gen. Karpukhin, agents infiltrated the crowd outside and were in the White House throughout the siege, and the barricades were flimsy and insufficient to stop an assault. The entire operation, planned for 1 A.M. on August 21, would have taken fifteen minutes, but it would have been a costly bloodbath. In the end, KGB commanders realized the gravity of the situation and the questionable legitimacy of the order, and refused to act.[13]

Vadim Bakatin, former Soviet Interior Ministry general and head of Gorbachev's stillborn Interrepublic Security Service, in late December 1991 gave Robert Strauss, U.S. ambassador to Moscow, blueprints showing the locations and designs of surveillance devices riddling the new American embassy structure, which still stands vacant behind the old embassy. This act occurred following alleged consultations with presidents Bush, Gorbachev, and Yeltsin; the data, Russian officials now acknowledge, provided a "key" to similar surveillance efforts worldwide as well as to the sensitive personnel who installed and maintained them. Some saw this "gift" as treasonous, causing billions of dollars in damage to Soviet security.[14] Bakatin's bold step, however, was instrumental in breaking a nearly seven-year deadlock over the issue, resulting in a June 19, 1992, agreement for the United States to build a new embassy on a more attractive Moscow lot.[15]

In March 1992, the KGB section responsible for codes and ciphers made public disclosures about its activities. Employing several hundred thousand people at a number of institutes and ten plants, the Eighth Directorate of the KGB built and maintained the "nuclear suitcase" carried at all times with the Soviet (and now the Russian) president. Captured cipher equipment was combined with unique Soviet algorithms to create a five-tier system of secure communications serving leaders at all levels. Now the directorate is looking for civilian applications, including protected communications for businesses. Despite the rise of new nations in the former USSR, Soviet Union, the same communications security system exists. For the new states, "Whether we like it or not, they will come to us [the KGB] for equipment."[16]

The KGB was also instrumental in carrying out special operations for party leaders. Archival materials have revealed how Lenin instructed that gold and other valuables of the Russian Orthodox Church be confiscated in 1922. Although the ongoing famine was the excuse, the wealth was used not for this cause, as was publicized, but to finance the new state. Gold seized during the Afghanistan war went for the same purpose. It is little wonder that Moscow's infusions of money to support the American, Italian, Spanish, and other Communist parties were not an unusual occurrence.[17]

Other KGB operations have come to light. Millions of dollars were expended to support insurgencies and Communist parties worldwide, including furnishing arms in 1975 for terrorist attacks by the Popular Front for the Liberation of Palestine against American and Israeli interests in third countries.[18] Another report revealed that then-KGB Chairman Yuri Andropov was able to rent a crowd of some 20,000 protesters in New Delhi, India, to demonstrate in front of the American Embassy for the equivalent of $500, with the remark, "Cheap and nasty, as they say."[19]

Some leftover affairs of state also persisted. Among them was cosmonaut Sergei Krikalev, who was stranded aboard the Mir space station until late March 1992. During his ten months in space, the Soviet Union collapsed, his native Leningrad became St. Petersburg, President Gorbachev retired, space controllers protested low pay, the food resupply was limited due to costs, and he had to endure reports that Mir itself was for sale. Krikalev's mission was doubled in length to save money, and he landed with a fellow cosmonaut, a Ukrainian, to find Ukraine independent and its new president, Leonid Kravchuk, engaged in prolonged disputes with Russia over assets and territory.[20]

No subject has done more to touch the soul of Soviet patriots than the fate of the country's soldiers missing in action after the ten-year war in Afghanistan. Special detachments of the army, the KGB, intelligence, and counterintelligence units succeeded in locating 12 missing servicemen, but at least 304 are still unaccounted for. Moscow claims to hold no Afghan prisoners of war, though it does concede that it has Afghan prisoners convicted of various crimes. Russia's parliament has been active in urging the United Nations and other former Soviet states to continue this painful search.[21] This concern comes at a time when Moscow's incarceration of 716 U.S. servicemen during World War II, interrogation of 59 men during the Korean war, and possible involvement with U.S. prisoners of war during the Vietnam war has generated new interest, and questions, about this entire dimension of Cold War angst.[22]

MILITARY/SPACE DEBRIS

Much of the debris of the former Soviet Union is connected with its seeming preoccupation with military affairs. This ranges from the tractor in Kazan struck by an accidentally launched surface-to-air missile[23] to countless stories of death and human tragedy associated with *dedovshchina* (the hazing of soldier conscripts), which kills and injures thousands of young men each year.

The immediate urgency and human impact of the debris associated with military affairs was first known in relation to the 1986 Chernobyl disaster.

Scientists are now discovering that the medical consequences have been more serious and widespread than originally reported: a deterioration of the health of hundreds of thousands of people due to radiation poisoning, heavy metals, chemical pollution, poor nutrition, and stress. Citizens of Belarus, which received 70 percent of the contamination, are experiencing large increases in cancer and other illnesses.[24]

A series of nuclear accidents elsewhere has eroded public confidence in the safety of nuclear power. In 1968, the malfunction of a reactor aboard a nuclear-powered experimental submarine led to at least nine deaths. In 1992 the Committee of Special Risk Subunit Veterans was formed in St. Petersburg to look after nuclear veterans "forgotten by the state that no longer exists."[25] In 1985 another submarine reactor explosion at Chazma Bay in the Far East killed the ten men aboard, and left contamination (still active) in playgrounds and beach areas.[26] And after a deliberate nuclear detonation to clear methane gas from a Ukrainian coal mine in 1979, thousands of miners were sent into the shaft the next day with no warning or safety precautions.[27]

The dumping of nuclear wastes from Soviet naval and icebreaker fleets in the shallow Kara and Barents seas could require an extensive and expensive cleanup of Arctic waters. This dumping occurred from the 1960s through the 1980s, with the Soviet navy terminating the practice only in 1991. Reports indicated that some twelve nuclear reactors had been scuttled off the island of Novaya Zemlya, Moscow's Arctic nuclear test range, and thousands of sealed containers of radioactive wastes produced by nuclear icebreakers and the Northern Fleet's more than two hundred propulsion reactors were dumped in the area. At least ten rusting nuclear-powered submarines await disposal, and tons of spent nuclear fuel are in temporary storage on barges in Murmansk.[28] More than fifty nuclear reactors on board submarines, including eight on submarines decommissioned as long ago as 1975, are within the city limits of Severodvinsk.[29] To Norway's prime minister, Gro Harlem Bruntland, this is a "security risk to people and to the natural biology of northern waters."[30]

A similar situation exists in the Soviet Far East, where some twenty-nine nuclear submarines awaiting disposal are tied to piers at the Pacific Fleet's base at Primorye. At present, there are no facilities for disassembling the reactors or for safely disposing the reactor fuel from sixteen submarines. Another three ships with damaged reactors are at anchor, some for as long as thirteen years. This situation has been termed "a delayed-action nuclear mine."[31]

Other seriously contaminated sites are the result of World War II activities, when toxic munitions were dumped at sea. One such site is in the Baltic Sea near the Latvian–Lithuanian border, where thousands of tons of war materials were reportedly dumped. This has been the subject of appeals for international assistance by the Baltic Council.[32] A second site is in the

Barents Sea, where up to sixty railcars of chemical munitions were dumped in the early 1960s.[33]

Authorities in Moscow do not have far to look when it comes to radiation pollution. It has been estimated that about 1,500 enterprises and institutes in the Moscow area work with radioactive materials. As a result, 630 radioactive sites have been identified where these materials have been dumped, leading to the discovery of fifty to sixty hot spots in the city each year.[34] In St. Petersburg, nine seriously contaminated spots are located within 300 meters of the Gulf of Finland.[35]

The question of safety has raised new concerns regarding health and the environment at the former Soviet Union's nuclear testing sites: Novaya Zemlya in the Arctic Ocean and Semipalatinsk in Kazakhstan. At Novaya Zemlya, the 82,000-square-kilometer (32,800-square-mile) archipelago was made the federal property of Russia on March 20, 1992, under a decree issued by Boris Yeltsin. It would remain a restricted area as Moscow's primary site for conducting underground tests to check the reliability of the Russian nuclear arsenal.[36]

The second major Soviet nuclear testing area, Semipalatinsk, was closed by Kazakh President Nursultan Nazarbayev on August 29, 1991, largely as a result of protests by an activist group called the Nevada-Semipalatinsk Movement. One of the scientist-members of the movement, which is dedicated to halting all nuclear testing, has claimed that millions of Kazakh citizens served as guinea pigs during the forty years of its use. Upon its closing, radiation victims were given three hundred to four hundred rubles, the equivalent of one dollar.[37]

The Kazakh Supreme Soviet in 1990 passed a decree banning the testing of nuclear and other weapons of mass destruction. President Nazarbayev described the reason for this decision: "I think Kazakhstan has discharged its duty to the country in full. And discharged it at a high price—the destruction of the health of tens of thousands of people, who are now finding it irritating to have to listen to the military almost go so far as to virtually insist that it's actually good for them to live around the test site."[38] In February 1992, after four decades of control by the Soviet Ministry of Defense, the 870,000 hectares (2,175,000 acres) of land comprising the Semipalatinsk Nuclear Test Site Command were being returned to the three surrounding oblasts for further disposition.[39]

Attention has also been directed at the two main centers for developing Soviet nuclear weapons, Arzamas–16 and Chelyabinsk–70, both in the Russian Federation. Both closed cities, identified by their military postal code numbers, formed the heart of the secret world of Soviet nuclear programs, employing the country's best scientists and resources to achieve and maintain the Soviet Union's superpower status. In February 1992, Arzamas–16 was visited by Boris Yeltsin, and U.S. Secretary of State James Baker toured Chelyabinsk–70.

The research center code-named Arzamas–16 is located on the Volga in the Russian Federation. Eighty kilometers (fifty miles) from the city of Arzamas (some 400 miles [640 kilometers] east of Moscow in Nizhniy Novgorod Oblast), it was founded in 1946 to spearhead Stalin's project to build the atomic bomb, which was successfully detonated in 1949. Its vast nuclear weapons complex has been compared with its U.S. counterpart at Los Alamos, New Mexico. Academician Andrey Sakharov, the noted physicist, used to work at Arzamas–16, and his house has been preserved as a museum.[40] Scientists there are now engaged in a host of projects to turn graphite into diamond dust and in subatomic particle research, in hopes of securing funding from foreign firms.[41] Arzamas–16 is currently engaged in dismantling the tactical nuclear weapons withdrawn from Belarus, Ukraine, and Kazakhstan in the spring of 1992.[42]

Arzamas–16 and Chelyabinsk–70 are both central to Moscow's nuclear program through designing and testing nuclear weapons and their components. Chelyabinsk–70, a secret city in the Urals with the geographical name of Snezhinsk, which is not listed on maps, was founded in 1955 and employs nearly 16,000 people who for years received special bonuses and incentives to remain isolated and perform their specialized work.[43] Located on the shores of Lake Sinara in the vicinity of Sverdlovsk (now Yekaterinburg) and Chelyabinsk, it was originally established as a backup should Arzamas–16 become damaged or destroyed. Top-secret research was conducted in its inner sanctum, Zone-B, in the late 1940s, where Soviet prisoners and captured German scientists reportedly tested the affects of radiation on live organisms.[44]

Chelyabinsk–70 was long considered a model scientific production center because of its vertically integrated theoretical research, its design center, and its production plants operating together under one command. Although it is still performing sophisticated research in fiber optics and computer-assisted devices for medical diagnosis, its significance has paled with the passing of the USSR.[45] According to its research director, "this transition from a feeling of being vitally needed people to people who are virtually useless is having a negative effect."[46]

Both Arzamas–16 and Chelyabinsk–70 were made into Russian federal research centers by a February 1992 decree of President Yeltsin. He described the scientists working at the research centers as similar to cosmonauts, specialists who should be treated as special and who "need to be protected—they have earned this through their self-sacrificing life over many decades."[47]

Tomsk–7 and Chelyabinsk–65 are other "relatives" of the nuclear weapons network. Located in Siberia some fifteen kilometers from the city bearing its name, Tomsk–7 was founded in 1949 by Lavrenty Beria, head of the secret police. It also produced weapons-grade plutonium and stood accused of contaminating the Tom River and eight holding basins for radioactive materials. Its production reactor was stopped on August 14, 1992, and residents' concerns of unemployment have created serious problems for local officials. Chelyabinsk–65 was the first center for producing weapons-grade plutonium. Known as the Mayak Chemical Combine, it was said to be the largest producer of plutonium in the world. It was responsible for an accidental explosion of improperly stored nuclear waste in 1957, leaving 16,000 hectares of land still contaminated. The large lake used by the production facility for holding nuclear wastes is considered the most polluted area in the world, with contamination levels some two and one-half times as lethal as the radiation released at Chernobyl.[48]

Another secret city, Krasnoyarsk–26, mined and produced nuclear materials for Soviet weapons. Located in western Siberia north of the city of Krasnoyarsk and not shown on maps, it is noteworthy for radiation dosimeters on its streets. It was founded in the late 1940s as the key location where uranium was mined and enhanced for the Soviet Union's atomic and thermonuclear weapons. Its large reactors are cooled with water taken directly from and returned to the Yenisey River, which has raised objections from environmentalists.[49] Its existence was publicly acknowledged only in 1988, and the first foreigners visited there in March 1992.

On June 30, 1992, a weapons-grade plutonium reactor there, which was built by prisoners deep underground, was shut down. The reactor had been operating since 1958, and the crater is to be sealed. Local officials and environmentalists, in August, sent a bill for more than 6.7 billion roubles to its director and Russia's atomic energy minister to pay for the contamination the reactor caused to the air, soil, and water, as well as damage to people's health.[50]

Other debris includes Yeniseysk–15, the Krasnoyarsk radar some sixty kilometers north of the city of Krasnoyarsk, considered by U.S. authorities to be in violation of the 1972 ABM treaty. The Soviet army started demolishing the tall radar structure and support buildings in 1989; further demolition was suspended in April 1992 at the request of local inhabitants, who wish to use the remaining buildings for commercial purposes. In the meantime, much of what remains is being looted by people seeking construction materials.[51]

The southern Urals city of Beloretsk, in the former Bashkir Autonomous Soviet Socialist Republic, is the general location of the secret facilities codenamed Beloretsk–15 and Beloretsk–16. Both were associated with a program to build underground shelters for the Soviet leadership in case of nuclear war. Started by Leonid Brezhnev in the mid 1970s at the cost of billions of rubles, the shelters and extensive supporting infrastructure required thousands of workers and technicans who were brought to the remote site and continue to work there.[52]

Other facilities kept from public view were associated with the Soviet biological and bacteriological warfare program. In Sverdlovsk, Military Installation No. 19, a subunit of the Soviet Defense Ministry's Scientific Research Institute for Microbiology, was the source of airborne anthrax that killed an unknown number of citizens in 1979. For years Soviet authorities insisted that sick cattle had caused the outbreak of the disease, rare in humans in its pulmonary form. Long-rumored reports that anthrax spores "leaked" from Compound No. 19 were confirmed by an April 4, 1992, presidential decree granting benefits to survivors and admitting violations of the 1972 bacteriological weapons convention.[53]

Another source of concern focused on a bacteriological test site on an island in the Aral Sea. Vozrozhdeniye Island, a part of Kazakhstan, was reportedly used to test live agents, including anthrax, for five decades. Based upon Boris Yeltsin's decree of April 24, 1992, "On Ensuring Compliance with International Obligations in the Field of Biological Weapons," reports of bacteriological experiments have been published in the Soviet press. In the 1970s, testing on live animals and agent research expanded dramatically through fear of falling behind the West, despite a 1972 international convention that the USSR ratified in 1975.[54] Beyond this, Russia informed the United Nations in July 1992 about its activities in the biological/bacteriological field.

According to a retired Soviet general involved in the biological weapons program, bombs and rockets had been prepared containing anthrax, tularemia, and Q fever. This was part of a weapons program, in contravention of international agreements, that reportedly ended in 1990. Decontamination of the island testing ground was begun in August 1992, and it is expected to be safe for civilian purposes in two or three years.[55]

Some 700,000 people live in the closed cities of the former Soviet Union. These cities include those listed above as well as Sverdlovsk–45, Sverdlovsk–44, Sverdlovsk–16, Nizhniy Tagil–39, and Penza–19. All are centers of secret work and are located at unmarked sites some distance from these postal addresses.[56] On August 10, 1992, President Yeltsin signed into law a bill that re-closed certain areas. This act stated that "territories with industrial enterprises developing, producing and storing weapons of mass destruction, or utilizing radioactive and other materials, as well as military facilities which need a special regime of security will be declared closed administrative entities."[57]

The final debris relates to the vast Soviet space program, which has been operated by the Soviet military. Ministry of Defense space facilities were constructed at Kapustin Yar, Tyuratam, and Plesetsk. Kapustin Yar is a test center near Volgograd, Russia, where captured German V–2 rockets were launched in October 1947. Tyuratam, in Kazakhstan, was the Soviet Union's principal missile test center. It became operational in June 1955, and the first Soviet ICBM was launched on August 26, 1957. The Sputnik launch of October 4, 1957, and Yuri Gagarin's epic orbital flight on April 12, 1961, originated from Tyuratam.[58]

Tyuratam has also been known as the Baykonur cosmodrome, a security precaution to divert attention to the city of that name some 200 miles (320 kilometers) east of Tyuratam. The third space city is Plesetsk, which began to function as a cosmodrome in 1960. Some 60 percent of all launches from the former Soviet Union were from Plesetsk, a site in Russia that is particularly convenient for launching polar-orbiting satellites.[59]

The Baykonur cosmodrome's location in Kazakhstan has led to disputes over soldier welfare and environmental protection. Hundreds of soldiers and junior officers assigned to military construction units at Baykonur were involved in a large-scale disturbance on February 23–25, 1992, over poor living conditions, that spread to Tyuratam and threatened an international space launch.[60] In addition, residents of Yakutia have protested that spent first- and second-stage booster rockets of intercontinental ballistic missiles and space rockets from launch sites fall on Kazakhstan and Yakutia, inflicting untold environmental damage.[61]

The future of the former Soviet space program is subject to speculation. Russia created the Russian Space Agency in February 1992, primarily focused on its space centers at Plesetsk and Kapustin Yar. Because 85 percent of all launches originated in Russia, there is widespread recognition that no other CIS member state can maintain a program of such dimension. The Baykonur cosmodrome may be located in Kazakhstan, but Kazakhs constitute about 1 percent of space unit personnel (and over 50 percent of construction unit personnel). According to the director of the Russian Space Agency, "if Baykonur is abandoned it will turn into a scrap metal dump. Kazakhstan does not have its own autonomous space and missile potential."[62]

These programs were financed by a defense budget that was the source of unending dispute in the West. Not unexpectedly, the budget was several times larger than the official figures. It was often asserted that Soviet expenditures were out of control and that no one knew their total cost. Indeed, a central accounting was in fact performed by a secret component of the state bank, Gosbank, in the "Second Department of the Directorate for Special Operations." It was openly called the Inventory Department, or Parkbank, and it was located next to the Ministry of Defense's Main Intelligence Directorate (GRU), known as the "aquarium." The office was established in 1978 to coordinate programs and to send directives to the military-industrial complex for research and production activities. Never audited, it has continued to provide a central accounting service for defense programs.[63]

OTHER DEBRIS

A final area of consideration is the vast ecological damage that Soviet carelessness and environmental neglect have visited upon this long-suffering land. In the west, a 1,000-kilometer (620-mile) "invisible wall" running from St. Petersburg in the northeast to Lübeck, Germany, in the southwest has separated Europeans with expensive and functional water purification systems from waves of human and industrial wastes originating in the former Soviet-dominated countries. This has led most Scandinavian programs for aiding Eastern Europe to focus on environmental projects.[64]

Soviet agriculture brought environmental neglect to citizens' dinner tables. According to Murray Feshbach, 30 percent of all food in the new republics is contaminated to the point that it should not be consumed. In addition, 42 percent of infants' food is contaminated by pesticides; and DDT has affected 25 million acres (ten million hectares) of arable land; and dioxin has been used freely. Large numbers of livestock are diseased, and in southern Russia desertification is claiming 100,000 acres (40,000 hectares) a year. It is clear that the abuse and neglect of agricultural lands will take enormous efforts to correct.[65]

Some deliberate contamination has further aggravated an already abysmal record. In the southern Urals, a local council has reported the presence of a secret dump of 123 tons of toxic chemicals that has been concealed since 1972. Leaching from the containers has apparently reached the groundwater, resulting in a high incidence of medical disorders.[66] Countless other sites exist, creating the need for one of the most enormous cleanup operations in history.

MOVING FORWARD

Boris Yeltsin, the Russian president, has stated that his country cannot afford to waste time by looking backward upon this legacy of waste, abuse, and human travail. He has acted quickly and aggressively to acknowledge past sins and to pledge compliance with international accords and understandings. Much of the debris of the Soviet era was connected with the vicissitudes of the Cold War, which left both principal parties wounded and in need of resuscitation.

Yeltsin unequivocally told the April 1992 session of the Russian Congress of People's Deputies that preoccupation with past events and tragedies is no longer Russian state policy:

> I can say quite definitely that the spirit of the "cold war" has no future in Russia. The Russian people will not allow themselves to be encircled by an Iron Curtain or dragged into imperialist adventures again. Russia is an active member of the world community and is mastering the tricky business of civilized relations. Russia is building an open and peaceful state. I am convinced that the shadows of the past are no longer able to impede this. In the West too, of course, not everyone has the same attitude to the Russian reforms, but it is possible to say with confidence that most of the world community is on our side, on the side of reforms and the renewal of Russia.[67]

For the debris of Russia and the other new nations of the former Soviet Union to be fully swept aside, the West must demonstrate its advantages in human terms: quality of life and livelihood, humane governance, and self-actualization. As former President Richard Nixon has acknowledged, "The communists have lost the Cold War, but the West has not yet won it. Today, the ideas of freedom are on trial."[68]

NOTES

1. D. Muratov and V. Fromin, "Gorbachev Goes, but Remains. Interview with USSR's First and Last President," *Komsomolskaya pravda,* December 24, 1991, 1–2, in FBIS-SOV–91–247, December 24, 1991, 18.

2. Ibid., 19.

3. Ibid.

4. Ibid.

5. Ibid., 20.

6. Ibid.

7. Ibid.

8. Ibid., 21.

9. "Address by USSR President Mikhail Gorbachev to the Soviet People from Moscow—Live," Moscow Central Television First Program Network, 1700 GMT, December 25, 1991, in FBIS-SOV–91–248, December 26, 1991, 20–21.

10. Ibid., 21.

11. "Security Officials on Banned Entry into Russia," Moscow TASS, 1220 GMT, February 27, 1992, in FBIS-SOV–92–042, March 3, 1992, 44.

12. "Novosti" newscast, Moscow Television First Program Network, 1500 GMT, February 11, 1992, in FBIS-SOV–92–030, February 13, 1992, 40.

13. Dmitriy Belovetskiy and Sergey Boguslavskiy, "They Refused to Storm the White House," *Literaturnaya gazeta,* August 28, 1991, 5, in JPRS-UMA–91–023, September 10, 1991, 69–70; Celestine Bohlen, "Russia Coup Trial is Yielding a Maze," *New York Times,* August 21, 1992, A3.

14. Yevgeniya Albats, "Walls Have Ears," *Moskovskiye novosti,* December 29, 1991, 15, in FBIS-SOV–92–004, January 7, 1992, 30–33; Andrey Zhdankin, "At First Hand: Bakatin Slammed the Door Behind Him," *Rossiyskaya gazeta,* December 31, 1991, 1, in FBIS-SOV–92–004, January 7, 1992, 33.

15. Thomas L. Friedman, "Deal Made on Bugged U.S. Moscow Embassy," *New York Times,* June 20, 1992, A4.

16. O. Volkov and V. Umnov, "Who Taught the President's Telephone to Hold Its Tongue. We have an Entire Industry Unknown to Anybody," Moscow *Komsomolskaya pravda,* May 1, 1992, 3, in FBIS-SOV–92–089, May 7, 1992, 31–34.

17. G. Solomatin, "Novosti" newscast, Moscow Television First Program Network, 1400 GMT, June 5, 1992, and " 'Terrible Impression' Made," Moscow Radio Rossii Network, 1800 GMT, June 5, 1992, in FBIS-SOV–92–110, June 8, 1992, 26–27; "Smirnov on Aid to Foreign Communist Parties," Moscow INTERFAX, 1926 GMT, July 29, 1992, in FBIS-SOV–92–148-S, July 31, 1992, 15.

18. "Moscow Plans Its Next Show Trial," *Time,* June 8, 1992, 26.

19. "Demonstration for Five Thousand," Moscow *Kuranty,* June 3, 1992, 2, in FBIS-SOV–92–108, June 4, 1992, 8.

20. William J. Broad, "For Two (Ex-Soviet) Astronauts, an Alien World Lies Ahead," *New York Times,* March 25, 1992, A20.

21. L. Gorovoy, "All Prisoners of War Must Be Freed. Today There Is No Reason to Detain Them," *Krasnaya zvezda,* May 15, 1992, 3, in FBIS-SOV–92–096, May 18, 1992, 5; "More on Efforts to Release POW's in Afghanistan," Moscow Radio Rossii Network, 1200 GMT, March 24, 1992, in FBIS-SOV–92–060, March 27, 1992, 18.

22. "A Presummit Gesture: Yeltsin Confirms That the Soviets Held American Prisoners in the 1950s," *Time,* June 22, 1992, 27.

23. Ye. Grigoryev, "Someone Pushed the Button," *Trud,* July 28, 1990, 1, in JPRS-UMA–90–020, September 10, 1990, 17.

24. James Brooke, "Chernobyl Said to Affect Health of Thousands in a Soviet Region," *New York Times,* November 3, 1991, A1.

25. V. Sikorskiy, "18 Years Before Chernobyl: A Similar Accident Occurred on a Northern Fleet Experimental Submarine and the Fates of Its Victims Are Still Hidden Behind a Curtain of Secrecy," *Krasnaya zvezda,* May 6, 1992, 2, in JPRS-UMA–92–018, May 20, 1992, 21–23.

26. Ye. Varshavskaya, "Explosion in Chazma Bay: About an Unknown Nuclear Catastrophe," *Trud,* October 21, 1991, 2, in JPRC-UMA–91–028, November 14, 1991, 32–36.

27. John Iams, "Coal Mine Nuclear Test Kept Secret," *Harrisburg (Pa.) Sunday Patriot News,* June 28, 1992, A17.

28. Patrick E. Tyler, "Soviets' Secret Nuclear Dumping Raises Fears for Arctic Waters," *New York Times,* May 4, 1992, A1, A8.

29. Lyudmila Zhukova, "We All Live Off a Yellow Submarine," *Moscow News,* July 12–19, 1992, 11, in JPRS-UMA–92–030, August 12, 1992, 11.

30. Tyler, "Soviets' Secret Nuclear Dumping," A8.

31. Pavel Smirnov, "Ecology: Nuclear Privatization," Moscow *Rossiyskaya gazeta,* May 25, 1992, 2, in JPRS-UMA–92–023, June 24, 1992, 20–22.

32. "Baltic Council Issues Appeal on Soviet Dumping," Vilnius Radio, 1800 GMT, June 26, 1992, in FBIS-SOV–92–126, June 30, 1992, 9.

33. "What Is at the Bottom of the White Sea?," Moscow *Komsomolskaya pravda,* June 13, 1991, 4, in FBIS-SOV–91–115, June 14, 1991, 35.

34. Y. Blokhin and V. Mikosha, "Novosti" newscast, Moscow First Program Network, 1700 GMT, June 16, 1992, in FBIS-SOV–92–122, June 24, 1992, 3.

35. "Briefly and Clearly," *Pravda,* June 16, 1992, 4, in FBIS-SOV–92–121, June 23, 1992, 46.

36. Yuriy Meshkov, "Environment: Will the Nuclear Test Site Start Operating? Another Decree Has Been Signed About Tests in Novaya Zemlya," *Nezavisimaya gazeta,* March 24, 1992, 6, in FBIS-SOV–92–060, March 27, 1992, 1; Sergey Ostanin, "Yeltsin Decrees Novaya Zemlya Russian Property," Moscow TASS, 1706 GMT, March 20, 1992, in FBIS-SOV–92–056, March 23, 1992, 31.

37. "Soviet Nuclear Horrors Uncovered," *Carlisle* (Pa.) *Sentinel,* May 4, 1992, A4.

38. Yuriy Luchin, "So Long, Test Site?" *Ogonek,* No. 51, December 1990, 25.

39. "News Item: Kazakhstan," *Rossiyskaya gazeta,* February 22, 1992, 6, in FBIS-SOV–92–039, February 27, 1992, 69.

40. Gennadiy Talalayev, "Decree on 'Federal Centers' Issued," Moscow TASS, 1357 GMT, February 28, 1992, in FBIS-SOV–92–041, March 2, 1992, 2.

41. John J. Fialka, "Russian Scientists Change Their Work, Not Always Along Lines the U.S. Likes," *Wall Street Journal,* May 5, 1992, A16.

42. Igor Mosin, "Arzamas–16 is Concerned...," *Pravda,* June 25, 1992, 4, in JPRS-UMA–92–025, July 8, 1992, 50; "Observers Check Arzamas–16 Weapons Destruction," Moscow Radio Rossii Network, 0300 GMT, June 23, 1992, in FBIS-SOV–92–124, June 26, 1992, 3.

43. Georgiy Shcherbina, "Baker Opens 'Closed Cities,' " *Izvestiya,* February 17, 1992, 1, in FBIS-SOV–92–032, February 18, 1992, 30.

44. "Black Box" program, Moscow Ostankino Television First Program Network, 1922 GMT, September 9, 1992, in FBIS-SOV–92–179, September 15, 1992, 14–16.

45. Georgiy Shcherbina, "Instead of the Bomb, Open Business," *Izvestiya,* November 25, 1991, 2, in JPRS-UMA–92–001, January 10, 1992, 47.

46. Dmitriy Yakushkin, "The Bomb, Baker and Salaries," *Moskovskiye novosti,* March 8, 1992, 15, in JPRS-UMA–92–011, April 1, 1992, 82.

47. "Yeltsin Visits Arzamas: Holds News Conference," Moscow Russian Television Network, 2020 GMT, February 28, 1992, in FBIS-SOV–92–041, March 2, 1992, 1.

48. A. Chelnokov, "Tomsk–7, What the Film 'The Resident's Mistake' Did Not Tell About," Moscow *Komsomolskaya pravda,* July 14, 1992, 3, in JPRS-UMA–92–029, August 5, 1992, 56–60; A. Pelt, "Utro" report, Moscow Television First Program Network, 1855 GMT, August 23, 1992, in FBIS-SOV–92–166, August 26, 1992, 33; "Utro" program, Moscow Television First Program, 1945 GMT, September 28, 1992, in FBIS-SOV–92–193, October 5, 1992, 29; Matthew L. Wald, "High Radiation Doses Seen for Soviet Arms Workers," *New York Times,* August 16, 1990, A3.

49. Steven Erlanger, "A Siberian Town: Not a Secret and Ready to Deal," *New York Times,* March 29, 1992, A1, A6; Yuriy Rogoshin, "Stopping Reactors in Krasnoyarsk," *Izvestiya,* April 18, 1992, 1, in FBIS-SOV–92–084, April 30, 1992, 45.

50. Nikolay Krivomazov, "A Couple of Questions From the Nether Regions," *Pravda,* June 30, 1992, 1, in FBIS-SOV–92–130, July 7, 1992, 47; Aleksey Tarasov, "People of Krasnoyarsk Demand 6.730 Billion from Atomic Specialists," *Izvestiya,* August 6, 1992, 2, in FBIS-SOV–92–154, August 10, 1992, 48–49.

51. Aleksey Tarasov, "Demolition of Krasnoyarsk Radar Station Buildings Suspended," *Izvestiya,* April 22, 1992, 8, in FBIS-SOV–92–084, April 30, 1992, 45–46.

52. M. Safarov, "...And Some Need Bunkers," *Komsomolskaya pravda,* March 14, 1992, 2, in JPRS-UMA–92–011, April 1, 1992, 2.

53. "Does a Cow Amount to a Bacteriologial Bomb?" *Komsomolskaya pravda,* May 14, 1992, 1, in FBIS-SOV–92–099, May 21, 1992, 6; A. Pashkov, "How We Got 'Inoculated' for Anthrax: Military People in White Coats Still Are Potentially Dangerous for the Society," *Izvestiya,* November 12, 1991, 8, in JPRS-UMA–91–032, December 17, 1991, 50–51.

54. "Closure of Bacteriological Test Range Demanded," Moscow Mayak Radio Network, 1200 GMT, January 13, 1992, in FBIS-SOV–92–010, January 15, 1992, 70; V. Umnov, "After 20 Years of Silence the Soviet Microbes Are Talking," Moscow *Komsomolskaya pravda*, April 30, 1992, 1, in FBIS-SOV–92–087, May 5, 1992, 4–6; " 'Top Secret' Bacteriological Test Site Noted," *Komsomolskaya pravda*, January 24, 1992, 2, in FBIS-SOV–92–016, January 24, 1992, 93.

55. R. Jeffrey Smith, "Russia Fails to Detail Germ Arms," *The Washington Post*, August 31, 1992, A1, A15.

56. Pavel Vanichkin and Andrey Shitov, "Additional Details of Talks," Moscow ITAR-TASS, 0510 GMT, June 17, 1992, in FBIS-SOV–92–117, June 17, 1992, 15; Sergey Mushkaterov, "Problems of Our Closed Cities Discussed in Norway," *Izvestiya*, May 20, 1992, 6, in JPRS-UMA–92–020, June 3, 1992, 53.

57. Galina Vinitskaya, "Parliament Adopts Law on Closed Territories," Moscow ITAR-TASS, 1631 GMT, July 14, 1992, in FBIS-SOV–92–137, July 16, 1992, 48.

58. Dino A. Brugioni, "The Tyuratam Enigma," *Air Force Magazine*, March 1984, 108–09.

59. Ibid.; Boris Konovalov, "Russian Space Agency Set Up," *Izvestiya*, February 28, 1992, 5, in FBIS-SOV–92–044, March 5, 1992, 57.

60. A. Ladin, "Disturbances in Military Construction Units. Many Demands of the Soldiers Are Just," *Krasnaya zvezda*, February 27, 1992, 3, in JPRS-UMA–92–010, March 18, 1992, 22–23; "Complaints of Baykonur Soldiers Confirmed," Moscow Mayak Radio Network, 0900 GMT, March 4, 1992, in FBIS-SOV–92–044, March 5, 1992, 71.

61. Dmitriy Khrapovitskiy, "Sakha (Yakutia) Suspends Treaty with Baykonur," *Izvestiya*, April 10, 1992, 1, in FBIS-SOV–92–073, April 15, 1992, 40–41.

62. A. Belousov and A. Dolinin, "Could Plesetsk Become the Central Russian Cosmodrome?" *Krasnaya zvezda*, April 29, 1992, 1, in FBIS-SOV–92–084, April 30, 1992, 39; "Baykonur Servicemen Want Single Strategic Force," Moscow POST-FACTUM, 1648 GMT, March 19, 1992, in FBIS-SOV–92–059, March 26, 1992, 17; Konovalov, "Russian Space Agency Set Up," 57.

63. Igor Stadnik, "Investigation: Parkbank—We Hid the Military Budget There," Moscow *Moskovskiye novosti*, July 19, 1992, 14–15, in JPRS-UMA–92–033, September 2, 1992, 5–6.

64. Soren Ostergaard Sorensen and Berlingske Tidende, "With Iron Curtain Gone, Littoral States Join to Clean up Polluted Baltic Sea," *Christian Science Monitor*, May 27, 1992, 15.

65. Murray Feshbach, "Russia's Farms, Too Poisoned for the Plow," *Wall Street Journal*, May 14, 1992, A12.

66. Yuriy Balandin, " 'Secret' Sverdlovsk Chemical Dump," Moscow Radio Rossii Network, 1000 GMT, February 3, 1992, in FBIS-SOV–92–024, February 5, 1992, 69.

67. "Yeltsin Addresses Congress," Moscow Radio Rossii Network, 1630 GMT, April 21, 1992, in FBIS-SOV–92–080-S, April 24, 1992, 14.

68. Richard Nixon, "The Challenge We Face in Russia," *Wall Street Journal*, March 11, 1992, A14.

8

Selected Biographies

A number of emerging leaders of the former republics of the Soviet Union will play an increasingly influential role in the new Eurasian states. Some of these individuals are already in political life, while others have just entered the limelight. The succession of elites in any political system can be a traumatic and, often, life-threatening experience. In the case of the former Soviet Union, some leaders who had been token representatives of an ethnic group in Soviet republics controlled and led by Russians are reaching a new prominence. The elite succession in progress, then, is the beginning of the ascension to political power of genuine ethnic elites, individuals who will lead and represent their peoples along the uncertain paths of the days ahead.

Geydar Aliyev: Aliyev, born on May 10, 1923, is chairman of the Supreme Majlis (parliament) of Nakhichevan autonomous republic, located within Armenia but under Azerbaijan's jurisdiction. Prior to holding this position, he was a full member of the Communist party's ruling Politburo. As a protégé of Yuri Andropov, his background has been in the security services. He rose to head the Azerbaijan KGB in 1967, and within two years he also became chief of the Azerbaijan Communist party, a position he maintained until 1982. He is a force in Azerbaijani politics and at the center of Turkey's efforts to improve its position in that part of the southern Caucasus.

Vladimir N. Chernavin: Admiral of the fleet Chernavin was born on April 28, 1928. This Russian naval officer commands all CIS naval forces. As elements of the Black Sea Fleet and the Caspian Sea Fleet are detached to form navies of the new nations, Admiral Chernavin has the difficult task of realigning naval forces and personnel. He is also presiding over the professionalization of naval personnel based upon their voluntarily signing personal contracts for periods of service. One of his most important responsibilities is as a nuclear commander, supervising ballistic missile submarines.

Victor S. Chernomyrdin: An experienced manager and technocrat who was in charge of the Soviet Union's gas and energy industry, Chernomyrdin has served four years as a member of the party's Central Committee staff. He entered the national limelight as minister of the gas industry in 1985 and, in 1989, became chairman of its new organizational form, the state corporation Gazprom. In June 1992, he was appointed as deputy prime minister in a move heralded as a conservative resurgence, but Chernomyrdin's abilities and inside knowledge have enabled him to move nimbly within the government and to get things done. Born in 1938 in the Orenburg region of Russia, Chernomyrdin now charts Russia's course in economic reform and privatization.[1]

Yegor T. Gaidar: Gaidar rose quickly on the Russian stage as a youthful economic adviser for the new Yeltsin regime and then as acting prime minister of the Russian Federation. When he was not confirmed as prime minister at the December 1992 session of the Congress of People's Deputies, Yeltsin appointed him as director of the Institute of Economic Problems and economic adviser to the Russian president. Born in Moscow on March 19, 1956, he has been at the forefront of Russian economic reform.

Mikhail S. Gorbachev: The former Soviet president and communist party general secretary was born on March 2, 1931, in the Stavropol area of southern Russia. A party member since 1952, Politburo member since 1979, and general secretary since March 1985, he won the Nobel Peace Prize in 1990 for the change he brought to Eastern Europe and for defusing global tensions. After the August 1991 conservative coup that tried to prevent the conclusion of a union treaty leading to a new constitution and the demise of the Communist party, he fought a rearguard action to maintain control of a disintegrating Soviet Union. According to his friend and architect of *glasnost,* Alexander Yakovlev, Gorbachev is a "great and tragic figure." On the day of Gorbachev's resignation, Yakovlev observed, "All talk about him having clung to or hanging on to power is rubbish, speculation. He has absolute power, but began to give it up voluntarily."[2] He has continued to criticize developments in the former Soviet Union following his resignation. Commenting upon the death of the Soviet Union, on December 27, 1992, Gorbachev observed: "This was a perfectly tragic mistake, the consequences of which we will have to suffer for a very long time."[3]

Pavel S. Grachev: Newly appointed minister of defense of Russia, this general won the Soviet Union's highest military decoration, Hero of the Soviet Union, for bravery during one of his two tours fighting the *mujahideen* in Afghanistan. Born on October 1, 1948, and a paratrooper and paratroop commander since 1965, he won acclaim during the August 1991 coup for refusing to use his troops against Yeltsin forces. Known as a serious military professional, Grachev is not noted for political intrigue. Instead, the army general (four-star) will lead the formation of a modern, rapidly deployed military force capable of moving quickly to the far corners of Russia, the world's largest nation. He will also be the man to watch as the Russian Federation emerges as the former Soviet Union's sole nuclear power by the year 2000.[4]

Boris V. Gromov: Born on November 7, 1943, Colonel General Gromov was appointed as Russia's Deputy Minister of Defense on June 30, 1992. A combined arms officer, he was the last commander of Soviet troops in Afghanistan before their February 1989 withdrawal. Gromov commanded the Kiev Military District from 1989 to 1990 and was appointed Deputy Minister of Interior in December 1990. A hero of the Soviet Union, he was deputy commander of Ground Troops prior to his current position.[5]

Andrey A. Kokoshin: Named by President Yeltsin as the first deputy minister of defense of the Russian Federation on April 3, 1992, Kokoshin is a doctor of historical sciences and deputy director of the Institute of the USA and Canada, where he had broad contact with the U.S. academic community. A specialist on political and national security issues, Kokoshin has taken a number of innovative stands on key policy issues relating to force structure, disarmament, and arms control. A native of Moscow, where he was born on October 26, 1945, he is the son of a military officer.

Leonid M. Kravchuk: Kravchuk was elected to a five-year term as Ukraine's first president on December 1, 1991. Born on January 10, 1934, this Ukrainian has spent his career as a Communist party apparatchik (functionary). In an election that set him against a leading nationalist from western Ukraine, Kravchuk surprised many observers with his staunch position on issues affecting Ukraine's sovereignty and independence. As leader of the former Soviet Union's second most populous state, Kravchuk can be expected to use his assertive personality and many years of experience as a Communist to ensure that a central authority that can control Ukrainian affairs does not exist beyond Ukraine's borders.

Konstantin P. Morozov: As Ukrainian minister of defense, the former Soviet air force officer—now a colonel-general (three-star)—is in charge of a new army for a new nation. Having served as a senior air force officer in the USSR, Hungary, Poland, and Czechoslovakia, he was in command of an arm of the air force in Ukraine when the CIS was created and Ukraine assumed control of its own defenses. Morozov was born on June 3, 1944; his father is Russian and his mother is Ukrainian.[6]

Nursultan A. Nazarbayev: Elected as president of Kazakhstan on December 1, 1991, in the republic's first such election, he is known as a staunch advocate of a market economy. Nazarbayev has hired foreign experts to serve as republic economic advisers, and he is committed to pursuing an independent path for realizing Kazakh greatness. Born on July 6, 1940, he became head of the republic's Communist party in June 1989. It is said that his first real acquaintance with socialism was on his wedding day, when he took his new bride to the apartment they had been allocated, only to find that construction had just begun. The couple spent their wedding night in the home of a friend's grandmother.[7]

Yevgeniy Primakov: Director of the Russian Foreign Intelligence Service since December 26, 1991, Primakov is a native of Kiev, born on October 29, 1929. He graduated from the Institute of Oriental Studies in Moscow in 1953 and worked ten years as a journalist and *Pravda* correspondent in the Middle East. In 1970 he joined the Institute of the World Economy and International Relations (IMEMO), was promoted to the rank of Academician, and eventually was named head of that organization in 1989. From 1989 to 1991 he served in parliament and was a member of the Presidential Council. In September 1991 he became head of the KGB's First Main Directorate, which is responsible for foreign intelligence and espionage.[8]

Yevgeny I. Shaposhnikov: A marshal of aviation born on February 3, 1942, this pilot emerged as the Soviet minister of defense when his superior, Marshal Dmitri Yazov, was implicated in coup activities. Shaposhnikov had the unenviable task of keeping the Soviet armed forces in one piece while the Soviet Union itself disintegrated. With the creation of the Commonwealth of Independent States on December 21, 1991, Shaposhnikov was appointed commander in chief of the joint CIS forces. His rank is equivalent to a five-star general in Western armies.

Marshal Shaposhnikov has been serving as an interim commander as the nature of the CIS forces, their disposition, and their missions evolve. While it seems certain that the CIS will continue to control borders, strategic forces, and some air defense, this position could evaporate if the CIS itself passes away, if Yeltsin assumes command of CIS forces, or as nuclear weapons are consolidated within Russia and a separate CIS command becomes superfluous.

Boris N. Yeltsin: This native of Sverdlovsk, born on February 1, 1931, gained national and international prominence during the August 19, 1991, coup, when he stood up against party and military leaders to maintain his new position as the first elected president of Russia. A construction engineer who prides himself on his early efforts to master the building trades, he confounds his personal security detail by wading into crowds and speaking directly to people who may oppose him. Many credit his stalwart performance following Mikhail Gorbachev's return to Moscow on August 24, 1991, with the stability that quickly returned to a changed capital and nation. Yeltsin has been both president and prime minister of Russia, though he gave up the latter office in December 1992. Reflecting on the year ahead in his 1993 New Year's address, Yeltsin noted: "Russia is at last returning to the path of common sense and real values. . . . It is not Russia's fault that she was swept from this path and turned into a testing ground for communism. Today we are rid of this delusion."[9]

NOTES

1. Steven Erlanger, "Kremlin's Technocrat: Viktor Stepanovich Chernomyrdin," *New York Times*, December 15, 1992, A16.

2. "Yakovlev: Gorbachev 'Tragic Figure,' " Moscow TASS, 2058 GMT, December 25, 1991, in FBIS-SOV–91–248, December 26, 1991, 25.

3. "Itogi" program, Moscow Ostankino Television Network, 1900 GMT, December 27, 1992, in FBIS-SOV–92–249, December 28, 1992, 4.

4. Daniel Sneider, "Turning Russia's Army into a Lean Machine," *Christian Science Monitor*, June 9, 1992, 7.

5. "Col Gen Gromov, Boris Vsevolodovich," *Krasnaya zvezda*, June 30, 1992, 1, in JPRS-UMA–92–025, July 8, 1992, 1.

6. "Defense Leaders of Key Republics," *Air Force Magazine*, March 1992, 48.

7. Y. Dotsuk and I. Sichka, "When He Plays the Domba, All Around Him Sing. Nineteen Unknown Facts from N. Nazarbayev's Life," Moscow *Komsomolskaya pravda*, February 22, 1992, 2, in FBIS-SOV–92–040, February 28, 1992, 55.

8. "Biography of Yevgeniy Primakov," Moscow TASS, 1950 GMT, December 26, 1991, in FBIS-SOV–91–249, December 27, 1991, 33–34.

9. "New Year's Address to the Nation by Russian Federation President Boris Yeltsin in Moscow," Moscow Russian Television Network, 1730 GMT, December 30, 1992, in FBIS-SOV–92–252, December 31, 1992, 18.

For Further Reading

Akiner, Shirin. *Islamic Peoples of the Soviet Union*. London: Kegan Paul, 1983.

Alstadt, Audrey L. *The Azerbaijani Turks: Power and Identity under Russian Rule*. Studies of Nationalities Series, edited by Wayne S. Vucinich. Stanford, Calif.: Hoover Institution Press, 1992.

Aslund, Anders, ed. *The Post-Soviet Economy: Soviet and Western Perspectives*. New York: St. Martin's Press, 1992.

Bailer, Seweryn, and Michael Mandelbaum, eds. *Gorbachev's Russia and American Foreign Policy*. Boulder, Colo.: Westview Press, 1988.

Bremmer, Ian, and Ray Taras, eds. *Nation and Politics in the Soviet Successor States*. Cambridge, U.K.: Cambridge University Press, 1993.

Brzezinski, Zbigniew K. *The Grand Failure: The Birth and Death of Communism in the Twentieth Century*. New York: Scribner, 1989.

Chew, Allen F. *An Atlas of Russian History: Eleven Centuries of Changing Borders*. rev. ed. New Haven, Conn.: Yale University Press, 1967.

Clemens, Walter C., Jr. *Baltic Independence and Russian Empire*. New York: St. Martin's Press, 1991.

Colton, Timothy J. *The Dilemma of Reform in the Soviet Union*. rev. ed. New York: Council on Foreign Relations Press, 1986.

Conquest, Robert. *The Harvest of Sorrow: Soviet Collectivization and the Terror-Famine*. New York: Oxford University Press, 1986.

Conquest, Robert, ed. *The Last Empire: Nationality and the Soviet Future*. Stanford, Calif.: Hoover Institution Press, 1986.

Davies, R. W., ed. *The Soviet Union*. 2nd ed. Boston: Unwin Hyman, 1989.

Dewdney, J. C. *USSR in Maps*. New York: Holmes & Meier Publishers, 1982.

Feshbach, Murray, and Alfred Friendly, Jr. *Ecocide in the USSR: The Looming Disaster in Soviet Health and Environment*. New York: Basic Books, 1992.

Fierman, William, ed. *Soviet Central Asia: The Failed Transformation*. Boulder, Colo.: Westview Press, 1991.

Fisher, Alan W. *The Crimean Tatars*. Studies of Nationalities in the USSR Series, edited by Wayne S. Vucinich. Stanford, Calif.: Hoover Institution Press, 1978.

Hajda, Lubomyr, and Mark Beissinger, eds. *The Nationalities Factor in Soviet Politics and Society.* Boulder, Colo.: Westview Press, 1990.

Hewett, Ed. A., with Clifford G. Gaddy. *Open for Business: Russia's Return to the Global Economy.* Washington, D.C.: The Brookings Institution, 1992.

Hovannisian, Richard G., ed. *The Armenian Genocide.* New York: St. Martin's Press, 1992.

International Institute of Strategic Studies. *Strategic Survey 1991–1992.* London: Brassey's for International Institute of Strategic Studies, 1992.

Kalbouss, George. *A Study Guide to Russian Culture.* Needham Heights, Mass.: Ginn Press, 1991.

Little, David. *Ukraine: The Legacy of Intolerance.* Series on Religion, Nationalism, and Intolerance. Arlington, Va.: United States Institute of Peace Press, 1991.

Mandelbaum, Michael, ed. *The Rise of Nations in the Soviet Union: American Foreign Policy and the Disintegration of the USSR.* New York: Council on Foreign Relations Press, 1991.

Medvedev, Grigori. *The Truth About Chernobyl.* New York: Basic Books, 1991.

Motyl, Alexander J., ed. *Thinking Theoretically About Soviet Nationalities: History and Comparison in the Study of the USSR.* New York: Columbia University Press, 1992.

Nahaylo, Bohdan, and Victor Swoboda. *Soviet Disunion: A History of the Nationalities Problem in the USSR.* New York: The Free Press, 1990.

New World Demographics. *The FirstBook of Demographics for the Republics of the Former Soviet Union, 1951–1990.* Shady Side, Md.: New World Demographics, 1992.

Olcott, Martha Brill. *The Kazakhs.* Studies of Nationalities in the USSR Series, edited by Wayne S. Vucinich. Stanford, Calif.: Hoover Institution Press, 1987.

Ralston, Richard E., ed. *Communism: Its Rise and Fall in the 20th Century.* Boston: Christian Science Monitor, 1991.

Rauch, Georg Von. *The Baltic States, The Years of Independence: Estonia, Latvia, Lithuania, 1917–1940.* Translated by Gerald Onn. Berkeley: University of California Press, 1974.

Raun, Toivo U. *Estonia and the Estonians.* 2d. ed. Studies of Nationalities in the USSR Series, edited by Wayne S. Vucinich. Stanford, Calif.: Hoover Institution Press, 1991.

Roberts, Brad, and Nina Belyaeva, eds. *After Perestroika: Democracy in the Soviet Union.* Washington, D.C.: Center for Strategic and International Studies, 1991.

Rorlich, Azade-Ayse. *The Volga Tatars: A Profile in National Resilience.* Studies of Nationalities in the USSR Series, edited by Wayne S. Vucinich. Stanford, Calif.: Hoover Institution Press, 1986.

Rubinstein, Alvin Z. *Soviet Foreign Policy Since World War II.* 4th. ed. New York: HarperCollins, 1992.

Solchanyk, Roman. *Ukraine: From Chernobyl to Sovereignty.* New York: St. Martin's Press, 1992.

Smolansky, Oles M. and Bettie M. Smolansky. *The U.S.S.R. and Iraq: The Soviet Quest for Influence.* Durham, N.C.: Duke University Press, 1991.

Suny, Ronald Grigor. *The Making of the Georgian Nation.* Studies of Nationalities in the USSR Series, edited by Wayne S. Vucinich. Stanford, Calif.: Hoover Institution Press, 1988.

Twining, David T., ed. *Beyond Glasnost: Soviet Reform and Security Issues.* Westport, Conn.: Greenwood Press, 1992.

Twining, David Thomas. *Strategic Surprise in the Age of Glasnost.* New Brunswick, N.J.: Transaction Publishers, 1992.

White, Stephen. *Gorbachev in Power.* 2d ed. New York: Cambridge University Press, 1991.

White, Stephen, Alex Pravda, and Zvi Gitelman, eds. *Developments in Soviet Politics.* Durham, N.C.: Duke University Press, 1990.

Wixman, Ronald. *The Peoples of the USSR: An Ethnographic Handbook.* Armonk, N.Y.: M. E. Sharpe, Inc., 1988.

Zickel, Raymond E., ed. *Soviet Union: A Country Study.* 2d ed. Area Handbook Series, Federal Research Division, Library of Congress. Washington, D.C.: U.S. Government Printing Office, 1991.

Index

About the Author

DAVID T. TWINING is Director of Eurasian and Commonwealth Studies, U.S. Army War College. Among his earlier publications are *Strategic Surprise in the Age of Glasnost* (1992) and *Beyond Glasnost: Soviet Reform and Security Issues* (Greenwood Press, 1992).